An Unseen Unheard Minority

New Directions in the History of Education

Series editor, Benjamin Justice

The New Directions in the History of Education series seeks to publish innovative books that push the traditional boundaries of the history of education. Topics may include social movements in education; the history of cultural representations of schools and schooling; the role of public schools in the social production of space; and the perspectives and experiences of African Americans, Latinx Americans, women, queer folk, and others. The series will take a broad, inclusive look at American education in formal settings, from prekindergarten to higher education, as well as in out-of-school and informal settings. We also invite historical scholarship that informs and challenges popular conceptions of educational policy and policy making and that addresses questions of social justice, equality, democracy, and the formation of popular knowledge.

Diana D'Amico Pawlewicz, *Blaming Teachers: Professionalization Policies and the Failure of Reform in American History*

Dionne Danns, *Crossing Segregated Boundaries: Remembering Chicago School Desegregation*

Sharon S. Lee, *An Unseen Unheard Minority: Asian American Students at the University of Illinois*

Kyle P. Steele, *Making a Mass Institution: Indianapolis and the American High School*

An Unseen Unheard Minority

Asian American Students at the University of Illinois

SHARON S. LEE

Rutgers University Press

New Brunswick, Camden, and Newark, New Jersey, and London

Names: Lee, Sharon Shockley, author.
Title: An unseen unheard minority : Asian American students at the
    University of Illinois / Sharon S. Lee.
Description: New Brunswick : Rutgers University Press, 2022. |
    Series: New directions in the history of education |
    Includes bibliographical references and index.
Identifiers: LCCN 2021009988 | ISBN 9781978824447 (paperback) |
    ISBN 9781978824454 (hardcover) | ISBN 9781978824461 (epub) |
    ISBN 9781978824478 (mobi) | ISBN 9781978824485 (pdf)
Subjects: LCSH: Asian American college students—Social conditions—Illinois—
    Champaign. | Asian American college students—Ethnic identity—Illinois—
    Champaign. | University of Illinois at Urbana-Champaign—Students—Political
    activity—History—20th century. | University of Illinois at Urbana-Champaign—
    Students—Political activity—History—21st century. | Student movements—
    Illinois—Champaign—History—20th century. | Student movements—
    Illinois—Champaign—History—21st century.
Classification: LCC LC2633.6 .L44 2022 | DDC 378.1/982995073—dc23
LC record available at https://lccn.loc.gov/2021009988

A British Cataloging-in-Publication record for this book is available from the British Library.

Portions of chapter 1 were previously published: Sharon S. Lee, "The De-minoritization of
Asian Americans: A Historical Examination of the Representations of Asian Americans in
Affirmative Action Admissions Policies at the University of California," *Asian American Law
Journal* 15 (2008): 129–152.

References to internet websites (URLs) were accurate at the time of writing. Neither the
author nor Rutgers University Press is responsible for URLs that may have expired or changed
since the manuscript was prepared.

♾ The paper used in this publication meets the requirements of the American National
Standard for Information Sciences—Permanence of Paper for Printed Library Materials,
ANSI Z39.48-1992.

www.rutgersuniversitypress.org

Manufactured in the United States of America

To all Asian American students who struggle to be seen and heard

Contents

Foreword

Sharon Lee and I have a lot in common. We share a doctoral alma mater, the University of Illinois at Urbana-Champaign. We struggled to make sense of ourselves and be successful in predominantly White spaces from kindergarten through our doctorates. Our undergraduate years opened our eyes to knowledge, experiences, and possibilities we'd never previously realized. It was there that we sought and found community, made a way, and found our voices. We research who we are as an Asian American woman and a Black American woman, respectively. And we've written books on students' racialized experiences at the University of Illinois as a way to, as Lee puts it, move beyond statistical parity as the sole measure in assessing minoritized student experiences and to center student voices in the discussion. Both of us chose these topics to write ourselves and our communities into history.

Some say that insider status creates blind spots for researchers. I've never found that argument convincing—and there is a lot of scholarship to back me up, particularly when it comes to communities of color. I think it makes a researcher more attuned to the issues at hand, to know the right (and hard) questions to ask of archives and interviewees. It's also a way to ensure that the stories of previously ignored communities get told.

We know very little about Asian American student activism. I suspect the model minority myth not only does personal and communal damage to those living it but also moves researchers away from the seeing the possibility of Asian Americans as activists. Why study that group if you believe they've encountered few struggles in higher education? Add to that the reality that definitions of activism often privilege direct action (e.g., sit-ins, protests, demonstrations), and the type of activism employed by Asian American students in the Midwest gets completely ignored. As I've argued in my own work, we need a more expansive way of understanding what activism looks like. That would not only provide nuance to discussions of institutional change efforts, but it would allow for a broader umbrella under which different tactics—and groups—would be included in the narrative.

This is one of the reasons I believe this book to be of great use. Lee uses her insider status to start the reader on the path of deeper understanding of the nature of, barriers to, and successes and failures of Asian American student activism. She is right that this is a regional narrative and that Asian American student activism will look different elsewhere (and I hope future researchers take up that topic). That doesn't undercut her analysis. Instead, it strengthens it by acknowledging the fact that the Asian American student experience is a varied one. It's the same way we should understand the Asian American community itself—as diverse, heterogeneous, and sometimes at odds.

Another reason I find this book worthwhile is that it offers another glimpse into the nature of institutional change and the role of youth in it. As one of Lee's interviewees noted about forthcoming institutional support for Asian American student demands, "These vital resources were not merely created by the university out of thin air; they were instituted as a direct result of student initiative and protest." I came to similar conclusions in my study of Black student protest, and the same can be said of Latinx student protest.

There should never be a straight line drawn from the past to the present—contexts, institutions, and people change—but what can we take from earlier activism and activists to inform what is happening on campuses today? In the year 2020, we began living through another huge wave of student activism spurred on by a health pandemic, anti-Black racism, and extreme economic decline. Students all over the country have been demanding that their institutions remove police from campus, enact antiracist policies, create a wider safety net for students, and become active agents in the amelioration of social ills. Some of their demands mirror those of their predecessors, while others are necessarily different. No matter the decade, though, student activism has been the catalyst that has forced institutions of higher education to wrestle with the divide between their reality as oppressive spaces and the promise of what they could become.

Lee's book reminds us that this is an uphill climb. Generating and maintaining momentum for institutional transformation is difficult work. At the same time, this book reminds us that there are productive avenues to enact lasting change. All hope is not lost. Progress was made in the past, and additional progress can be made in the future. Student activists play a pivotal role in that, and those of us in academia should be exhilarated and proud to be pushed forward by our students. Partnering with them in this work will spark disagreements and tension, but it will also force us to work toward making our institutions the welcoming, collaborative, and excellent places we know they can be. Now let's get to work.

Joy Williamson-Lott
Professor, College of Education
Dean, The Graduate School
University of Washington, Seattle

Preface

I am an Asian American Midwesterner—I was born and raised in Cleveland, and I earned my educational degrees in Ohio, Wisconsin, and Illinois. I have always known that Asian Americans were minorities, a concept I was made painfully aware of at an early age, growing up in the suburbs in the 1970s and 1980s. A U.S.-born, middle child of Korean immigrants who benefited from the 1965 Immigration Act, I grew up in a predominantly White community where there were scarcely any other Asian families. I never saw anyone who looked like me in the classroom, in textbooks, or on television. Children teased me for my small eyes and short stature. Teachers expected me to be smart, the model student for others. I was drawn to learning about African American history in high school because I viscerally understood the pain of stereotypes, racism, and discrimination. I knew that I was not in the majority, as I was not seen or heard as a multidimensional person. I was not White.

As an undergraduate at Oberlin College, I learned a language to articulate my racialized experiences. I devoured books on immigration history, Asian American history, and race and ethnic relations. I was incensed that I had never learned about the Japanese American internment and felt deceived for having that history erased from my public schooling. I began to fully understand how historical, institutional, and structural barriers privileged Whiteness in the United States and how policies created racial categories that have no biological basis yet profoundly limited opportunities for non-White communities.

When I earned a master's degree at the University of Wisconsin, I felt isolated in my program that did not enroll a large number of students of color. I cofounded an Asian American graduate student organization through which I met another Asian American student from California. She joked that she had learned how to "become" Asian American once she was in the Midwest, to reach out beyond her Chinese ethnic community due to the sheer invisibility of Asian faces in Wisconsin. Her entry into the Midwest came with a culture shock of being starkly isolated as a minority. For me, it was second nature.

When I was hired by the University of Illinois at Urbana-Champaign (UIUC) in 2000 to help build a burgeoning Asian American studies program, it was the first campus I had been to where Asian American students (U.S. domestic, not international students) were not classified as minorities. Because of their high enrollment numbers relative to their percentage of the state population, they were deemed overrepresented by university polices. Thus, UIUC did not target Asian American students in minority services or programs. Due to my personal experiences with racism, I was perplexed by this presumption. Thus began my research on higher education policies and Asian American student struggles for minority recognition.

A Few Caveats

Asian American students are diverse, so any study cannot claim to represent the entirety of their experiences. My study focuses on Asian American student leaders at the University of Illinois who advocated for Asian American academic and student affairs resources—those who were part of the historical record and who were willing to be interviewed. It is not my intention to disregard the many other students who contributed to this movement in countless other ways. I also acknowledge that not all Asian American students advocated for such resources.

I also recognize my study's focus on East Asian American students. Within the field of Asian American studies, scholars have critiqued how the term "Asian American" has centered East Asian American voices at the expense of South Asian, Filipino, and Southeast Asian Americans. Yet as Yen Le Espiritu and William Wei show, documenting Asian American movements is important, as doing so demonstrates an important political response to issues that affect many individuals along broad racial categories.[1]

In addition, while some scholars in Asian American studies are moving toward a more transnational and diasporic perspective that includes Asian perspectives, and while I am not denying the historical, cultural, and contemporary connections that Asians in the United States maintain with Asia, this study focuses on American experiences and does not address the experiences of international Asian students (beyond in the early historiography), who are also present in large numbers at the University of Illinois. For terminology, I use the term "Asian American" without the hyphen between words; however, I quote archival documents that use the hyphen. I also quote and cite documents that use the conflated terms "Asian Pacific American" (APA) or "Asian Pacific Islander" (API), although this study does not address Pacific Islander student experiences and needs.[2]

I have one note on the usage of the term "minority." Claiming a minority status may come with a sense of being less than or disadvantaged. University of Illinois student affairs staff expressed this notion in a strategic plan in 1991. A task force recommended replacing the term "minority" with "multicultural," "because the current language does not serve us well and the terms 'minority' and 'majority' are inadequate and pejorative."[3] The report went on to cite dictionary definitions of "minority" as the smaller of a group or one that is different from others, and "majority" as being greater or superior. In this study, however, I frame minority status as a political strategy accompanied by benefits. As minority groups have mobilized around a shared history and to contest discrimination, minority rights have been one way to gain compensation and assistance through policies such as affirmative action, particularly in the 1960s and 1970s. For Asian American students at UIUC, claiming minority status was a critical argument to justify gaining university resources.

Lastly, I acknowledge that challenging a Black-White racial paradigm and expanding minority needs to include Asian Americans (a high-achieving group in the aggregate) comes with risks. It is urgent and necessary to address the economic and educational disparities that have never been rectified for the African American community in the United States. In my critique of underrepresentation as a measure for minority status, I do not support diverting resources away from race-conscious admissions and support programs that focus on these goals. Rather, my aim is to critique the opposite—that parity or overparity signals equity. My intent is to challenge the exclusion of Asian American students from diversity and minority discussions on the presumption that they are akin to White students. Anti-Asian sentiment persists today, in different forms as anti-Blackness, but just as insidious. Asian American students at UIUC claimed their racialized experiences as students of color and learned from and supported the efforts of their African American, Latinx, and Native American peers. They took part in student-led movements that challenged the university to address their needs, changing higher education policies along the way for generations to come.

Abbreviations

AAA	Asian American Association
AAS	Asian American studies
AATF	Asian American Task Force
ACCORD	Asian-Pacific American Coalition to Combat Oppression, Racism, and Discrimination
APA	Asian Pacific American
APAC	Asian Pacific American Coalition
APARB	Asian Pacific American Resource Board
APARC	Asian Pacific American Resource Committee
EOP	Educational Opportunities Program
HKSA	Hong Kong Students Association
IBHE	Illinois Board of Higher Education
ISA	Indian Student Association
KASA	Korean American Students Association
KUSA	Korean Undergraduate Students Association
MAAS	Midwest Asian American Students
MAASU	Midwest Asian American Students Union
OAR	Office of Admissions and Records
OMSA	Office of Minority Student Affairs
PSA	Philippine Student Association
SEOP	Special Educational Opportunities Program

TASC   Taiwanese American Students Club
UIUC   University of Illinois at Urbana-Champaign
VSA   Vietnamese Student Association

Select Timeline of Asian American Student Activism at the University of Illinois at Urbana-Champaign (UIUC)

1940s	Indian Student Association (ISA) founded by international students. ISA reorganizes in 1987.
	Philippine Student Association (PSA) founded (with roots back to the 1919 Philippine Illini). PSA restructures in 1985 to focus on undergraduates.
Summer 1968	UIUC establishes Special Educational Opportunities Program (SEOP or Project 500) to recruit disadvantaged (especially Black) students to campus.
January 1971	The Asian American Alliance, the first pan–Asian American student organization at UIUC, forms.
April 1971	Members of the Asian American Alliance attend the national anti–Vietnam War march in Washington, D.C.
5 May 1971	Asian American Alliance members lead a local march against the Vietnam War.
Fall 1972	Asian Studies 199 is offered, the first course on Asian American issues at UIUC. The course continues in the fall 1973 and spring 1974 semesters.

February 1973	The Asian American Alliance submits a proposal for an Asian American studies program at UIUC.
1979	Korean Undergraduate Students Association (KUSA) founded. KUSA changes its name to Korean American Students Association (KASA) in 1995.
1983	Vietnamese Student Association (VSA) founded.
Spring 1986	Asian American Association (AAA), the second pan–Asian American student organization at UIUC, forms, with assistant dean of students Yuki Llewellyn as its first sponsor.
April 1989	The first Midwest Asian American Students (MAAS) conference is sponsored by the Asian American Association at UIUC.
January 1990	Vice chancellor for student affairs Stan Levy creates the Asian American Task Force, which meets through the fall of 1991.
Spring 1990	The Asian Council founded as an umbrella student group; includes representatives from the Asian American Association, the Philippine Student Association, the Korean Undergraduate Students Association, the Indian Student Association, and the Hong Kong Students Association.
6–8 April 1990	The second MAAS conference held at UIUC.
Spring 1991	The Asian-Pacific American Coalition to Combat Oppression, Racism, and Discrimination (ACCORD) founded to promote Asian American community needs and concerns. Taiwanese American Students Club (TASC) founded.
March 1991	UIUC's first Asian American Awareness Month held, coordinated by the Asian Council.
1–3 March 1991	The third MAAS conference held at UIUC.
Fall 1991	Asian American Programming Committee of Illini Union Board's cultural programming division formed.
Spring 1992	Asian American Artists Collective founded.
26 March 1992	Members of ACCORD protest anti-Asian racism in front of the Alpha Tao Omega fraternity.

3–5 April 1992   The fourth MAAS conference held at UIUC, in conjunction with the meeting of a new network—the Midwest Asian American Students Union (MAASU).

5 May 1992   Latinx students and supporters hold sit-in at the Henry Administration Building for eight hours and demand improvements to recruitment and retention of Latinx students and faculty, developing a Latina/o studies program, increasing resources for La Casa Cultural Latina, and eliminating Chief Illiniwek as the university mascot.

Fall 1992   Anthropology professor Clark Cunningham and other invited guest lecturers teach the first semester of Sociology/Anthropology 296C (Asian American Experiences).

14 October 1992   State senate hearings held at UIUC to discuss the university's response to the 5 May protest and the campus climate for students of color. Asian American students testify to anti-Asian sentiment at UIUC.

December 1992   Coalition of Asian American students submits petition for an Asian American cultural center to the UIUC chancellor.

Spring 1993   Asian Pacific American Coalition (APAC) founded.

9–11 April 1993   The fifth MAAS conference held at UIUC, cosponsored by the Asian American Association and the Indian Student Association.

25–27 March 1994   The sixth MAAS conference held at UIUC, cosponsored by the Asian American Association, the Indian Student Association, and the Philippine Student Association.

May 1994   Student-written proposal for an Asian Pacific American cultural center presented to the administration. The proposal is rejected.

Fall 1994   Students prepare legal documents against the university, claiming that by denying Asian American students support services, the university is violating state law defining Asian Americans as minorities in public institutions of higher education.

The first "Asiantation," a new-student orientation for Asian Pacific Americans, is conducted.

September 1994	Asian Pacific American Resource Board (APARB) formed, funding $30,000 annually for Asian American programming; renamed the Asian Pacific American Resource Committee (APARC) in 1997.
23–26 March 1995	The seventh MAAS conference held at UIUC.
April 1995	Students at Northwestern University undergo a hunger strike to advocate for an Asian American studies program.
January 1996	Asian American students at UIUC hold a daylong teach-in to advocate for an Asian American studies program.
29–31 March 1996	The eighth MAAS conference held at UIUC.
Fall 1996	First assistant dean of students for Asian Pacific American student affairs hired.
	First "Unseen Unheard" annual Asian American activism conference held.
	Ad hoc committee formed to investigate the possibility of starting an Asian American studies program at UIUC.
Fall 1997	Asian American Studies Committee (AASC) established. The three-year building phase focuses on hiring six faculty in Asian American studies, a university commitment that receives national attention.
Fall 1998	University clinical counselor position specializing in Asian American needs and issues created.
Fall 2000	The AASC becomes the Asian American Studies Program under the College of Liberal Arts and Sciences.
Fall 2002	The Ad-hoc Committee on Asian Pacific American (APA) Student Life is appointed and charged with examining the personal, social, and academic needs and concerns of APA students on campus. Its report, submitted in April 2003, highlights nine recommendations, the top being the creation of an APA cultural center.
9 September 2005	UIUC Asian American Cultural Center grand opening at 1210 West Nevada Street in Urbana.

An Unseen Unheard Minority

Introduction

The Invisibility of Asian Americans in Higher Education Diversity Discussions

In 2019, Students for Fair Admissions (SFFA) sued Harvard University, claiming the prestigious school discriminated against Asian Americans. Conservative legal strategist Edward Blum founded SFFA in 2014 and purposefully recruited Asian litigants for lawsuits against high-profile universities with a goal of dismantling racial considerations in admissions. Earlier cases such as *Regents of the University of California v. Bakke* (1978), *Grutter v. Bollinger* (2003), and *Fisher v. University of Texas* (2013, 2016) featured White plaintiffs who argued that racial considerations injured them in favor of underrepresented racial minorities with allegedly lower credentials (such as test scores). The claiming of Asian Americans as victims further extended the anti–affirmative action argument. *SFFA v. Harvard* embraced Asian Americans, a racialized non-White group with stellar academic achievements (the model minority), as "proof" that race no longer mattered and should not be considered in the admissions process.

This narrative of Asian American achievement is not new. The statistically robust presence of Asian Americans in higher education is undeniable. In 2016, Asian Americans had the highest percentage of 18-to-24-year-olds enrolled in college (57.2 percent) of any racial group, including Whites (41.9 percent). In 2017, Asians had higher levels of educational degree attainment than any other group, with 30.7 percent having bachelor's degrees and 24.7 percent advanced degrees.[1] Asian American statistical representation at highly selective schools also outpaces their national numbers. In 2016, Asian American enrollment rates at highly selective colleges were nearly 18 percent, with 22 percent at Harvard and Yale in 2017–2018.[2]

What can be denied, however, is the claim that all Asian Americans, a vastly diverse group, are high achieving. In addition, the claim that Asian Americans no longer experience racial obstacles, are akin to honorary Whites, and are proof that race is no longer an obstacle must be repudiated.[3] The fact that Asian Americans are racially positioned as model minorities to argue that affirmative action should be abolished exemplifies how racial narratives infuse Asian American lives. This model minority narrative negates the racial experiences of Asian Americans, dividing them from other students of color and erasing them from higher education discussions about diversity and minority students. Asian Americans are the fastest-growing racial population in the United States and their presence on college campuses is incontrovertible, yet higher education administrators and policy makers assume Asian American students have no educational needs. Thus, Asian Americans are misguidedly rendered invisible in higher education discourse about minority students or diversity writ large.

Are Asian Americans Minorities?

Why have higher education administrators disregarded Asian Americans in discussions about minority students? The first reason is the alluring model minority narrative—the image of Asian Americans as hardworking, noncomplaining, and able to pull themselves up by their bootstraps through cultural values of education and respect for authority, which has a long history in the United States.[4] Scholars have refuted this model minority image, calling it a myth because it overgeneralizes success for a diverse group that has wide variation across ethnic lines. The category "Asian American," along with its often-conflated corollary "Pacific Islander"—which refers to a large population not covered in this study—consists of a heterogeneous group encompassing many ethnicities, languages, cultures, religions, and histories.[5] The term "Asian American" refers to Americans of East Asian (Chinese, Japanese, Korean, Taiwanese), South Asian (Indian, Pakistani, Sri Lankan, Bangladeshi), Southeast Asian (Thai, Vietnamese, Laotian, Cambodian, Indonesian), and Filipino descent. Certain subgroups such as Southeast Asians and Pacific Islanders still struggle with educational access.[6]

Because the model minority myth attributes culture and individual hard work to upward mobility (think: Asian students raised by culturally strict "tiger moms") rather than historical and structural barriers, it is used to pit Asian Americans against other minority groups. Asian American success stories are used to shame African Americans and Latinx communities for not working hard to succeed in the same way and to argue that programs such as affirmative action are unnecessary.[7] In addition, the model minority myth overlooks persistent racial discrimination against Asians in the United States and the ways race continues to inform their experiences. A deeper look at Asian American experiences reveals the ways anti-Asian racism persists and needs to be interrogated to fully understand the nuances of race in America.

A second reason for Asian American exclusion from minority discussions is a policy focus on parity. Affirmative action policies developed with proportionality as a goal, and the concept of proportionate representation is one measure of affirmative action's progress; in other words, a primary measure of minority status is parity.[8] If a group is not represented in an institution or workplace at equivalent rates as its available population, it is defined as disadvantaged. As Dana Takagi notes, "Strict adherence to parity and representation in diversity talk reinforces the notion that diversity should be more focused on under-represented groups."[9] Because in the aggregate they are demographically overrepresented in institutions of higher education, Asian Americans are not considered to be experiencing discrimination. And as they have exceeded parity, administrators presume the diversity goal for Asian Americans has been reached, thus excluding Asian Americans from minority and diversity discussions. However, while underrepresentation remains a critical measure for assessing racial inequity, overrepresentation or parity/over parity does not connote that equity has been achieved.

Related to a focus on parity, a third reason why Asian Americans are overlooked in minority discussions is the predominance of a Black-White racial paradigm. When educational institutions began addressing the challenges facing minority students, the focus was on African Americans. Historically, Black-White relations have informed educational discourses and policies for racial equity such as in the landmark *Brown v. Board of Education* (1954) ruling and with affirmative action policies aimed to benefit African Americans.[10] Because of this nation's oppressive history of slavery, Jim Crow segregation, and anti-Black racism, as well as the advances made by the African American–led civil rights movement, it is no surprise that racial discourse begins in Black and White. And in regional areas such as the Midwest where racial demographics are not as diverse, this Black-White paradigm of race relations predominates. However, a Black-White binary marginalizes racial minorities who are neither White nor Black and overlooks the increasing complexity of race in the United States.[11]

The Realities of Race

The erasure of Asian American student experiences as racial minorities and the presumption of their honorary Whiteness obscure the realities of race in the United States. A 2019 Pew Research Center study found that approximately the same percentage of African American and Asian American respondents reported personal experiences with racial discrimination.[12] During 2020–2021, anti-Asian violence proliferated, revealing an unyielding pattern of hate that blamed Asians for the COVID-19 pandemic.[13] The history of Asians in the United States (which I will detail in chapter 1) reveals that time and time again, Asians in the United States have been racialized as foreigners and disloyal despite generations of citizenship, through anti-Asian immigration restriction (first targeting Chinese immigrants in the 1850s and then expanding to Japanese, Koreans, Indians, and Filipinos); racial restrictions on land ownership, equal education, and naturalization rights (as Asians were deemed ineligible for citizenship); and wartime internment of Japanese Americans during World War II.[14] The super student–model minority narrative effectively erases the historical and present-day realities of Asian American students as racialized non-White minorities.

Asian Americans' continued experiences with racism reveal the different ways that groups are racialized in the United States. Claire Kim describes how Asian Americans and African Americans are racialized in relation to each other; in particular, Blacks have been racialized as inferior and Asians have been racialized as aliens, which subordinates them both as non-White groups.[15] Asian American foreigner racialization manifests itself in instances of anti-Asian tension and backlash, creating an inhospitable campus environment. For instance, as Asian American college enrollments began to rise in the 1980s, anti-Asian backlash and tension rose on campuses, evidenced by racist nicknames denoting prestigious schools (MIT became Made In Taiwan; UCLA was United Caucasians Lost Among Asians). In addition, White students expressed racial resentment against Asian American students, complaining that they were curve breakers. Asian Americans' status as honorary Whites does not protect them from anti-Asian hostility or resentment. In time of economic or wartime crisis, Asians Americans are painted as spies, terrorists, and harbingers of insidious pandemic viruses.[16]

Due to shared racial experiences, Asian American panethnicity emerged as an adaptive political strategy during the 1960s when Asian American communities began to work together.[17] Following 1960s civil rights legislation, demographic acknowledgment was critical, as numbers were the basis for determining eligibility for federal funding and services. Population statistics identified disadvantage and underrepresentation and outlined eligibility for affirmative action programs in education, employment, and public services. Hence, a system that foregrounded enumeration for minority benefits provided an incentive for Asian ethnic groups to come together, form an Asian American identity, and advocate for minority eligibility. By embracing a racial minority identity, Asian Americans aligned themselves with other communities of color in the fight against institutionalized racism.

Beyond Black and White: Making Asian Americans Visible

Because of their racialized experiences, Asian American students have argued against university policies that exclude them from minority services and programs. In doing so, Asian American students and their allies pose a critical counternarrative of minority experiences that rejects the model minority myth, standard measures of underrepresentation, and a narrow Black-White racial lens. They contest policies that ignore them, advancing the minority discourse in order to establish resources such as Asian American studies programs and Asian American cultural centers at universities across the nation.

The ways Asian American students actively challenge and reframe minority discussions reveal important new ways to think about race on college campuses, especially considering demographic shifts in America. Particularly propelled by the liberalization of immigration policies after 1965, Asian American and Latinx students have increased in number on university campuses and have also been a part of activist movements for culturally and racially relevant curricula and support services.[18] These populations do not fit well into a Black-White dichotomy, as outlined by Eileen O'Brien, who calls Latinxs and Asian Americans the racial middle. O'Brien and scholars of critical race theory point out that Latinxs and Asian Americans encounter stereotypes and discrimination that peg them as un-American, suspicious, illegal, and disloyal; they face issues around language, immigration, and biculturalism; and they do not fit in simple Black or White categories.[19] Thus, it is imperative to disrupt simple binaries of White and Black in order to reveal the deeper complexities of race in the United States. So limited is the public's understanding of Asian American student experiences that researchers often describe Asian Americans as invisible, unseen, and misrepresented.[20]

I acknowledge that my critique of the emphasis on underrepresentation and a Black- White racial paradigm within minority policy discourse is risky. By bringing in other students of color into a higher education diversity discussion, it is not my intention to dismiss underrepresentation and to engage in competition for resources, comparing Asian American and African American oppressions. The founding of the United States was built on anti-Black oppression that denigrated Black lives for centuries. Jim Crow segregation and discrimination persisted long after the passage of the Thirteenth Amendment, which abolished slavery, and continues on despite gains made in civil rights legislation in the 1960s. Protests against police brutality through the Black Lives Matter movement continue to reveal the insidious and oppressive nature of anti-Black racism. My goal instead is to complicate our racial narratives that have overlooked experiences of Asian American students. By mining Asian American educational history, one can glean insights into the experiences of Asian American students and how they interpreted, negotiated, and challenged university policies that excluded them—experiences that diverged from those of African American students yet addressed similar struggles with racial isolation, backlash, and hostility.

Asian American Students at the University of Illinois at Urbana-Champaign

Since the early 1970s, when they began appearing on campus in large numbers for the first time, Asian American students at the University of Illinois at Urbana-Champaign (UIUC) challenged higher education's definitions of minority status. They contested the model minority myth, the university's focus on underrepresentation in defining minority status, and the Black-White racial paradigm, all of which erased their experiences on campus. In doing so, these students demanded their inclusion in minority student and diversity discussions and were able to gain significant campus resources.

UIUC struggled with providing access to racial minorities and focused its efforts on improving the underrepresentation of African American and Latinx students in enrollment and retention. At this institution, as at many others, Asian Americans matriculate and persist in high numbers. UIUC never defined Asian Americans as an underrepresented minority and does not include Asian Americans in minority student services.

Despite this policy construction of Asian Americans as nonminorities, the campus is home to the largest Asian American studies (AAS) department in the Midwest. Established in 1997, it is housed in the College of Liberal Arts and Sciences and has twenty-five faculty and forty-nine permanent courses, according to the fall 2019 course catalog. It is also home to an Asian American cultural center, established in 2005. With a $1.3 million construction budget, the 6,800-square-foot center is one of the largest of its kind in the Midwest.[21] Students, faculty, and staff advocated for these academic and student affairs units beginning in the 1970s, with renewed activism in the 1990s, challenging the university rationale that Asian Americans were not minorities.

UIUC provides an important Midwestern site to examine, one where a Black-White model is prevalent. Much research on higher education policies and Asian American college students has focused on California; however, two million Asian Americans live in the Midwest, and from 2000 to 2010 Asian Americans grew by 48 percent in the region. In particular, the state of Illinois is a prime site, as it is home to the largest number of Asian Americans in the region and the sixth-largest concentration in the country.[22] Asian American studies and student support services have grown on Midwestern campuses since the early 1990s. UIUC, as a public flagship, land-grant, and predominantly White university, provides a significant case study for Asian American student movements in the region from the 1970s through the 1990s and reveals Midwestern experiences of identity and community building. This research strives to recognize the Midwest as a "typical and authentic site of Asian America."[23]

Coming together to form pan–Asian American organizations, Asian American students at UIUC argued that their cultural and racial needs were not being met on campus; however, they could not do so through a traditional minority paradigm argument, as they were not underrepresented. Instead, they advocated for programs, faculty and staff positions, and academic courses, using discourses and strategies that argued that Asian Americans were a minority even though they were overrepresented. One of their activist conferences was titled "Unseen Unheard," referring to their invisibility as the campus's unseen and unheard minority. They challenged policies and pushed the boundaries of minority status that were solely measured by underrepresentation and a focus on African Americans and were informed by the model minority myth, shattering their silence from university discussions of minority students.

The Study Outline

This book begins with an Asian American higher education historiography that reveals how anti-Asian racism affected Asian American students, regardless of their socioeconomic status and academic abilities. It documents how Asian and Asian American students formed campus organizations and articulated their critique against racism they experienced. It also reviews how higher education policies, particularly affirmative action, shifted in the 1970s to remove Asian Americans from minority programs due to parity measures.

Chapter 2 provides a historical backdrop of Asian American students at the University of Illinois at Urbana-Champaign, starting with the university's first minority services. It begins with the late 1960s, examining the campus's Special Educational Opportunities Program (SEOP), also known as Project 500, which was established in 1968 to recruit disadvantaged (especially Black) students to campus. While the primary focus of SEOP was on African American students, administrators began paying more attention to Latinx students' needs in the 1970s due to student activism. The presence of Asian American (or Oriental, as they were called then) students in the program was minimal. Japanese American and Chinese American students from Chicago established the first pan–Asian American student organization, the Asian American Alliance, at UIUC in 1971. Their history reveals the voices of Asian American students who articulated their racial experiences on campus, challenged their invisibility, advocated for academic courses in Asian American studies, and protested the Vietnam War.

Following chronologically, chapter 3 moves into the 1980s, documenting the rise of a new Asian American student population at UIUC. This new cohort of Asian American students (whose parents had immigrated to the United States after 1965) began to coalesce, and this synergy created new opportunities to work together and define a shared Asian American identity despite challenges in doing so given the growing diversity of the population. New Asian American organizations came together to address the racial hostility that was rampant on college campuses at the time, and Asian American students began to critique the model minority myth and their exclusion from minority programs at UIUC.

Chapter 4 documents mid-1990s student activism at UIUC, which flourished for students of color, widening racial discourse beyond a Black-White racial lens. Latinx students were vocal in pushing for their programs and mobilized a multi-racial coalition to stage a sit-in of the administration building in 1992, a pivotal event that would have repercussions on administrative responses to other activists. In addition, the early 1990s saw an emerging movement by Native American students for visibility and for the elimination of the racist school mascot Chief Illiniwek. After 1992, Asian American students began to pressure administrators to create culturally and racially relevant academic and student services resources, primarily an Asian American studies program and an Asian American cultural center. Their forms of activism emerged within a larger context of campus protest and included behind-the-scenes actions such as crafting petitions, proposals, activist programs, and legal strategies to compel the university to recognize their minority experience. It was a time when Asian American student leaders navigated their own routes of activism distinct from the confrontational sit-ins of the time to gain resources.

Chapter 5 discusses the ways this history reveals how students came together in a pan–Asian American movement to challenge minority discourses that led to the creation of an academic program in Asian American studies in 1997 and an Asian American cultural center in 2005. It examines the ways diverse Asian American student leaders united to articulate their shared racial experiences and how they engaged in specific activist strategies within a larger Midwestern context. Ultimately, this study rejects higher education's narrow goal of statistical parity as the sole measure in assessing minority student experiences and brings Asian American voices back into minority student discussions.

Asian American students at UIUC challenged simplistic measures of adjustment and success and pushed the racial and minority discourse beyond the model minority myth, statistical underrepresentation, and a Black-White racial paradigm. In doing so, they testified that racial and cultural differences affected their experiences, despite their high rates of academic achievement and socioeconomic status, revealing a more complex reality of racism on college campuses. By listening to these histories and voices, one can ultimately see and hear Asian American students.

1

The Historiography of Asian American College Students

Historians of higher education have documented how colleges in the United States emerged as selective institutions, starting with colonial colleges that were not a viable option for the majority of early settlers due to familial needs for labor.[1] The social origins of the college in the United States were such that only a small minority, namely White males, could attend. In particular, access to college was not readily afforded to racialized non-White students—African Americans, Latinxs, Native Americans, or Asian Americans. As James D. Anderson notes, "Racism was imbedded in the nation's foundations, affecting its major institutions, including the institutions of higher education."[2]

The historiography of Asian Americans in higher education is relatively sparse, as outlined by Eileen Tamura.[3] Of the historical work that has been done, it is clear that racial inequity was embedded in Asian American college students' lives. In reviewing higher education historiography, Michael Hevel and Heidi Jaeckle outline three key moments of historical research on Asian and Asian American students: pre-World War II era Asian students from China, Japan, and the Philippines who attended colleges in the United States; World War II era Japanese American college students who resettled outside of internment camps; and 1960s era Asian American college student activists who protested for ethnic studies and against the Vietnam War.[4] This chapter will review and expand on this historiography, in particular adding an analysis of higher education affirmative action policies in the 1970s–1980s, when some campuses began to deny Asian Americans minority services based on their overrepresentation. This historiography sets an important foundation and context for Asian American student activism at the University of Illinois.

Asian Students in U.S. Colleges

Immigration from China, Japan, Korea, India, and the Philippines to the United States rose in the mid-nineteenth to early twentieth centuries, meeting labor demands in sugar cane fields in Hawaii and in gold mines and on railroads in the American West. Missionaries also convinced Asian students to attend American colleges and universities, with messages of social reform, education, and democratic values.[5] While Asian laborers and Asian students came to the United States under vastly different circumstances, they were both subject to anti-Asian sentiment and racism.

Asian student immigration to the United States coincided with a rise of anti-Asian legislation. White workers rallied against Chinese labor, subjecting Chinese workers to penalties such as the 1850 Foreign Miners Tax that limited their ability to earn a fair income. In 1913, California Alien Land Laws barred Japanese and other Asian farmers from owning land. Nativist and racist ideologies fueled anti-Asian imagery; Ronald Takaki notes how the Chinese were described with "slanted eyes, a pigtail, dark skin, and thick lips." Furthermore, "like Blacks, the Chinese were described as heathen, morally inferior, savage, childlike, and lustful."[6] Anti-Asian violence grew increasingly common in the 1880s in the American West.

Legislation racialized Asians as foreign and unassimilable. The Supreme Court ruled in *Ozawa v. United States* (1922) and *United States v. Bhagat Singh Thind* (1923) that, respectively, East and South Asians were not eligible for naturalization or citizenship rights. Ultimately, legislation ended Asian immigration through the 1882 Chinese Exclusion Act, the 1907–1908 Gentlemen's Agreement, the 1917 Immigration Act that created an Asiatic Barred Zone, and the 1934 Tydings-McDuffie Act that set quotas on Filipino immigration.[7]

During this time, a small number of Asians were allowed entry to the United States as foreign students, an elite category exempt from immigration restrictions that targeted laborers. The first Asian students to enter U.S. colleges were from China. Luping Bu describes how Yu Wing came to the United States in 1847 with missionary support, earning his degree from Yale in 1854. He then persuaded the Chinese government to send 120 Chinese boys to study in the United States in 1870. Around this same time, the first Japanese students educated in the United States graduated from Amherst.[8] In 1903, the Pensionado Act provided scholarships to Filipino students studying in U.S. colleges to prepare them for future government jobs in the Philippines; the Philippine government sponsored about 200 students from 1903 to 1907.[9]

Asian college students found social support through internationally minded campus Cosmopolitan Clubs in the early twentieth century, which had a close affiliation with the Young Men's Christian Association (YMCA). Asian students created their own chapters of the Chinese Students' Christian Association (CSCA), Japanese Students' Christian Association (JSCA), and the Filipino Students' Christian Movement (FSCM). As Stephanie Hinnershitz documents, these Christian organizations created a space for Asian international students to come together and discuss their shared panethnic racialized experiences with discrimination on and off campus in housing, dining, and student club membership.[10] These organizations also grew their U.S.-born Asian American membership through the 1920s and 1930s. This second generation also voiced their frustrations with racism, such as documented in the national Survey of Race Relations led by University of Chicago sociologist Robert Ezra Park.[11]

Chinese, Japanese, and Filipino students experienced similar conditions of discrimination on and off campus. At a time of heightened anti-Asian sentiment and racism, their advantaged class status (relative to Asian labor) did not shield them from racism. Weili Ye notes, "Being the Other to the laborers in terms of class and modernity, the students nonetheless found themselves inseparable from the lower-class immigrants around the issue of race. And race mattered in America."[12] Thus, despite their socioeconomic status and educational attainment, Asian students were still racialized as non-White, foreign, and inferior and were subjugated as such.

In response to these experiences, Asian students created organizations to share resources, build community, and advocate for their needs. Asian American students in organizations like the CSCA and JSCA discussed issues of racism and discrimination that affected Asians and Asian Americans in the late 1920s, and they wrote about their experiences in student bulletins and newspapers and organized student conferences, arguing for equality. In one instance, Chinese, Japanese, and Filipino students worked together to propose a new curriculum in 1927 to add more Asian history and language courses in California universities.[13] This type of activism—pan-Asian community building, critique of racial discrimination, and demand for curricular inclusion—would be embraced by later generations in the 1960s through the 1990s.

Asian International Students at Illinois

During this time period, Asian students chose to attend the University of Illinois at Urbana-Champaign (UIUC). University president Edmund James played an important role in recruiting Chinese students to campus, inviting Chinese diplomat Wu Tingfang to give the commencement speech in 1909. Eighteen Chinese students came to Illinois from 1909 to 1911, and the Urbana

FIG. 1.1 UIUC Chinese Students' Club, an early Asian international student organization, from the 1919 *Illio*. (Photo courtesy of Illini Media/*Illio*.)

campus hosted the national conference of the Chinese Students Alliance in 1913.[14] During James's presidency (1904–1920), Chinese students comprised the largest international student population on campus, which also included students from Japan, Brazil, the Philippines, and India. James was also the first university president to fund a position for an advisor for foreign students. By 1920, UIUC had 300 Chinese and 150 Japanese students, more foreign students than any other state university in the United States.[15] UIUC also welcomed Filipino pensionado students, one of fifty universities that had significant Filipino student populations in the early twentieth century. From 1906 to 1907, there were thirteen Filipino students at UIUC, the highest single number of Filipino students in the United States.[16]

What was life like for these Asian students on campus? University records show a history of Asian student clubs at UIUC, including the Chinese Students' Club (with its roots as early as 1911) and the Philippine Illini (1919), although a Japanese Student Association did not form until 1976. In addition, campus yearbooks showcase international performances put on by these students[17] (see figs. 1.1, 1.2, and 1.3).

At the same time, anti-Asian racism persisted on and off campus. Carol Huang notes that Chinese students in the early twentieth century tended to cluster in housing near campus, some of which was owned by the university. Chinese alumni recounted their experience with racial hostility in the student union and from other students. And as late as 1945, over 92 percent of landowners in Urbana-Champaign would not rent to Chinese students.[18]

FIG. 1.2 A Korean student performing at the UIUC International Fair, from the 1963 *Illio*. (Photo courtesy of Illini Media/*Illio*.)

FIG. 1.3 Filipino students performing at the UIUC International Fair, from the 1966 *Illio*. (Photo courtesy of Illini Media/*Illio*.)

Japanese American College Students during World War II

The second period of Asian American higher educational historiography moves into the World War II era and focuses on Japanese American students. Gary Okihiro discusses how a U.S.-born second-generation Japanese American Nisei population came of age in the 1930s and 1940s and was Americanized in public schools. At the announcement of Executive Order 9066 in 1942, college administrators on the West Coast were concerned with how to transfer Nisei students to receptive colleges and universities. By May 1946, there were an estimated 2,300 Nisei college students in internment camps.[19]

Those able to attend colleges in the nation's interior were limited in their options. Allan Austin documents how these students were pioneers in Japanese American resettlement. Among this group, 4,000 Nisei enrolled in over 600 colleges and universities through the assistance of the National Japanese American Student Relocation Council, which functioned from 1942 to 1946.[20] The council gathered student data, selected qualified students, secured necessary releases, contacted colleges, placed students, raised scholarship monies (through foundations, churches, and fund-raising drives), and facilitated student adjustment. Despite these efforts, college administrators resisted admitting Japanese American students, and most large, prestigious universities were not open to them. Even for schools who admitted these students, most set quotas to limit their numbers due to concerns about a racial backlash. Okihiro notes that among the first group of 402 Nisei students relocated in the fall of 1942, most attended college in the Rocky Mountains and Midwest, with high numbers at the University of Nebraska, Washington University, the University of Utah, and the University of Denver. On the East Coast, Nisei attended small liberal arts colleges such as Haverford, Smith, and Swarthmore.

Access to prestigious research universities was still hampered for Japanese American students during World War II. Historical records show that while these students experienced incidents of racism on campus, the council emphasized their assimilation and acceptance with the larger White community by focusing on educational success.[21] A national postwar focus on success and assimilation through education remained a major strategy for Japanese Americans to move on after the war.

The historical record is unclear as to the experiences of resettled Japanese American students at UIUC during World War II. Okihiro notes that in 1942, university president Arthur C. Willard was hesitant about admitting relocated Nisei students to campus, expressing concern with how the board of trustees and the public would feel. Carol Huang notes that President Willard outlined specific polices in considering the admission of a Japanese American graduate student in 1944, including seeking clearance by the Provost Marshall General of the U.S. army.[22]

There is some evidence that Nisei students were eventually admitted to Illinois in 1945; however, additional research needs to be conducted to unearth these histories. Given its Midwestern locale and government research concerns, it is likely that these students encountered similar trepidation as at other inland campuses in the nation, accepted with a level of friendliness yet also feeling racially isolated.

Asian American Student Activism in the Sixties

The third area of established Asian American higher education historiography explores the role of Asian American college students in activist movements in the 1960s and 1970s, in particular for ethnic studies and against the Vietnam War, both issues that affected Asian American students at Illinois, as will be discussed in chapter 2.[23] Demographically, a post–World War II Asian American baby boom resulted in 107,366 Asian Americans in colleges and universities by 1970, the majority of whom were Chinese American and Japanese American.[24] As this second-generation Asian American population arose, their shared racialized experiences led groups to come together to discuss Asian American history, identity, and consciousness. In articulating their experiences with racism, many Asian American student groups embraced a new racial self-pride, rejecting an emphasis on assimilation and a model minority ideal, and aligning themselves with other students of color, such as African Americans, and with Asian nations struggling for self-determination.

Asian American college students advocated for self-determination and a relevant university curriculum. Formed in the spring of 1968, the Third World Liberation Front (TWLF) at San Francisco State College was comprised of the Black Student Union, the Latin American Student Organization, the Mexican American Student Coalition, the Pilipino American Collegiate Endeavor, the Asian American Political Alliance, and Intercollegiate Chinese for Social Action. This multiracial coalition led the call for an autonomous ethnic studies program, the hiring and retention of minority faculty, and increased admission of students of color.[25] Ethnic studies rejected a Eurocentric curriculum and instead centered the voices and communities of color. A student strike from 6 November 1968 to 27 March 1969 (the longest student strike in U.S. history), culminated in arrests and violence but ultimately led to the founding of the first school of ethnic studies in the country. Berkeley saw a similar strike from 19 January 1969 to 19 March 1969. Other campuses followed suit, such as at the City College of New York where activists staged a three-day takeover in March 1971 on the issue of access for Asian American students. These protests led to the establishment of Asian American studies (AAS) courses and programs throughout the country.

Protesting the Vietnam War was another major political issue facing students of color. The unpopular Vietnam War gave rise to an antiwar movement in the 1960s that began in the South and expanded east and west, spreading to liberal Midwestern cities with large universities such as Ann Arbor, Bloomington, Chicago, Columbus, Madison, East Lansing, and Minneapolis.[26] Antiwar teach-ins, marches, and protests of Reserve Officers' Training Corps (ROTC) and recruitment visits from the Central Intelligence Agency (CIA) and Dow Chemical Company took place on college campuses.

Nationally, people of color also began to infuse a racial critique of the war, of the imperialist role of the United States against a Third World country, and on the drafting of African American and Latinx men who lacked the resources to evade the military. Organizations such as the Black Anti-Draft Union and Afro-Americans against the War in Vietnam formed in the mid-1960s. In the summer and fall of 1970, Chicano activists protested the high proportion of Hispanic casualties among soldiers and a discriminatory draft. In an April 1967 march in New York, a group of Native American protestors held a sign reading, "Americans—Do not do to the Vietnamese what you did to us."[27] Asian Americans were also involved in the antiwar movement, forming organizations such as the Bay Area Asians Coalition against the War in 1972, which had sister groups in Los Angeles, New York, and Sacramento.

The connection of the Vietnam War with anti-Asian racism writ large was something new to the antiwar movement. The war united Asian Americans because of shared experiences of being called a "gook," a racial slur used against Asian nations during times of war. William Wei writes, "'Gookism' made no distinction between the Vietnamese, Laotians, and Cambodians (among other Asians) encountered overseas and Asian Americans at home just as no distinctions had been made between Japanese and Japanese Americans during World War II. The term was even used to refer to Asian Americans serving in the US military."[28] The slaughter of Asian bodies, shown on nightly television reports, also conveyed the message that Asian lives were disposable. By aligning themselves with the Vietnamese in an anti-imperialist struggle for self-determination, Asian American students infused the antiwar movement with a new lens of transnational Asian identity.

Access Widens: The Civil Rights Movement and Affirmative Action

Asian American higher educational historiography would be remiss if it did not include the historical evolution of minority policies and affirmative action. The racialization of minority groups steadily changed to exclude Asian Americans based on statistical parity, the model minority myth, and a Black-White racial paradigm. Importantly, Asian American student and community members contested this shifting removal of Asian Americans from minority student considerations at various historical moments.

Higher education began to widen for racialized groups due to the civil rights movement. The 1954 landmark *Brown v. Board of Education* case, which banned racial segregation in education, struck down the concept of separate but equal set forth by *Plessy v. Ferguson* in 1896. The *Brown* ruling was tested in higher education in 1956 in the case of *Florida ex rel. Hawkins v. Board of Control*, as African American students sought admission to the University of Florida Law School. Striking down the segregated law school system in the state, the Supreme Court ruled that state universities must not discriminate by race, extending *Brown* to higher education.[29]

As a result of these policy changes, racial minority college student enrollments began to grow. From 1954 to 1969, enrollment at private Black colleges increased from 25,569 to 48,541; enrollment of Black students at predominantly White colleges in the South also increased by a factor of four between 1947 and 1964.[30] Black undergraduate enrollment continued to rise through the 1970s (with smaller increases at the graduate level). The 1960s and 1970s were also a watershed for Latinx and Native American college students.

Affirmative action policies in higher education employment and admissions became important tools in diversifying campuses across the nation. President Lyndon Johnson's proposed Civil Rights Act included various titles that would desegregate public schools and public places; prohibit discrimination based on race, color, or national origin in federally funded programs (Title VI); and end discrimination based on race, national origin, sex, or religion in employment (Title VII). Starting in 1966, the Equal Employment Opportunity Commission (EEOC) required employers with over 100 employees to report their employees' race and gender. Minorities included "Negro, Oriental, American Indian, and Spanish Americans."[31]

Title VI of the 1964 Civil Rights Act was an important mechanism to address racial discrimination by denying federal funding to institutions that discriminated based on race. In addition, the act ordered all colleges and universities to report racial and ethnic data of students, which provided consistent racial data for the first time.[32] Title VII prohibited employment discrimination on the basis of race, color, religion, gender, or national origin. Universities began to actively recruit African American students and employees as a result. Administrators felt that past discrimination had excluded minorities, and they were taking affirmative action to compensate.[33]

However, affirmative action as a program remained unclear; employers were encouraged to hire minorities, a process that considered race. In 1970, secretary of labor George Schultz signed Order No. 4, which expanded affirmative action plans to businesses with a $50,000 federal contract and over fifty employees, with hiring goals based on the minority workforce. Terry Anderson writes of Order No. 4's significance, "It directly linked the ratio of minorities in a locale with those working on contracted employment, which subsequently established proportional hiring as a way to prove compliance with affirmative action. It protected four minority groups who could receive affirmative action remedies: 'Negro, Oriental, American Indian, and Spanish Surnamed Americans.'"[34]

This shift from equal opportunity to equality of results with proportional hiring as a goal is one irony of affirmative action, as John Skrentny points out. Originally, color-blind policies were the focus of the 1964 Civil Rights Act, and yet racial classifications overcame this taboo. Race-conscious hiring was thought to be a way to address the crisis of urban unrest. By 1967–1968, business elites were also supporting racial hiring as a way to prevent violence.[35] Thus, the concept of parity or proportionate representation became one measure of affirmative action's progress. Yet this measure also raised issues for groups that were exceeding their parity. For instance, Jewish organizations spoke out against affirmative action, remembering the quotas that kept Jewish students and faculty out of elite colleges in the 1920s and 1930s.[36] Concerns over of overrepresentation would also plague Asian American students at the University of California.

Affirmative Action Efforts at the University of California in the 1960s

The evolution of minority policies at the University of California (UC) reveals how administrators shifted their definitions of minority student needs. Chartered in 1868 as a land-grant university, UC served as a model for public institutions of higher education. During the 1960s and 1970s, public institutions such as UC also focused on affirmative action policies to maintain access. Wanting to increase minority enrollment in the 1960s (especially after adopting the SAT in freshman admissions in 1968), UC administrators established Educational Opportunity Programs (EOPs)—initiated in 1964 and implemented on all campuses by 1968—that sought to increase enrollment and retention rates of low-income and minority students through community outreach, junior high school recruitment, and tutoring for enrolled college students.[37] EOPs targeted disadvantaged students primarily from racial minority backgrounds—which included Asian Americans.

The 1978 *Regents of the University of California v. Bakke* case brought issues of quotas in university admissions to the forefront of the affirmative action debate. Allan Bakke, a White male rejected from the medical school at the University of California, Davis, claimed that his denial was due to affirmative action admissions that set aside admissions slots for minority candidates. The high court struck down the use of such set-aside quotas, though it still affirmed the flexible use of race as one factor in admissions. Accordingly, in 1979, UC president David Saxton instructed UC chancellors that they could consider race and ethnicity in regular as well as special action admissions.

During this time, Asian Americans were included among minority groups targeted by affirmative action programs at UC Davis and UC Berkeley. However, this inclusion would end by the mid-1980s, due to rationales based on the statistical overrepresentation of Asian Americans and ideologies of them as a model minority. The University of California began to remove Asian Americans from minority considerations, and Asian American students and community organizations contested these changes, arguing that they still had minority experiences.[38]

Asian Americans and Affirmative Action

With the rising statistical representation of Asian Americans at the University of California, the late 1970s was a time of changing university policies. For instance, whereas in 1970 the UC Berkeley law school (Boalt Hall) had established an Asian special admissions program due to Asian American student activism, just five years later the Asian American Law Students Association was defending it. The law faculty had submitted a proposal to eliminate the school's special admissions program for Asian Americans "on the grounds that Asians have 'made it' in American society and that sufficient numbers of Asians were being admitted through the regular process."[39]

The students submitted an eighty-three-page report in protest. They challenged the model minority image and pointed to the needs of the Asian community that still struggled with poverty and faced pressing issues with immigration law, housing, labor, and limited English proficiency. Asian Americans were also underrepresented among the nation's and Bay Area's attorneys, and Asian communities needed bilingual and bicultural attorneys to serve them. Despite these efforts, Boalt Hall faculty members adopted a policy in 1975 that eliminated Japanese Americans from special admissions and limited Chinese, Korean, and Filipino applicants to less than 3 percent of special admits of each year's entering class.[40]

The issues raised at Boalt Hall—those of Asian American success in regular admissions (hence no longer needing special admissions consideration) and Asian American protest against a simplistic model minority rationale—reemerged in fuller detail during the *Bakke* case. For instance, in preparation for deliberation of the Supreme Court case, sixty-one amicus briefs were filed. One of those briefs was from the Asian American Bar Association (AABA) of the Greater Bay Area in support of the University of California, Davis.[41] Citing instances of historical and persistent discrimination, the amicus brief argued for the constitutionality of race-conscious admissions policies at UC Davis, which should include Asian Americans, a population in dire need of attorneys able to address their legal and social needs.

The Justice Department filed its own amicus brief in the *Bakke* case, and solicitor general Wade McCree made oral arguments before the court, representing the government's position in support of the University of California's race-conscious admissions policies. While the *Bakke* case was not specifically about Asian American admissions, the government questioned the inclusion of Asian Americans in minority programs because Asian Americans were excelling in the regular admission process. The government compared Asian Americans with other minority groups: Asian Americans (Japanese, Chinese, and Filipinos) were doing quite well, statistically speaking. Asian medical school entrance exam scores and grade point averages were also higher than those of their White peers. Thus, it remained unclear why Asians were still included in the special admission programs at UC Davis medical school.[42]

The Asian and Pacific American Federal Employee Council (APAFEC) challenged these interpretations of Asian American parity and argued that the government had used misleading statistics. For instance, the fact that more Asians had completed college than Whites did not translate into income parity, Asian unemployment was understated due to the undercounting of limited-English-proficient unemployed persons, and while there was a high percentage of Asians in professional, managerial, and administrative positions, few were in policymaking positions. The government's amicus brief also revealed little insight into Asian American subgroups of Koreans, Asian Indians, Samoans, Vietnamese, Hawaiians, Pakistanis, and Cambodians. The APAFEC foreshadowed: "By singling out Asians as not needing one minority program, the Government opens the possibility that Asian/Pacific American participation in any or all minority programs could be eliminated."[43] This elimination would have made it extremely difficult to meet the continuing needs for this community.

While the Supreme Court did not decide on the status of Asian special admissions at Davis, deliberations during the *Bakke* case signaled a shift in the understanding of Asian Americans' unquestioned inclusion in affirmative action admissions, with the introduction of the idea that Asian Americans had outgrown the need for affirmative action protections due to their statistical representation. Asian American groups protested this presumption and the ideological underpinnings of the model minority that collapsed the experiences of a diverse community.

Asian American De-Minoritization and the Admissions Controversy

Colleges and universities learned from *Bakke* that quotas were unconstitutional but that race could still be considered as one factor in the admissions process.

The University of California continued to support policies to foster diversity in admissions and outreach. The 1980s, however, witnessed an increasing selectivity in student admissions. For the first time, a large number of eligible students were turned away from UC campuses, primarily UC Berkeley and UCLA, which were rejecting approximately two out of every three eligible applicants.[44]

Asian American numbers at Berkeley had been on the rise since the 1970s. Given the constraints in admissions slots, administrators at Berkeley decided that their goal was "general parity between the racial and ethnic composition of the undergraduate enrollment and that of the state population in general."[45] Increasingly, administrators equated underrepresentation with disadvantage. Based on this concept of parity, John Douglass notes, "In 1984, the admissions office stopped considering Asian Americans eligible for special consideration outside of academic achievement because, in short, their numbers at Berkeley far exceeded their proportional share of the available undergraduate pie. They had become over-represented, and hence no longer a 'disadvantaged' group."[46] Prior to 1984, Berkeley policies included Asian Americans as an underrepresented group, which bestowed on them special admissions considerations and minority-oriented outreach and support programs. In redefining who was underrepresented, most Asian American groups were no longer considered in Educational Opportunity Programs (EOP) and special consideration admissions.[47] Hence, they were de-minoritized.

As a result of the 1984 policy change at Berkeley, the admission rates of Asian American students began to decline. With the redefinition of Asian Americans as no longer a disadvantaged group, Asian American applicants were no longer protected from redirection to other UC campuses through a central admissions system as other EOP (Black, Hispanic, and Native American) applicants. Originally, EOP programs had protected eligible applicants based on their disadvantaged socioeconomic status; however, they shifted their foci to race-based programs that no longer included Asian Americans. The change disproportionately affected Asian American EOP students: in 1983, there were 62 White and 248 Asian American EOP students; one year later there were 55 White and 136 Asian American EOP students; in 1985 there were 24 White and 83 Asian American EOP students.[48]

A decline in Asian American admissions occurred at other institutions across the nation. Between 1983 and 1986, despite the growing Asian American college applicant pool, figures revealed that declining percentages of Asian American students were being admitted to prestigious universities. In response, Asian American professors, students, and activists levied charges that these universities were setting quotas on the number of admitted Asian American students. Major controversies and investigations ensued at Brown, Harvard, Stanford, Princeton, UCLA, and Berkeley. The charges centered around two basic issues: the admission rate for Asian Americans was lower than that for

Whites, and Asian American enrollments had not risen in proportion to their sharp increases in the applicant pool. A task force at Berkeley also charged that Berkeley administrators had instituted policy changes such as weighting of supplemental criteria that hurt Asian Americans.[49]

Administrators responded to allegations of quotas by using statistics—in short, Asian Americans were overrepresented at Berkeley. In a 12 December 1986 Associated Press story, UC president David P. Gardner stated, "Asian students have been so successful they have become over-represented at the university."[50] Changes in admission policy were needed because Asians comprised more than 20 percent of the undergraduate enrollment at UC campuses but made up only 6 percent of the state's population. This overrepresentation and racial imbalance were of concern to Gardner, who stated that they created new racial tensions and signaled for the reconsideration of policies that called for enrollment patterns that accurately reflected the state population.[51]

Within a few decades, Asian Americans were no longer categorically presumed to be minorities at the University of California because of their overrepresentation (and policies that focused on a Black-White racial lens), which was bolstered by an ideological model minority myth. No longer protected by minority programs, they were facing ceilings on their admissions. As Dana Takagi articulates, the rhetorical shift from quotas against Asian Americans (to protect White students) pivoted to an anti–affirmative action argument that claimed affirmative action protected less-qualified African American and Latinx applicants to the detriment of the hardworking model minority Asians.[52]

The focus on Asian Americans as model minorities and victims of affirmative action persists today, as outlined in the introduction. This simplistic narrative conveys that Asian Americans have achieved success, thus proving that race is no longer a barrier to educational advancement. This message also equates Asian Americans with Whiteness and proclaims that Asian Americans do as well as, even better than, Whites, enjoying all the privileges as such. This narrative has effectively removed them from minority programs that have prioritized underrepresentation for African Americans and Latinx communities. While underrepresentation is an important measure to assess equity, an overrepresentation argument to effectively de-minoritize Asian American students and imply their honorary Whiteness is highly problematic.

Reviewing the educational historiography reveals that Asian and Asian American students have always experienced racial barriers as non-White people in the United States. Even the privileges of class status, adherence to Christian beliefs, and attempts to assimilate could not shield early Asian students or the second generation of Asian Americans from racial intolerance on college campuses. Asian American students and community members protested the ways that university policies questioned their minority status, arguing that Asian Americans were still underrepresented in the pipeline and still experienced racial barriers. In addition, the admissions controversy in the 1980s questioned if universities used strategies that limited the admission of Asian American students, to the benefit of White students.

Thus, despite Asian American success in higher education, fallacious model minority stereotypes overlook educational needs and the realities of racial backlash that obstruct Asian American student integration on campuses. The history of Asian American college students reveals the important ways these activists challenged their invisibility, spoke out against racism, and advocated for Asian American resources. Their activism led to the creation of significant resources for Asian American students on campuses across the country. Such was the case for Asian American students at the University of Illinois.

2

Making Noise in the Background

Asian American Students at Illinois, 1968–1975

Frank Bing and Herman Moy, both Chinese Americans from Chicago, graduated from the University of Illinois at Urbana-Champaign (UIUC) in 1971 with degrees in engineering. Growing up in the city, Bing played basketball with Chinese American and Japanese American friends and was part of an Asian American social scene that included school, sports, drum and bugle corps, and church life. Similarly, Moy had some Chinese American friends from his church in Chinatown. When they arrived at UIUC they could not find an equivalent social space, due to the small numbers of Asian American students there. So they began to socialize with international Asian students. Moy recalled playing basketball and baseball and practicing kung fu with overseas Chinese graduate students, as well as being the disc jockey for their parties. It would not be until their senior year when Chinese American and Japanese American students came together to form the first Asian American student organization at UIUC, the Asian American Alliance. The Alliance filled an important void. Bing recalled, "That was what was missing when we went to school because there was nothing like that. It was nice having a bunch of second-generation kids to hang out with again like back home."[1]

Second-Generation Asian Americans in Chicago

Bing and Moy were part of a growing second-generation (U.S.-born) Asian American student community in the Midwest. While much of Asian American history examines Asian labor immigration during the gold rush on the West Coast and on sugar plantations in Hawaii,[2] there was a substantial secondary migration of Chinese and Japanese settlers to Chicago before 1965 legislation liberalized immigration from Asia. These settlers, along with Chinese, Japanese, and Filipino international students attending college in Chicago, laid down roots in the Windy City, giving rise to a second generation of Asian Americans who would attend colleges throughout the state, such as the University of Illinois.[3]

Due to increasing anti-Chinese sentiment on the West Coast during the late 1870s (outlined in chapter 1), Chinese immigrants began looking for alternative employment opportunities in Chicago, New York City, and Boston. The 1893 Chicago Columbian Exposition attracted a number of Chinese laborers to work in laundries and restaurants, giving rise to the city's first Chinatown in the 1880s. By 1900 there were 1,209 Chinese in Chicago, and the community continued to grow in the 1920s and 1930s.[4]

Chicago's Chinatown provided an important hub for Chinese American life in the Midwest, serving as a center for Chinese business supplies and information to surrounding cities such as Minneapolis, Duluth, Indianapolis, Milwaukee, and St. Louis.[5] The majority of the Chicago Chinese American community worked in laundries or restaurants. Just as on the West Coast, the laundry business was a viable option, given low requisite start-up capital, demand for services, and lack of competition with European immigrants. The first Chinese laundry in Chicago opened in 1870. In 1928 there were 794 Chinese laundries in the city, though this number declined by the 1960s.[6] Chinatown continued to grow during the twentieth century. Spurred by international events such as the communist takeover of China in 1949, a new wave of immigration doubled the Chinese population in Chicago from 3,000 to 6,000. Another wave of immigration drew ethnic Chinese from Southeast Asia during the Vietnam War, fueling Chicago's Chinese population to 12,000 by 1970.[7] A sizeable U.S.-born Chinese American population also came of age in Chicago after World War II who "helped transform the Chinese American community through active participation in mainstream politics and the civil rights movement."[8]

Before World War II, there was also a small Japanese community in Chicago. Like the Chinese, the earliest Japanese resettlers came to work during the 1893 Columbian Exposition to build the Japanese exhibit. In 1927 there were 300 Japanese nationals in Chicago, working in businesses and restaurants.

However, it would not be until the relocation of Japanese Americans from World War II internment camps that the Japanese American community would grow in Chicago. In 1940 there were 390 Japanese recorded in Chicago; this number had grown to 10,829 by 1950. Of the 110,000 Japanese Americans interned, nearly 30,000 moved to Chicago in the 1940s (though almost half returned to the West Coast).[9] Just as it stood as a safer environment for Chinese resettlers, Chicago was a more racially tolerant place for Japanese Americans after the war and also offered plentiful jobs in domestic service, factories, offices, and small businesses. At the same time, workplace and housing discrimination were not uncommon. Japanese Americans congregated on the Near North and South Sides of the city, with suburban landlords unwilling to rent apartments to them.[10]

The University of Illinois and Minority Students in the 1960s

While there had been a presence of foreign students at UIUC since the early 1900s, the university struggled with providing access to minority students. The state of Illinois, while admitted to the Union as a free state in 1818, had a Southern culture. Its state constitution allowed current slaves to remain indentured, and its numerous Black Codes enacted between the early 1820s and through the passage of the Fifteenth Amendment in 1870 required those termed "Negros" or "mulattos" to produce a certificate of freedom and pay a bond to prove they would not be a charge to the state. Indictments and fines penalized anyone harboring a Negro, bringing a slave to the state for emancipation, or allowing Negroes to assemble. As Frank Cicero notes, by the late 1830s African Americans were free in Illinois but had no real legal rights.[11]

The few African American students who attended predominantly White flagship universities in the Midwest such as UIUC faced racism by anxious and resentful White students. Richard Breaux documents incidents of blackface, minstrel campus shows, and racial caricatures in yearbooks on these campuses from 1882 to 1937. At UIUC, students established honorary Ku Klux Klan organizations in 1915–1916. During this time period, membership rolls of the Invisible Empire grew to over 95,000 in Illinois, with roots in Champaign and nearby cities such as Pekin.[12]

UIUC's 1867 charter did not limit enrollment by race, and the university first admitted women in 1870; however, it did not admit its first African American student until 1887, and the first African American student to graduate would not do so until 1900. Racial segregation was the norm for the university and its surrounding Urbana-Champaign community until after World War II. Campus residence halls were not open to Black students until 1945, and Black students could not eat in university dining halls until the Illini student union opened in 1942.[13] Black enrollment grew slowly and did not exceed 1 percent of the student body through the 1940s.[14] Racial segregation in restaurants and theaters was common in Urbana-Champaign until the mid-1960s. These racist policies and practices did not begin to change until student activists protested campus-approved minstrel shows and segregated facilities in the 1950s.

Statistics of the three largest racial minority groups at UIUC (African American, Latinx, and Asian American) show that the numbers of students of color were miniscule in the 1960s and 1970s, with emerging growth in the 1980s and 1990s. The self-reported racial statistics also show that, compared to the state population of Illinois, there have been a few notable patterns over time (see table 2.1). The first is that, as on many campuses across the country, African American and Hispanic students (as described then) have always been under-represented at UIUC compared to their numbers in the state. Second, also as on many campuses across the country, Asian American students (this counts domestic students, not foreign) have always been overrepresented at UIUC compared to their state numbers. Thus, unlike at the University of California, as discussed in chapter 1, Asian Americans were not de-minoritized at Illinois; rather, they were never initially minoritized, or defined as minorities. Third, African Americans numerically composed the largest minority population at UIUC until the mid-1980s, when Asian American numbers surpassed them.

Thus, even though African American students warranted significant attention given their underrepresentation at UIUC, other groups such as Latinxs and Asian Americans were also marginalized on campus, composing smaller numbers of undergraduate enrollment in the 1960s and 1970s. These students advocated for curricula and support services that were overlooked by the university's focus on African American students. This policy focus is evident in the university's first coordinated effort to recruit minority students, the Special Educational Opportunities Program (SEOP).

The Special Educational Opportunities Program at the University of Illinois

UIUC began to recruit racial minority students in the 1960s. Students on the campus organized chapters of the Congress on Racial Equality (CORE) in 1966, the same year as a three-day race riot in Chicago. In 1967 the Black Students Association (BSA) formed to push the UIUC administration to increase the number of Black students on campus to reflect state population statistics and to improve the campus's racial climate.[15] The BSA also demanded more Black professors, a Black cultural center, and equal wages for all university staff.

The 4 April 1968 assassination of Martin Luther King Jr. energized Black power sentiment at Illinois and intensified the need for more proactive affirmative action programs. UIUC policies had begun to address racial inequities as early as 1963, but it was not until King's assassination that efforts intensified,

Table 2.1
Percentage of African American, Hispanic, and Asian Americans in the state of Illinois, compared to their percentage in UIUC undergraduate student enrollment

	African American		Hispanic or Latina/o		Asian American	
Year	Illinois	UIUC	Illinois	UIUC	Illinois	UIUC
1967	10.0%[a]	1.0%	. . .	0.1%	0.2%[a]	0.6%
1970	13.0%	3.8%	3.2%[b]	0.5%	0.42%	1.3%
1980	15.0%	3.9%	5.5%[c]	1.4%	1.5%	3.1%
1990	14.8%	7.1%	7.7%	4.3%	2.5%	9.7%
2000	15.1%	7.0%	12.3%	5.7%	3.4%	13.2%

SOURCE: Campbell Gibson and Kay Jung, "Historical Census Statistics on Population Totals by Race 1790 to 1990 and by Hispanic Origin, 1970 to 1990 for the United States, Regions, Divisions, and States," U.S. Census Bureau, September 2002, Working Paper Series No. 56, accessed 3 March 2009, http://www.census.gov/population/www/documentation/twps0056/twps0056.html#desc.; University of Illinois at Urbana-Champaign Office of Equal Opportunity and Access, "Undergraduate Enrollment by Racial/Ethnic Category, University of Illinois at Urbana-Champaign, Fall 1967 to Fall 2008," accessed 15 October 2009, http://oeoa.illinois.edu/Undergraduate%20Enrollment%20 by%20Race.pdf; U.S. Department of Commerce, "Census of Population: 1960. Advance Reports: General Population Characteristics, Illinois," accessed 25 February 2007, http://www2.census.gov /prod2/decennial/documents/15611114.pdf; U.S. Department of Commerce, "Census of Population: 1970. Characteristics of the Population, Illinois, Section 2," accessed 25 February 2007, http://www2 .census.gov/prod2/decennial/documents/1970a_il2-01.pdf; U.S. Department of Commerce, "Census of Population: 1980, Characteristics of the Population, General Social and Economic Characteristics, Part 15 Illinois," accessed 25 February 2007, http://www2.census.gov/prod2 /decennial/documents/1980a_ilC-01.pdf; U.S. Department of Commerce, "Census of Population: 1990, Social and Economic Characteristics, Illinois," accessed 25 February 2007, http://www.census .gov/prod/cen1990/cp2/cp-2-15-1.pdf; U.S. Department of Commerce, "Illinois 2000, Census 2000 Profile," accessed 25 February 2007, http://www.census.gov/prod/2002pubs/c2kprof00-il.pdf.
NOTE: International students are counted separately.
[a] Taken from the 1960 Illinois census.
[b] "Spanish language" population in the 1970 Illinois census.
[c] "Spanish origin" population in the 1980 Illinois census.

leading to the creation of the Special Educational Opportunities Program (SEOP) in 1968. (The program removed the word "special" from its title in 1971 to become the EOP.)[16] The SEOP's goal was to "recruit more disadvantaged students, especially Blacks, to the campus."[17] With the assistance of BSA, the goal that summer was to recruit 500 students for the program; hence, the program was also known as Project 500.

While Project 500 began with a focus on African American students, the program was open to all racial groups. For instance, a faculty letter from the Office of the President dated 3 February 1969 described the goals of the program as "increasing the number of minority group students" and assisting students "from disadvantaged backgrounds."[18] In addition, admission to the program was based on financial need. Administrators presented the SEOP as a program to serve economically and educationally disadvantaged students writ large, and smaller groups of Latinx, Asian American, and poor White students from inner-city Chicago high schools participated in the program.

However, from the beginning, Black students were the primary population served. An all-university committee met on 17 May 1968 to discuss the admission of disadvantaged students to the Chicago Circle, the medical center, and the Urbana-Champaign campuses and to recommend that "minimum admission goals for disadvantaged students shall be no less than 15 percent at each campus, and of this number at least two-thirds should be Negro."[19] This focus manifested itself in statistics in the 1970s and early 1980s. For instance, a memo listed the estimated racial breakdown of EOP students as of 16 March 1972 as 85 percent Black, 7 percent Spanish-speaking, 5 percent White, and 3 percent "other."[20] In an April 1977 report on minority student programs written by the Office of Academic Affirmative Action, it was noted that since the SEOP's founding, 601 students had earned degrees from the university, of which 90 percent were Black, 6 percent were Latinx, 1 percent were Asian American, and 3 percent were Caucasian.[21] In the fall of 1981, the program served a reported 712 Black, 178 Latinx, 121 Asian, and 28 White students.[22]

SEOP letters and publications also articulated this focus on Black students. In a letter regarding a campus event to honor mothers of Black university students in 1971, SEOP founding director Clarence Shelley wrote, "Although the SEOP has a multi-ethnic population including Puerto-Rican Americans, Mexican Americans, Indian Americans, Asian Americans, and White Americans, the largest minority represented are the Black Americans."[23] In addition, other materials described minorities as those who were underrepresented. An undated SEOP brochure listed admissions eligibility as such: "You are eligible for consideration if you have had limited economic or educational opportunities, and if your cultural heritage is greatly under-represented on this campus. The composition of this group will be primarily Afro-American, Hispanic-American and American Indian."[24]

Thus, even with a focus on socioeconomic disadvantage, UIUC minority programs began with a specific focus on African Americans, and this policy remained true for subsequent minority programs that developed under the university's Office of Minority Student Affairs (OMSA). Recruitment efforts targeted high schools with Black (and later Latinx) populations. If Asian American students happened to attend that targeted high school, they would also hear about minority programs; however, no concerted effort was made to recruit Asian Americans. The fact remained that the highest proportion of students (as well as graduate student counselors and administrators) in SEOP were African American. While the university emphasized that SEOP eligibility was based on socioeconomic disadvantage rather than race, and "that African

Americans would dominate the program only because their economic situation was worse than any other group's," the perception persisted that SEOP was only for Black students.[25] In this way, Joy Ann Williamson notes that the terms "minority," "disadvantaged," and "African American" became conflated, leading to a racialization of programs such as the SEOP at UIUC.

Latinx Students' Needs Emerge

SEOP's focus on African American students marginalized Latinx students, who felt their minority experiences were overlooked. In December 1970, Diann Geronemus of the School of Social Work interviewed Cuban, Mexican, Puerto Rican, and White SEOP students from Chicago, whom she termed to be "minority groups within a minority group program."[26] Most of the students interviewed considered SEOP as primarily for Black students, felt that non-Blacks were overlooked in the program, and observed the predominance of SEOP Black administrators, advisors, and graduate assistants. Geronemus concluded, "It is important to recognize the intra-group differences within the SEOP. The program must serve the varying needs of Black, White, and Latin-American students." In addition, some Latin American students "feel that they are the forgotten students in the program. They want an SEOP dean and advisors representing their own interests and needs, their cultural heritage, their background, and their values. Such a person would be better able to view and understand the problems they face in the university."[27]

Latinx students in the SEOP began to mobilize for greater services and representation in the early 1970s. Luis Esquilin was appointed assistant dean of SEOP and assigned to work with Latinx students during the 1970–1971 and 1971–1972 academic years. On 27 October 1971, Esquilin wrote a memo to Barry Munitz in the Office of University Vice President and Provost. He outlined the challenges facing Latinx students, which included an Anglo-centered curriculum that regarded Latinxs as culturally deficient; a lack of bilingual college admissions or financial aid information; few courses on Puerto Rican or Mexican experiences; low numbers of Latinxs at the undergraduate, graduate, and faculty/staff levels; and poor funding of Latinx student organizations on campus.[28]

When Esquilin announced his resignation for the fall of 1972, the Urban Hispanic Students Organization (UHO) and other students wrote letters of concern to EOP director Shelley and dean of students Hugh Satterlee, articulating their marginalization in the EOP as Latinx students, as well as requesting the right to search for, interview, and select Esquilin's replacement.[29] The members of UHO fully embraced their status as minority students, stating, "We feel that all demands must be met in order for the EO Program to function properly as a program for the aid of minority students; that any refusal on any demand would be in complete contradiction with the original idea of the program."[30]

Other students reflected on the need for this expansion as well. In a 29 September 1972 editorial titled "Hispanics Left Out," editors of the student newspaper the *Daily Illini* declared, "EOP has been successful in bringing many Black students to campus, but has largely ignored the other major racial minority in Illinois—Hispanic students. We believe the EOP program should be expanded to include more Hispanics. . . . Simple justice demands that Illinois' underprivileged Hispanic people be offered the same opportunity for a college education as the state's underprivileged Blacks."[31] Administrators began to acknowledge the different but equally important needs of Latinx students. At a meeting on 9 January 1973, Chancellor Jack Peltason acknowledged Latinx students' complaints with EOP and articulated the need "to deliver more programs related to the Latina/o's and [be] more responsible to all minorities, not just the Black minorities."[32]

Latinx students also expressed a desire for a cultural center. On 23 April 1974, the Urban Hispanic Students Organization, now renamed La Colectiva Latina, submitted a proposal for a Latinx cultural center to the administration that would serve the entire university as a space for intellectual and cultural activity and be a site for a Latinx library, tutorial services (an extension of EOP tutoring), informal counseling and advising, seminars for faculty and students, speakers, and events of the College of Education's bilingual-bicultural program. Such activities would also support curriculum development on Latinx experiences, foster solidarity among students, and enhance recruitment efforts.[33]

UIUC administrators were concerned with political protest in the spring of 1974, given recent Latinx activism at UIUC's sister campus in Chicago. In the spring of 1973, Latinx students expressed their concern over the very low numbers of Puerto Rican students at the Chicago Circle Campus. On 27 September 1973, thirty-nine Latinx students were arrested for occupying an administration building.[34] Such activity propelled administrators to investigate space for a potential Latinx cultural center in Urbana. Dean of Students Satterlee wrote to Chancellor Peltason on 29 April (six days after La Colectiva Latina's proposal was written), informing him that a vacant property on campus on Armory Street was a possible space and would act as a symbol of good faith. Satterlee reminded Peltason of the unrest at Circle Campus and how he had earlier warned, "Don't let that sort of thing happen here." Satterlee also advised, "Now we are at a point where we can make some real steps forward, not just to avert difficulty, but to add some penicillin, not a band-aid."[35] As a result, in September 1974 the *Daily Illini* announced that a Latinx cultural center—La Casa Cultural Latina, located at 510 East Chalmers—was in operation.[36] In its first year, La Casa sponsored lectures, a steel-drum band workshop, bilingual-bicultural workshops, visits by Latinx high school students, receptions, a Latina/o Day, outreach programs, fund-raising for student scholarships, and student publications.[37]

As a result of this student activism, administrators at numerous universities in the state began to acknowledge Latinx concerns in the 1970s. A 1974 report to the Board of Higher Education regarding special support services at select university campuses listed the needs of Latinx students and changing minority student demographics as prime concerns. Programs for minority and disadvantaged students at Circle Campus, Northern Illinois University, UIUC, Illinois State University, and Western Illinois University were highlighted.[38] All of them asserted the need for more Spanish-speaking staff, recruiters, counselors, and efforts to increase Latinx enrollments in the face of a poor economy and state budget. Though university minority programs had started with a focus on African American students, this recognition of Latinx students' needs revealed that a shift had occurred in UIUC's understanding of minority students. Latinx students articulated that they too were minorities, and little by little, they gained inclusion in SEOP advising, in Office of Admissions and Records (OAR) recruitment, and in support from the university, with the creation of La Casa Cultural Latina.

Asian Americans in Illinois

Asian American students had a different struggle on campus, as they were not underrepresented along measures of admission and retention. Asian American students were invisible to administrators, who often mistook them as international students. While the numbers of Asian American undergraduate students at UIUC were miniscule in the early 1970s—averaging about 300 total—a vibrant community emerged outside of institutional spaces and allowed for the expression of Asian American needs. If Latinx students pushed minority definitions from the margins of SEOP and OAR, Asian American students worked from the margins of the margins to articulate an Asian American identity.

UIUC was a predominantly White campus; thus, racial equality and awareness were hard to come by during the 1960s and 1970s, and not only for African American students. Asian American undergraduate student numbers never reached over 1,000 until 1982.[39] While anti-Asian racism was not as institutionalized or legalized as Jim Crow segregation for African Americans, Asian Americans encountered racial ignorance on campus and in the community. The local communities did not have much awareness of Asian or Asian American issues, evidenced by the nearby town of Pekin, whose high school claimed the athletics nickname "Chinks."

The small town of Pekin lies just south of Peoria, less than 100 miles northwest of Urbana-Champaign. The town was surveyed in 1829 and named Pekin after China's city Peking (now Beijing).[40] James Loewen identifies Pekin as a sundown town—a town that kept African Americans and other minorities from living there and had written and unwritten rules keeping African Americans out of the city after sunset.[41] Sundown towns emerged throughout the Midwest after Reconstruction, and residents employed a number of techniques to keep their towns White, including zoning, ordinances, harassment, and violence. Pekin was a center for the Ku Klux Klan in the 1920s. Pekin Community High School began to use the racial slur Chinks as a name for its athletic teams in the 1940s, though the exact origins of the term are unclear. Students represented the Chinks through costumes as part of athletic events, and school publications featured drawings of the mascot dressed in a conical hat, a robe, and with a queue hairstyle.[42]

The Pekin Chinks received national attention when the boys' basketball team won the Illinois state championship in 1964 and 1967; Chinese Americans began to complain about the offensive name in 1970. In particular, the founder of the Organization of Chinese Americans (OCA), K. L. Wang, traveled to Pekin in August and October 1974 to demand the name change, and his efforts included a teach-in with students.[43] Despite these efforts, the name did not change until 1980, to the Pekin "Dragons," and only after considerable protest by students, alumni, and community members.[44]

Ross Harano (BS, finance, 1965) recalled being a student at UIUC in the late 1960s. A third-generation Japanese American from Chicago, Harano had a social network with the few American-born Asians (mostly Chinese and Japanese Americans from Chicago) on campus. Estimating their numbers to have been around 100, he remembered that Asian Americans were viewed as a novelty. While he did not recall any blatant anti-Asian racism on campus, he said, "Most of these folks from southern Illinois had never seen an Asian!"[45]

At the time, the racist terms "Oriental," "Jap," "Gook," and "Chink" were not viewed as derogatory and were commonly used in conversations. Harano recalled feeling shocked when he learned about the Pekin Chinks basketball team during the state basketball tournament held in Urbana as he was walking through campus town: "I was walking down Green Street and there were all these signs in the store windows saying, 'Welcome, Pekin Chinks!' And nobody had a clue! I would walk into a store and say, 'What's with the sign?' They thought I was nuts! So I couldn't organize anything; it was just everybody was oblivious to it."[46]

Asian Americans were invisible at UIUC, and they were never targeted specifically for inclusion in SEOP or other minority programs. A few Asian Americans were part of the SEOP, but their presence was coincidental, as when they attended predominantly Black high schools visited by SEOP recruiters. Clarence Shelley, SEOP director from 1968 to 1972, said of this time period, "Asian American students were almost like a non-entity."[47] They were not identified as a pool of students to recruit.

Anecdotal evidence sheds some light on this situation. Rose Moy (BS, marketing, 1974) was a part of SEOP by chance. Moy had grown up in the Austin area of Chicago and attended Austin High School, which was predominantly Black by the time she graduated in 1970. Her immigrant parents ran a Chinese laundry, where the family lived in back of the storefront, and she was the first person in her family to attend college. Moy graduated in the top 15 percent of her senior high school class but was rejected by UIUC. She had heard about SEOP from a classmate the day before graduation in the lunchroom. Moy recalled, "No one bothered to tell me about any special college admissions programs that were available. But I thought about it and went to see my counselor, whom I probably saw maybe twice my whole lifetime there in high school. And so he gave me some information. I filled out the form. I guess I somehow was accepted, but I know I was originally rejected through the regular U of I admission process."[48]

After reapplying to UIUC through SEOP, Moy gained admission to the College of Business and matriculated in the fall of 1970. Her memory of the program was also that it was predominantly Black. She remembers of her incoming SEOP cohort, "When I arrived on campus and I went to the first orientation, I was really surprised. It was all African American, and they had a few Hispanics. Not too many at that time. It had one other White Polish girl. And I think I was the only Asian, period."[49] In retrospect, she described her admission to SEOP as just luck, of being in a high school where recruiters were targeting African American students and hearing of the program through a friend, not through a counselor or recruiter.

The Asian American Alliance

The rise of a U.S.-born Asian American population after the 1960s facilitated the coalescing of an Asian American student movement on college campuses. For the first time, Asian American students began joining pan-Asian organizations that transcended ethnic lines at schools on the coasts: Berkeley, San Francisco State, Yale, and Columbia. The Midwest was also a site for Asian American student organizations in the early 1970s, such as at Oberlin College and the state universities in Minneapolis, Madison, Ann Arbor, and Urbana-Champaign.[50] A new sense of Asian American identity emerged in these spaces, and students raised new challenges to university administrators' understandings of minority student needs.

With little institutional space, Asian American students came together at UIUC in January 1971 to create the Asian American Alliance, the first pan–Asian American student organization at UIUC. The Alliance articulated the political, social, and cultural concerns of a U.S.-born generation of students who were navigating a campus that had just begun to consider minority issues. While the Alliance only existed for about four years, it provided an important space for Chinese and Japanese American students to discuss identity issues, articulate their educational needs, and engage in the political issues of the time.

Asian American Alliance alumni credit the founding of the organization to Paul Wong and Patricia Hirota (Wong), a then-married couple who had been involved in the Third World Liberation Front strike for ethnic studies at UC Berkeley in 1969. In the fall of 1970, Wong came to UIUC as an assistant professor of sociology and Asian studies. Having been involved in Asian American political movements in California, the couple became aware of the presence of Asian American students on campus from Chicago as well as a few students from Hawaii. Wong recalled, "As soon as we got there, Patty and I felt that, wow, there were quite a few Asian American students. And then there were already Asian clubs for foreign students. But there was no organization of Asian Americans."[51]

Hirota (Wong)'s adjustment to the Midwest motivated her to help bring an Asian American community together. As she had been born and raised in Berkeley, she had grown up with a strong network of extended family and a Japanese American community. Also at Berkeley, she had been involved in the Asian American Political Alliance, which was part of a larger coalition of students who went on strike for ethnic studies in 1969. Coming to the Midwest was a culture shock; she now lived in a rural Midwestern, predominantly White town where there was one Asian market and one Chinese restaurant. The Midwestern Asian American experience was completely different, and she felt an urge to help create an Asian American space for support.[52]

Hirota (Wong) posted a letter in the *Daily Illini* on 19 January 1971 with the heading "Asian Students." She wrote,

> At a campus with over 400 Asian-Americans registered, I find it strange that there is not one organization for and of this ethnic group. Could it be that Asian-Americans here do not consider themselves different so do not find a need for any "special" organizations or services? Have they really "melted" into the American pot and lost the unique features of their people? I hope this is not so, but rather than [*sic*] Asian-Americans have never had an opportunity to express or define their differences. . . . Asians all over this country are coming together to relate to their common problems and to discover the beauty of being Asian. They are reaching out to each other and to their Black, brown, and red brothers and sisters in struggle. We here cannot afford to sit idle. Anyone interested in forming an Asian alliance call me.[53]

Several students contacted her upon reading this call, including three senior Asian American engineering majors from Chicago who were friends—Michael Imanaka (Japanese American), Frank Bing, and Herman Moy (both Chinese

American). Bing and Herman Moy recalled contacting Hirota (Wong) and meeting to discuss plans for a group. Soon thereafter they established the Asian American Alliance as a registered student organization. The request form, dated 24 January 1971, listed the purpose of the organization as this: "To stimulate awareness of the history, contributions, and travails of Asian Americans in the United States." Michael Imanaka was listed as president and Patricia Wong as treasurer.[54] The university recognized the Asian American Alliance as a new student organization on 29 January 1971.

The small group proceeded to make flyers announcing the formation of the organization and inviting others to join; they also passed out flyers to students during spring registration on February 3–5.[55] Hirota (Wong) announced the new group in the *Daily Illini* on 16 February. She wrote, "The Asian American Alliance has been formed to provide Americans of Asian ancestry with a vehicle for expressing that part of themselves which is uniquely Asian. . . . This is the first organization on campus formed expressly for and by Asian Americans."[56] She also announced the first meeting of the Alliance, which took place on 17 February 1971 and featured four film shorts about San Francisco's Chinatown.

The Alliance met frequently in the spring of 1971.[57] Word spread beyond the announcements in the campus paper. Asian American students also found each other through a mix of informal networks based on high school networks and dorm assignments. While Asian American students hailed from a variety of schools in Chicago, the ones who came to UIUC already steeped in an Asian American social network came from two main high schools: Lane Technical High School, at that time an all-male magnet school with a focus on science located at Addison and Western Avenues (Near North Side), and Senn High School (northeastern Chicago). Thus, some Asian Americans came to campus with other Asian American friends they had known in high school and with established social and support networks.

For those who grew up not knowing other Asian Americans and without a high school Asian American network, simply being Asian American elicited a connection, often one that was initiated by strangers. Warren Nishimoto (BA, history, 1972) transferred to UIUC from the University of Hawaii in 1970 and recalled learning about the Asian American Alliance during course registration: "I was in the Armory, they were having an orientation there, and I was kind of wandering around. Then Mike Imanaka came up to me, and he says, 'Excuse me, are you an Asian brother?' I never batted an eyelash and said, 'Yeah.' He told me they were starting up an Asian American Alliance and asked if I was interested in coming to the meeting. That's how I joined the group."[58]

For Asian American students from suburban Chicago or cities outside of Chicago, having an Asian American community was not the norm growing up. Steve Lee (BS, chemistry, 1975) attended high school in suburban Evanston, in a predominantly White neighborhood; he interacted with very few Asian Americans before college. He recalled that on his first night on campus he met another Chinese American student from Chicago, Doug Lee: "He and I were both kind of homesick and looking for anyone who looked familiar. And he walked up to me, and he said, 'Are you Chinese?' I said, 'Yeah.' He said, 'I am too.' So we kind of hung out and we helped each other adjust in the first weeks of college. . . . Doug knew folks from Chinatown, which really helped me to adjust. And that eventually helped me too because he introduced me to some of those folks, and that's how we eventually joined the Asian American Alliance."[59]

Suzanne Lee Chan (BS, biology, 1972), a Chinese American student from Peoria, also approached other Asian American students. Growing up in a predominantly White area, she did not have an Asian American network before college. She recalled, "I know when I talked to some other people who were Asian, because they were from Chicago, it wasn't so unique. But for me, certainly it was! And so that was the first thing I did. When I was at the dorms, I saw two people sitting outside of Allen Hall, and they were Lynn Ishida and Anne Shimojima [two Japanese American students]. And I made a point of going to introduce myself, because I said 'Wow! There's somebody like me!' It was really nice."[60]

Alliance members made concentrated efforts to find new members. Several alumni said that Herman Moy (BS, engineering, 1971) called them from the student directory. Moy recalled that Alliance members would comb the student directory and call students based on their surname.[61] In addition, the Alliance had informational tables at orientation, where they told students about the organization. On a predominantly White campus, and at a time when the total number of Asian American undergraduate students totaled around 300, it was also easy to find other Asian American students. Wanda Kawahara Lee (BS, microbiology, 1975) remembered that in a big dorm of about 700 students, there were only five Asian American students, and she could still name them.[62] Thus, Asian American students would see each other in the dorms or cafeteria.[62] They began to meet together to discuss similar experiences.

The new organization had a broad mission, which was reflected in discussions about what to name the group. Wong and Hirota (Wong) had been part of the Asian American Political Alliance at Berkeley and had played an important role in founding the organization. Conscious of building an inclusive Asian American space, Wong recalled, "We actually thought about, should we call this an Asian American Political Alliance, or should we just call it an Asian American Alliance? At that time we thought we shouldn't use 'political,' because some people might be scared away from an Asian American Political Alliance. So we made it an Asian American Alliance—so it was political but also cultural and social."[63] Hirota (Wong) also noted it was important to "cast as broad a net as possible" for this new community.[64] The Alliance created a wide range of activities for members. According to minutes from the 17 March 1971 meeting, five committees were formed: social (coordinating picnics and dinners); political/historical (protesting the Vietnam War, discussing Asian American history, gathering information about the lettuce boycott to support farmworkers); service (tutoring Asian children, gathering library resources); culture (planning demonstrations of martial arts and flower arranging); and awareness (facilitating discussions on discrimination, assimilation, gender issues).[65] Throughout the Alliance's existence, members participated in social events such as potlucks, parties, and picnics, as well as intramural sports, forming powder puff football and baseball teams (see figs. 2.1., 2.2, and 2.3).

While the Alliance was open to numerous activities, it was also founded with a critical view of racism and an urgency to embrace pride in being Asian American. Fostering an Asian American identity was an important starting point. In an early flyer, dated 5 February 1971, a call was made to fellow Asian Americans critiquing the melting pot ideal of assimilation and pointing out that Asians in Chinatown suffered poverty and that Japanese Americans were interned during World War II. The flyer challenged a complacent identity to its "Oriental"/Asian American readers:

> You may say, "But I'm American. My friends accept me as I am." Let's not fool ourselves. Our color difference is always noticed. We are constantly reminded of our difference by people who ask, "Are you Chinese, Japanese, or Filipino?" Do you feel embarrassed when your friends see you with your Oriental friends? Do you feel better dating a Caucasian than an Oriental? Are you Asian or are you American—or are you both? Why reject your heritage, your mother culture? Are you ashamed of the American stereotype of the docile, humble Chinese, the laundry-restaurant people? Are you embarrassed of your Issei grandparents? Do you know the contributions of our people have [sic] to America? We must become aware of them!! Asian pride and self respect are synonymous. We are Americans, but we are different and should be proud of it! BE YOURSELF!!—BE ASIAN AMERICAN!![66]

With its focus on Asian American issues, the Asian American Alliance filled an important need. Paul Wong reflected, "I think that most of the people were looking for a sense of community, a sense of identity. There was just nothing else there in Champaign-Urbana at that time for Asian Americans. So some of the students actually had belonged to Chinese clubs for foreign students and things like that."[67] As noted in chapter 1, organizations for Asian ethnic groups at UIUC had existed for some time; often these organizations began as a support for Asian international students but also provided spaces for U.S.-born Asians. Within these groups there was some interaction between Asian and

FIG. 2.1 Members of the Asian American Alliance at a picnic at Allerton Park, Monticello, Illinois, in 1974. (Photo courtesy of Asian American Alliance.)

FIG. 2.2 Members of the Asian American Alliance at a picnic at Allerton Park, Monticello, Illinois, in 1974. (Photo courtesy of Asian American Alliance.)

FIG. 2.3 Members of the Asian American Alliance at a picnic at Turkey Run, Marshall, Indiana, in 1974. (Photo courtesy of Asian American Alliance.)

Asian American students. In particular, some Chinese American students from the Asian American Alliance were involved with the Chinese Students Association (CSA), even though the latter organization conducted its meetings in Mandarin, was composed primarily of international graduate students, and focused on Chinese issues. The two organizations interacted through joint social dances, basketball tournaments, and cultural performance nights, which featured Chinese culture, music, and dance and involved students from mainland China, Taiwan, and Hong Kong (see fig. 2.4).

The small number of Asian American students on campus and their interaction with Asian international students may have led administrators to blur the two populations. Because Asian Americans have been historically racialized as foreign and un-American, a focus on the U.S. experience was critical. Thus, the importance of distinguishing between the needs of Asian international and Asian American students was paramount. The Asian American Alliance focused on U.S. issues and identity struggles, forming a bond across Japanese and Chinese ethnic lines (the two largest ethnic groups represented) to build a pan–Asian American community based on shared racial experiences. Two such experiences the Asian American Alliance addressed were the racially unjust Vietnam War and the need for an Asian American studies curriculum. These two issues were of critical importance to the first Asian American student movement at UIUC.

FIG. 2.4 Members of the Asian American Alliance performing at an international fashion show at the Illini Union in 1972. (Photo courtesy of Asian American Alliance.)

Protesting the Vietnam War

College students across the country were active in the antiwar movement of the 1960s and 1970s, staging protests, burning draft cards, walking out on classes, and traveling to marches in Washington, D.C. Urbana-Champaign was a hub of antiwar activism, which included student demonstrations and sit-ins.[68] National protests against the war also became a staple in Washington, D.C. through the 1960s and 1970s. On 17 April 1965, Students for a Democratic Society (SDS) led a march of 20,000 in Washington, "the largest single antiwar demonstration yet organized in America."[69] By 24 April 1971, this number was eclipsed by an estimated 200,000 to half a million protestors. These events were part of a week of peaceful demonstrations in San Francisco and Washington, D.C., organized by the National Peace Action Coalition in protest of the war.[70]

UIUC Asian American students and community members were involved in the 24 April 1971 national march against the Vietnam War in Washington, D.C. Paul Wong notes that during the march, the coordinating committee refused to adopt the Asian contingent's antiracist statement; thus, the Asian contingent marched as its own separate group.[71] Minutes from a UIUC Asian American Alliance meeting record that ten members planned to march on Washington.[72] There they met with other Asian contingents from across the country.

Alliance member Warren Nishimoto recalled how being involved with other Asian contingents protesting the war facilitated his own Asian American identity process, which he had not thought about growing up in Hawaii. Being a part of an Asian American group also helped him feel a stronger sense of purpose. He described the significance of attending the march: "Going out as part of the Asian contingent, part of this Asian American Alliance that had just started at U of I, I really felt personally involved in it, because a lot of these issues relating to the war did relate to Asian Americans. So it was all part of the identity-building process for me.... I felt a stronger sense of purpose being Asian and being part of an Asian American contingent than if I wasn't."[73]

A few days after the national protest, UIUC students took part in a number of events on campus in support of a two-day student strike against the war. An antiwar coalition organized a large local march on 5 May 1971, when more than 1,000 demonstrators proceeded from campus to Champaign's Westside Park for speeches, music, and theater performances.[74] The march commemorated the first anniversary of the invasion of Cambodia and the shootings at Kent State and Jackson State. A rally followed in the evening. On 6 May, students taught liberation classes on the quadrangle, held more meetings, and picketed numerous campus buildings. University police arrested thirty-nine antiwar protestors that day for occupying a marine recruiting station in the student union.[75]

The Asian American Alliance participated in the 5 May activities and requested to lead the march to address racist issues in the war, which were overlooked in the antiwar movement.[76] As an organization, the Alliance was now only three months old, but its members led the march holding specific Asian-related signs reading, "Stop the Racist War," "Asian Lives Are Not Cheap," "Stop Killing Our Yellow Brothers," "This Is a Gook. . . . Is It True What They Do to People Who Look Like Me?" and a yin-yang peace sign[77] (see fig. 2.5). This racial critique was part of a new discourse against the war that was taking place across the nation. In an article describing the emergence of the Asian American movement, Paul Wong wrote, "White protests had signs 'Give peace a chance' or 'Bring the GIs home.' The Asian-American movement, in contrast, emphasized the *racist* nature of the war, using such slogans as 'Stop killing *our* Asian brothers and sisters,' and 'We don't want *your* racist war.'"[78]

A flyer urging Alliance members to join the Champaign march also powerfully articulated a racial critique of the war. It read, "As Asians and Asian Americans we have the duty to speak out against the brutal slaughter of Asian men, women, and children. The time has come for the 'quiet Asian American' or the 'nice Asian' to end his passive acceptance of this *racist* and genocidal war. . . . The Asian American Alliance feels it is appropriate for us Asians to head the campus antiwar march. After all, they are killing people that look like you and me."[79] The flyer argued for the right of Asian countries for self-determination, for the need to support Southeast Asian people, and that racism was at the root of the war.

FIG. 2.5 The Asian American Alliance leads a local anti–Vietnam War protest, 5 May 1971. (Source: *The Daily Illini*; photographer, Ron Logsdon. Photo courtesy of Illini Media/*The Daily Illini*.)

Alliance member Terry Shintani (BS, business administration, 1972), a Japanese American student from Hawaii, recalled: "We started talking about how the Vietnam War had taken on an insidious racist feature. No one could imagine American soldiers going to a European town and gunning down White children, the way they wasted everyone including women, children, and elderly at My Lai. We reasoned that the soldiers were being influenced by the military's support or condoning of looking at the Asian-faced enemy as 'gooks,' subhuman beings whose lives weren't worth much."[80] These activists connected racism against Asians in America with that on the international front.

The Early Push for Asian American Studies at Illinois

The war was a driving force for activism during the late 1960s and early 1970s, though other issues also concerned students. Antiwar activism began dying down once Saigon fell to the North in 1975. Meanwhile, demands for ethnic studies became an important movement in the late 1960s, culminating at San Francisco State College and UC Berkeley in 1968 and 1969, as outlined in chapter 1.

The Asian American movement articulated a distinct Asian American identity, and a relevant curriculum was part of that goal, as education would challenge stereotypes and reclaim an ignored history. Raising awareness about the

Asian American experience was also a part of the Alliance's activities. Alliance cofounder Patricia Hirota (Wong) had also been involved in the Bay Area's coalition of students who went on strike for ethnic studies. From its inception in spring 1971, the organization screened films about Asian American experiences—on 4 March it showed the film *Nisei: The Pride and the Shame* on the internment experience, and on 20 April it showed films about Hiroshima, Nagasaki, and the U.S. war in Vietnam.[81] Discussions about Asian American experiences also took place during potluck dinners, such as on 8 May 1971, when small groups discussed issues regarding Asian stereotypes, cultural values among different generations of Asians and Asian Americans, interracial marriage, racial discrimination, and women's liberation.[82]

Asian American students had wanted courses at UIUC that reflected their histories and experiences, which were invisible in the Midwest. Herman Moy recalled the efforts that Alliance members took to ask for a course on Asian American experiences. They researched information from other universities that had similar courses, which were nonexistent in the Midwest. He also recalled approaching various departments such as Asian studies and anthropology to sponsor a class on Asian American experiences.[83]

One such course was offered by Bill MacDonald of the Center for Asian Studies as Asian Studies 199 in fall 1972, as a course overload. UIUC offered courses under the 199 rubric for areas that were not covered in the traditional curriculum; these courses needed only a sponsoring instructor and permission from a department head.[84] Approximately twenty students enrolled in Asian Studies 199 and wanted more courses. In the spring 1973 semester a similar course was proposed, but there was no instructor to teach it.

With their desire for courses and for a permanent structure, the Alliance proposed a formal Asian American studies program on 1 February 1973. The proposal read, "The university has an obligation to provide an opportunity for the educational growth of its students. This obligation can be fulfilled by offering appropriate educational programs. . . . There is a definate [*sic*] need for an adequate Asian American Studies Program to be developed. Several students have indicated that they wish to major in Asian American Studies. Unfortunately, there is no existing curriculum in Asian American Studies at this university, or at any other university in the Midwest for this purpose. The Program must be researched and a curricula [*sic*] developed."[85] The Alliance requested that a half-time staff position be created for the Asian American studies program for instruction and curriculum development and that $5,000 be released for acquiring necessary materials such as ethnic newspapers, journals, films, and reference books.[86]

While no formal program was established, some headway was made for a course. In the fall 1973 semester, the course continued under the sponsorship of the anthropology department. Clark Cunningham, professor and head of the department from 1972 to 1975 and from 1980 to 1982, collaborated with Bok-Lim Kim, a faculty member in the department of social work, in teaching Anthropology 199: The Asian-American Experience. This course had twenty-five students enrolled. Despite a handful of offerings, however, this course did not continue at UIUC in the long run due to the lack of full-time faculty committed to offering the course and the lack of widespread administrative support.

Fighting the Foreigner Stereotype

Despite the issues that the Alliance sought to raise, the perception of Asian Americans as foreign students persisted, limiting the ways the administration and other students understood Asian American experiences. Paul Wong, then assistant professor of sociology and Asian studies, recalled, "At that time, the university was used to having foreign students, a lot of students from Asia. So they looked at Asians as all pretty much foreign. So the concept of 'Asian American' was not in their minds at all. You know, they had no understanding of what that was."[87] The racialization of Asian American as foreigners erases the historical contributions of Asian Americans to the United States and pigeonholes Asian Americans as outsiders.

This racial ignorance manifested itself on many levels across campus. The *Daily Illini* incorrectly described the Alliance several times as a foreign-student organization, much to the dismay of Alliance members. For example, in March 1971 the paper announced that the Undergraduate Student Association had funded the Alliance $75.00 in support of its activities, under the description of money given to "foreign students."[88] A few months later in coverage of a local march, the *Daily Illini* described "foreign student representatives" who spoke at the antiwar rally. On 18 May 1971, Patricia Hirota (Wong) wrote a letter to the editor objecting to the paper's representation of Asian American students as foreigners. She wrote, "I suppose this mistake was due to the ignorance of the fact that there are hundreds of thousands of Asians who were born in America, descendants of the Chinese who built the railroads in the 19th Century and the Japanese who made California the rich agricultural state it is. Many of us are third or fourth generation, which should make us as American as anyone else. Still, we of yellow skin are asked, 'Where did you come from?' or 'How did you learn English?' and are considered foreigners because we do not look 'American.'" She continued: "The Asian American Alliance, as the name implies, is composed mainly of Asians born in America. We feel deep bonds with the peoples of Asia, but we are different from them, and we want to be recognized. We must stop this form of racism. America is not just Black and White."[89]

Sometimes UIUC staff did not know what to do with Asian American students, who were presumed to be foreign. Terry Shintani (BS, business administration, 1972) recalled seeking office space for the Alliance, as the Black Students Association (BSA) had office space in the student union. He recalled, "Because BSA was given office space, I thought I was justified in asking for the same thing for the Asian American Alliance. When I went to the student affairs office, I asked for similar space. The clerk there immediately told me that the foreign students' office was across the hall. When I explained that I was American, the clerk did not know what to do and said they would call me back—which they never did." For Shintani, coming from Hawaii, this experience was new. He explained, "Asian Americans from Hawaii are different from Asian Americans on the mainland in that Asian Americans are a plurality in Hawaii and are not accustomed to being treated like foreigners or being looked at in a strange way."[90] Perhaps the presence of Asian students on campus since the early twentieth century affected administrators' interpretation of these Asian American students; regardless, these experiences reveal the university's lack of understanding of Asian American student experiences. Asian Americans seemed to be barely on the radar of administrators, and there was little discussion as to their experiences and needs as a racial minority.

Asian Americans Don't Fit Minority Concepts

African American and Latinx students fit the university's definitions of minority students because they were underrepresented along some measure. A harder rationale came for Asian Americans. Were Asian Americans a minority on campus? UIUC followed guidelines from the U.S. Department of Health, Education, and Welfare, which defined four main minority groups as Black, Hispanic, Asian, and American Indian. Racial data on these groups were kept in concordance with these categories. However, the university's focus was on Black and Latinx students.[91] Reporting on the four groups and having university recognition of minority status were two different things, as this recognition led the way to gaining services such as recruitment and retention as well as counselors, cultural centers, advisors, and the like. Since UIUC's focus was on underrepresentation, Asian Americans did not qualify due to their parity, despite their miniscule numbers on campus in the 1970s and 1980s. In addition, UIUC began its minority programs and services with a focus on African American students and never targeted Asian American students.

Alliance members unequivocally felt they were a minority during their time at UIUC, challenging these notions of nonminority status. Alliance documents reveal concerns about navigating a predominantly White campus. At a potluck dinner on 8 May 1971, small groups discussed issues specific to racial comfort, with the following questions posed: "How do you feel when attending an all-White social function? Do you act the same or different with White friends as you do with friends of the same racial/ethnic backgrounds? Do you have friends among other minority groups? How do you feel when being among them?"[92] It is clear that members were concerned about navigating White spaces.

Alumni also recalled how it was obvious they were a minority given their small presence at UIUC. Debbie Shikami Ikeda (BS, elementary education, 1974) reflected, "I remember going to [an Alliance] meeting, and someone said, 'Look around your classes—are there other people that look like you?' And it dawned on me that there weren't. Particularly in the College of Education there were very few of us. In fact, I remember looking around the classroom, and it was all White people!"[93] Frank Bing (BS, engineering, 1971) also described the situation succinctly on campus relative to their small numbers: "I mean we're smaller than a minority. At 300 you're not even a minority, you're the background noise!"[94]

On the administrative side, not only was "minority" conflated with "Black" (and then expanded to include Latinx), but it also centered on issues of underrepresentation in admissions and retention. In particular for the SEOP, Clarence Shelley explained, "We focused so much on enrollment that I think it may have hurt our efforts to work with Asian American students in terms of programming and support because enrollment numbers for Asian American students were never an issue. Because they were never an issue, serving them was not an issue either. We were never called to account for that."[95] This focus on underrepresentation left Asian American students out of minority student discussions.

While the Asian American student community was diverse (with not all coming from middle-class backgrounds), the presumption that they were academically successful model minorities prevailed. Steve Lee (BS, chemistry, 1975) recalled, "I think our situation was kind of different because not as many of us came from disadvantaged backgrounds, and we tended to be more successful academically, so it was kind of hard for them to think of us as a special-needs group in the same vein as African Americans and Latinos."[96] Debbie Shikami Ikeda also noted, "I think we were such a small group that administrators really didn't know our history at all. Whereas the Black student groups and the Latino groups—there seemed to be more general knowledge about their struggles. And I think they had that whole model minority myth, and that was one of the things we would talk about in our [Asian American studies] class. And so there was not a recognition that there were any issues for Asian Americans."[97]

Thus, Asian Americans at UIUC were silenced from campus minority discussions due to the model minority image, the focus on statistical underrepresentation, and the focus on African American and Latinx students. Visibility for African Americans and Latinxs was also greater because of the forms of organizing and protest that these groups took on that generated university attention, forms that were uncomfortable for some Asian American students. While the Alliance was involved in activist marches, there was also a hesitation in approach. Steve Lee remembered, "One of the things we used to joke about was, maybe because of our cultural upbringing, we were just not into confrontation and being demanding. And it was just not comfortable for us. I think that our parents being more recent immigrants, certainly there were Confucian ideals of respecting authority and civil obedience; it just wasn't part of the cultural makeup." Lee continued: "In fact, my parents, I remember, were alarmed that I was with a group [the Alliance] that had any possible social-political agenda, because their recollection was when you're in China, that the government would crack down even before the communists, that civil disobedience was not a smart thing to do, so they kind of passed that down to me. They'd say, 'Don't make waves.'"[98]

These cultural pressures and hesitancy to embrace confrontational protest would arise at various moments for Asian American students through the 1980s and 1990s. At the same time, this hesitancy did not mean Asian American students were politically passive. They embraced a strong critique of university policies and emphasized that their experiences did not fully resemble those of Black or Latinx students.

There were other challenges to Asian American visibility as well, including the youth of the Alliance as a student organization, its struggles to build unity among Asian American students, and the lack of administrative and faculty support. While some professors such as Clark Cunningham taught an early Asian American studies course, Steve Lee recalled obstacles to advocating for Asian American resources without the large-scale support of faculty: "There weren't a lot of Asian American faculty. Most of the faculty were immigrants themselves, and I don't think they necessarily saw themselves as relating to our goals and needs. It's kind of hard to get an engineering professor, for example, to see that as something he'd want to take on, whereas he's probably more research oriented."[99]

Thus, Alliance members struggled to navigate campus life on their own without institutional support or a broad coalition of faculty and staff allies. Asian American activism also was new and those involved were small in number. These factors, along with the university's misperception of them as either foreign students or a problem-free group since they were not underrepresented, kept Asian Americans invisible to UIUC administrators.

Asian American Student Movements in Midwestern Context: The 1970s

It is important to note the tenor of Asian American activism in the Midwest, which took place in a more racially isolated community compared to the West

Coast. Particularly for Paul Wong and Patricia Hirota (Wong), this change of scenery was blatant, having come from Berkeley and having been involved in the Third World Liberation Front. Hirota (Wong) commented on her impressions of the differences between Berkeley's Asian American movement and the one that was forming in Illinois. She recalled of the Berkeley group:

> They were so much more advanced politically, they had read all these things and they had been involved with things like the Young Socialist Alliance and the Black Panther Party. So they had been politically around for much longer and they were more sophisticated in so many different ways. And their whole sense of being Asian and being a revolutionary was really very strong. And then moving to the Midwest, it just felt more like . . . it was like finding who they were. The whole identity thing was a huge part of it; that's why the sports and the cultural events were really important because we were isolated away from where we had grown up. So it just felt like a much more, in a way, innocent, less sophisticated group. But then, that was really important; in a way it was more virgin territory from where I came out of, from the Bay Area. So I felt like the whole social part was more important there than in Berkeley.[100]

Alliance members from Chicago also commented that Wong and Hirota (Wong) had a more advanced knowledge of the issues. Hailing from California, they came to the Midwest with a stronger sense of pride in being Asian American, having grown up around a larger Asian American community. In addition, their involvement in the Third World Liberation Front and push for ethnic studies at Berkeley connected them directly to the Asian American studies movement, to resources for curriculum, and to information on how to start Asian American studies programs; such information was not readily available in the Midwest.

For Asian Americans from Hawaii, the Midwest also opened their eyes to a new Asian American identity framed in mainland racial categories. Warren Nishimoto hailed from Hawaii and had never had to think about an Asian American identity, having grown up in a multi-ethnic neighborhood and school, with neighbors and classmates who were Hawaiian, Japanese, Chinese, Korean, and Filipino. Coming to Illinois was a new experience, and Nishimoto said that his initial impression of campus was that it was more White and Black, with everyone else marginalized.[101] When other students in the dorms inquired about his background, he had to articulate a whole string of identities for the first time: he had to explain that he was from Hawaii (but not ethnically Hawaiian) and that he was Japanese American (not from Japan; he was a U.S. citizen). He also had to outline the history of Asian labor migration to Hawaii in order to explain why there were so many Japanese Americans in Hawaii. He described the process as forcing him to articulate who he was for the first time, which in the long run was a positive thing because it helped him think about his identity in a new place with other Asian Americans.

The Midwest was a new site of Asian American identity and activism, in contrast to California. As William Wei writes in his assessment of the Asian American movement in the Midwest, "Except for those living and laboring in such places as Chicago's Chinatown, most Midwestern Asian Americans had disappeared into suburbia. Without a physical community to relate to, Midwestern Asian Americans found it difficult to start and sustain an ethnic-consciousness movement. Accordingly, Asian American activism started later in the region and Asian American groups had a harder time recruiting and retaining members."[102] Despite these challenges, Asian American students formed Asian American student organizations on campuses such as Oberlin College, the University of Minnesota (Minneapolis), the University of Wisconsin–Madison, and the University of Michigan (Ann Arbor), along with UIUC.

As Asian students did so in the 1920s and 1930s, Asian American student groups began convening at regional conferences in 1974 to network and support each other. The first Midwestern Asian American conference was held in Chicago on 12–14 April 1974. As a result, students from the Madison Asian Union issued *Rice Paper*, a resource packet to serve as a voice to help unify Asian Americans in the Midwest. In its first issue, editors wrote, "Certainly one of the great obstacles in organizing Asians in the Midwest is our geographic and spiritual isolation. Our invisibility is so total that Asian Americans are not thought to exist in this 'vast banana wasteland.' As of yet there has been no coherent analysis defining our regional identity. This void not only stunts our individual understanding of our role in the Midwest, but also greatly handicaps the Asian American Movement in general."[103] A list of contacts included those at the universities of Michigan, Illinois, Wisconsin, and Minnesota, as well as Michigan State, Washington University (St. Louis), Northwestern University, Carleton College, Bowling Green State University, Oberlin College, and community groups in Chicago.

The first issue of *Rice Paper* contained resource articles, graphic art, and poems about Asian American identity. It reprinted articles about economic issues in Chinatown and critiques of the racist media depictions of Charlie Chan. *Rice Paper* also included voices from representatives from college campuses who discussed their experiences at the April conference, echoing the need for a Midwestern network to keep each other informed and provide community support. Oberlin students stated that the conference "came as a welcome revitalization. . . . The energy and camaraderie displayed and the earnestness with which brothers and sisters posed and attempted to answer important questions reinforced our confidence that Asian-Americans in [the] Midwest will develop unity and can work and struggle together."[104]

A second Midwestern conference was held in Madison, Wisconsin, on 26–29 September 1974, with the theme of "Getting beyond Identity." It covered issues such as Asian American sexuality, community activism, and Asian American college student experiences. Over seventy Asian American students and professionals attended, including members of the Alliance.[105] Thus while evolving later than on the West Coast, an Asian American identity was emerging in the 1970s across Midwestern college campuses.

These Asian American student spaces in the Midwest provided a critical source of support. Steve Lee recalled that his experience in the Alliance was significant because it provided him a community he had never had: "It meant a lot to me because being out in the suburbs you could count on one hand how many other Asians were in your high school class. In fact, in my class I think there might have been two other people, out of a class of 1,000. So that was really meaningful for me. So from my perspective being a suburban Chinese American, that made a big difference."[106]

The Decline of the Asian American Alliance

Records of the Asian American Alliance fade after 1975. In 1974, at the second Asian American Midwestern conference in Madison, the Alliance had a position paper included in *Rice Paper*. In it, Steve Lee reported on the challenges facing the Alliance. He wrote, "Externally, there is a failure to attract concerned Asians. Internally, the group lacks direction. Cohesiveness is lacking among the members and communication is poor. The burden of holding A³ [Asian American Alliance] together and promoting it has fallen on too few concerned Asians. As a result, the group is in the midst of reorganization and an assessment of itself." He went on to state that few Asian American students were interested in Asian American educational activities (such as promoting the Asian American studies course and program) and concluded, "These efforts have been limited by, once again, our lack of concerned Asians willing to devote the time towards these activities."[107]

This concern over leadership of Asian American-related events (aside from those just social), revealed itself even earlier, in a 1972 letter to the *Daily Illini*. The Asian American Week Planning Committee wrote an open letter to Asian Americans, describing the Alliance's history (now one year old) and a desire to plan an Asian American Awareness Week for April 1972. However, the committee expressed frustration at the lack of interest.[108] A lack of Alliance leadership was particularly an issue by the end of the spring 1974 semester. By this time, a large cohort of active members had graduated. The last record of the organization's registration on campus was dated September 1974, and the last public listing of an Alliance meeting was on 6 November 1974 in The *Daily Illini*.[109] Alliance alumni, especially those of the class of 1974, recalled the challenges of building new leadership before graduation, as outlined by Steve Lee in *Rice Paper*. Members recalled struggling to pass on leadership positions with little success. The momentum built up by Asian American students in the Alliance from 1971 to 1974 had begun to fade.

Given the locale and time, the Asian American movement at UIUC focused on identity and community building and was limited in size, as the Asian American undergraduate student population in the 1970s at UIUC totaled about 300. While the small numbers of Asian American students may have been background noise on campus, their coming together to create an Asian American space and articulate Asian American issues widens the higher educational historiography. Asian American students at UIUC created an important community of support to foster a distinct racial Asian American identity, which university administrators did not understand.

Recognition of minority needs at UIUC came from students who pushed the envelope, challenging university policies. The push first came from the Black Students Association, which was involved in the efforts for what would become SEOP. SEOP's specific focus on recruiting and supporting African American students marginalized other racial minority students on campus, most notably Latinx students. Then the push came from Latinx students who sought a bilingual recruiter, staff, and a cultural center of their own.

Asian American students were never specifically recruited for the program and were never considered a minority group. Asian American students also advocated for Asian American studies courses, raised awareness on campus for Asian American issues, and protested the Vietnam War, operating in marginal spaces outside of SEOP. These students made noise even if they remained in the background of minority student programs. Their concerns would reemerge with a new generation of student leaders at UIUC through the 1980s and 1990s—leaders who broadened the understandings of minority needs to make room for Asian American students.

3

We Are Not Model
Minorities

A New Asian American
Student Movement,
1975–1992

In 1991 student leaders Jody Lin and Karin Wang wrote an editorial in the University of Illinois's student newspaper the *Daily Illini* with the title "'Model Minority' Tag Hurts Asian-Americans." In it, they rejected the view of diversity as simply a Black-White issue and described the invisibility of Asian American experiences. They charged that the model minority myth ignored continued discrimination facing Asian Americans and fostered anti-Asian resentment and backlash. They wrote of this problem and of the lack of campus resources to rectify it:

> As applied to this campus, the effects of the "model minority" stereotype and
> the invisibility of Asian-Americans as people of color is painfully apparent.
> Even though Asian-Americans have been in the United States since 1763, one
> can find few courses that relate in any way to Asian-American history. No
> Asian-American studies course exists, and very few sociology, history, or
> literature courses at this University deal in any way with Asian-American
> history or contributions to American culture. There is also a very obvious lack

of administrative and University support for Asian-American needs and concerns on this campus.[1]

Lin and Wang represented a new generation of Asian American student leaders at the University of Illinois at Urbana-Champaign (UIUC) in the mid-1980s. While the Asian American Alliance had dissolved by the mid-1970s, the need for Asian American spaces at UIUC did not fade away. About a decade later a new generation of Asian American students, children of post-1965 immigrants, would come together to articulate their educational needs and experiences with racism, critique the lack of university resources and support, and reject an insidious model minority stereotype.

Asian American College Student Growth in the 1980s and 1990s

Though Asian American visibility was low on campus during the early to mid-1980s, a few things are clear about this population. During the early 1980s, the enrollment of Asian American students at UIUC nearly tripled in size. In 1976 there were a reported 392 Asian Pacific Islander American undergraduate students (1.6 percent). By 1985 this figure had risen to 1,508 (5.5 percent).[2] In 1982, Asian American students outnumbered African American students for the first time, when there were 981 African American undergraduate students (3.7 percent) compared to 1,043 Asian Americans (4.0 percent).

The Asian American model minority image was popular in the 1980s. In 1987, *Time* magazine touted images of successful Asian American students with the cover title "Those Asian-American Whiz Kids." While David Brand's feature article provided a somewhat critical analysis of the model minority image—pointing out the problems of the stereotype that all Asian Americans excelled in math and science, the consequences of pressure from Asian parents to meet high educational expectations, and anti-Asian backlash—he ultimately reinforced the model minority message that anything was achievable through hard work. He stated, "If assimilation and other trends mean that the dramatic concentration of super-students has peaked, talented young Asian Americans have already shown that US education can still produce excellence. The largely successful Asian-American experience is a challenging counterpoint to the charges that US schools are now producing less-educated mainstream students and failing to help underclass Blacks and Hispanics."[3]

Asian American enrollment in higher education rapidly increased in the 1970s through the 1980s, coinciding with the widening access to college for all racialized minority groups. In 1976 there were 198,000 Asian Americans at all levels of higher education. By 1988 that figure had increased to 497,000. Put another way, Asian American representation in higher education grew from 2 percent to 4 percent in that time.[4] This growth occurred at both competitive private and public institutions—from 1976 to 1986, the proportion of Asian Americans in freshman classes grew from 3.6 percent to 12.8 percent at Harvard, from 5.3 percent to 20.6 percent at MIT, from 5.7 percent to 14.7 percent at Stanford, and from 16.9 percent to 27.8 percent at Berkeley.[5]

The demographic rise of Asian American students in higher education in the 1980s and 1990s was a result of the liberalization of immigration laws in 1965, as well as the decline of residential segregation, fueling the growth of Asian American communities. Thus, as the number of Asian American college students increased nationwide in the 1980s, life on campuses differed greatly from the 1960s and 1970s. As William Wei points out, Asian American college students were now more ethnically diverse than those whose parents had immigrated before 1965. In addition, their immigrant parents benefited from 1965 legislation that favored professional groups; thus, more students came from families with educational and professional training, with the exception of Southeast Asian refugees.[6]

These changes were reflected in demographic shifts in the state of Illinois. While there were earlier histories of some Asian groups in Chicago (as noted in chapter 2), after the 1965 Immigration Act and the fall of Vietnam, Asian immigration and refugee resettlement to Illinois increased significantly. Before the 1960s, the major Asian American groups in Chicago were Chinese, Japanese, and Filipino. After the 1960s, there was significant growth in Chicago of Bangladeshi, Cambodian, Indian, Indonesian, Korean, Laotian, Nepalese, Pakistani, Thai, Tibetan, and Vietnamese communities, as well as continued immigration from China and the Philippines. By the end of the 1980s, there were 285,000 Asian Pacific Americans in Illinois; by 1990, that number had grown to 292,421.[7]

Asian American students began to come together at colleges and universities across the country at this time. While the 1960s and 1970s civil rights, antiwar, and ethnic studies movements had faded on a large scale, a new awareness and activism began to take shape. Wei notes that after the 1970s, Asian American generations came to college with a sense of social justice, garnered from the political gains made in the 1960s. Thus, a new spirit of Asian American student activism began to grow on college campuses such as UIUC in the 1980s and 1990s.[8]

UIUC Minority Programs in the 1980s

While Asian American student demographics were changing in the 1980s, some things remained the same. UIUC still did not acknowledge Asian Americans as a minority group; in fact, the growing numbers of Asian Americans and their aggregate academic success on campus reinforced a model minority stereotype. University minority programs maintained their focus on improving the academic success of underrepresented students by focusing on enrollment and retention, particularly for African Americans and Latinxs.

This focus on African Americans and Latinxs continued as the Educational Opportunities Program (EOP) expanded. As the EOP grew, the need for a permanent campus program to develop its services became clear. In 1988 the EOP was renamed the Office of Minority Student Affairs (OMSA).[9] Through the 1980s and 1990s, OMSA oversaw a number of programs focused on outreach, recruitment, and retention of underrepresented students. OMSA also provided an orientation program, tutoring and skills classes, and referrals to other campus units such as the counseling center and career development office.[10] While some individual Asian American students could partake of services if they were admitted through its programs based on socioeconomic qualifications, in general OMSA's focus was on African American and Latinx students due to their underrepresentation.[11]

From a policy perspective, Illinois state legislation defined minority populations more broadly, which included Asian Americans. For instance, in 1985, the Illinois General Assembly passed Public Act 84-726 requiring public institutions of higher education to develop plans to increase the participation of underrepresented groups, including women and the students with disabilities. This act was amended in 1988 by Public Act 85-283 and outlined the following:

> To require public institutions of higher education to develop and implement
> methods and strategies to increase the participation of minorities, women and
> handicapped individuals who are traditionally under-represented in education
> programs and activities. For the purpose of this Section, minorities shall mean
> persons who are citizens of the United States and who are: (a) Black (a person
> having origins in any of the Black racial groups in Africa); (b) Hispanic
> (a person of Spanish or Portuguese culture with origins in Mexico, South or
> Central America, or the Caribbean, regardless of race); (c) Asian American
> (a person having origins in any of the original people of the Far East, Southeast
> Asia, the Indian Subcontinent or the Pacific Islands); or (d) American Indian
> or Alaskan Native (a person having origins in any of the original people of
> North America).[12]

Illinois statute 9.16 also held the same wording and required public institutions to report to the Illinois Board of Higher Education (IBHE) on their programs for underrepresented groups.

While Illinois state law defined Asian Americans as a minority group (which Asian American students would emphasize in the 1990s), the IBHE focus remained on African American and Latinx students. In 1986, an IBHE annual report cited that racial and ethnic minorities included Black, non-Hispanic; Hispanic; Asian or Pacific Islander; and American Indian or Alaskan. However, the report also stipulated, "These categories have been established and defined by the federal government for purposes of various policies and data reports. For purposes of this report, data about Black and Hispanic groups are highlighted because these two groups are most under-represented in Illinois higher education compared to their proportions in the state population."[13] Additional findings were that Black and Latinx students' representation declined at each educational level, they were better represented in community colleges, and they did not complete their degrees at equivalent rates to their enrollment.

In the following year's IBHE report, there was an additional explanation of why minority programs focused on Black and Latinx students: "In the 1980 census, Asians or Pacific Islanders accounted for 1.4 percent of the state's population and American Indians or Alaskans accounted for 0.1 percent. These groups are represented to this extent or greater in most aspects of Illinois higher education."[14] UIUC chancellor Morton Weir was also quoted in the *Daily Illini* regarding why the focus of minority services was on African Americans and Latinxs, compared to Native Americans. He stated, "We try to spend money where there is clear under-representation. Native Americans are not under-represented on this campus."[15] And in 1990 a campus report further elaborated, "Given the significant representation of Asian students on campus and the very small proportion of American Indians in the state's population (0.1 percent to 0.2 percent for the campus), UIUC has targeted its minority recruitment efforts on increasing Black and Hispanic enrollments."[16] Because the Native American population in the state was so low, their enrollment figures did not signal underrepresentation; thus, they were not a focus population for UIUC minority programs. Asian Americans, clearly overrepresented in enrollment figures compared to state population statistics, were also disregarded.

While Asian American students were not included in university minority programs, they were still counted in reports that tabulated minority student populations at UIUC. This inclusion followed federal guidelines established by the U.S. Office of Education and the U.S. Office of Civil Rights, which outlined racial/ethnic categories in the late 1960s as American Indian, Black American, Oriental American, Spanish surnamed, and Caucasian. These categories were revised in 1976 as American Indian or Alaskan Native; Black non-Hispanic; Asian or Pacific Islander; Hispanic; and White non-Hispanic.[17]

This inconsistent inclusion of Asian Americans as minorities was disconcerting—Asian Americans were counted in minority student reports but not targeted for minority student services. For instance, in a 1986 *Daily Illini* article about minority student numbers, Weir, who was then vice president for academic affairs, cited that minority students made up 11.6 percent of undergraduates, although 5.5 percent of that number was Asian Americans.[18] In a 1990 university report, administrators reported that minority enrollment was on the rise in the 1980s, and Asians "had experienced the most rapid growth and represent the largest minority group at 8.5 percent in 1989."[19] The inclusion of Asian Americans in minority student tabulation increased the total numbers and made the campus appear diverse, yet there were no diversity programs or resources targeted for Asian American students.

This inclusion in reports that recognized and grouped Asian Americans with other minority groups contradicted UIUC policies that did not offer any Asian American–specific services. When turned away from OMSA, Asian American students in the 1980s and 1990s did not have an alternative institutional support space, and they began to question why the university counted Asian Americans as minorities in name but not in practice. They even began to question if minority program funding from the state or federal governments was being garnered through inflated minority numbers but not being funneled down to Asian American students, a criticism that emerged from a growing Asian American movement on campus. For instance, in 1991, student leaders Jody Lin and Karin Wang articulated, "The invisibility of Asian-Americans is almost a double standard at this University. On the one hand, the administration considers Asian-Americans as a minority when reporting minority-student enrollment figures to the federal government, but when it comes to actual support services for Asian-Americans or supporting programs put on by Asian-American student groups, the administration offers little more than verbal support."[20] Thus, they began challenging the situational claiming of Asian Americans as minorities when reporting enrollment to state and federal agencies but not in providing minority services to Asian American students at UIUC.

The Asian American Association

Ironically, a focus on numerical representation haunted Asian American students when they were both small and large in number at UIUC. In the 1970s, there were too few to garner administrative attention, while still technically being overrepresented. In the 1980s and 1990s, their growing numbers lent weight to the sense that they needed nothing special or unique. At the same time, the prospect of the mobilization of this critical mass of Asian American students did move administrators to pay them more attention. Forming a new pan–Asian American community began to take on a greater importance in the 1980s and 1990s, as students intensified their political advocacy for campus support.

After the Asian American Alliance folded, Asian American students (now more likely to be children of post-1965 immigrants) did not come together again as a registered organization at UIUC until 1986, when they created the Asian American Association (AAA). That year, two Chinese American students— Loretta Chou (BS, chemical engineering, 1989) and Rebecca Li (BS, chemical engineering, 1989) founded AAA, the second pan–Asian American student organization at UIUC. According to its constitution, AAA's purpose was to "act as a support group of Asian Americans at the University of Illinois." Its objectives were to provide social activities and cultural awareness for Asian American students and to promote awareness of Asian American issues to the campus community.[21] The need for such an organization was clear, just as the absence of an Asian American space had prompted the creation of the Asian American Alliance in 1971. Chou recalled thinking of the idea for the organization after visiting friends at the University of Michigan, which had its own Asian American Association. She was intrigued that at Illinois there were no organizations for Asian American students at the time, though there were Chinese and Korean student clubs for international students. She said, "There was nothing for people born in the U.S. yet were Asian and raised between two cultures: American and Asian. When I heard about this Asian American Association at the University of Michigan, I thought how it's interesting that the University of Illinois has been around for so long and has such a huge population of Asian Americans, but they don't have anything like this group. . . . So Rebecca and I started exploring ideas and talking to people about how to actually start up a club."[22]

AAA held its first informational meeting on 10 April 1986 to discuss plans for the new organization that included social dances, movies, picnics, sports activities, ski trips, and a banquet. One idea included having speakers come to talk about Asian American issues.[23] Chou was the first president, with Li serving as one of two vice presidents. The group also had a secretary, an art and graphics chair, a publicity chair, social chairs, and a sports coordinator.

In its first newsletter, AAA acknowledged the Asian American Alliance as an important part of UIUC history and presented the need for a new organization for Asian American students:

> Ten years ago there was an organization called the Asian American Alliance at the University of Illinois. Unfortunately, because of administration problems, it ended a couple of years later. Since then the more than 1,000 Asian-Americans on campus have gone without such a group. We all feel that there still is a need for a similar group on campus which would provide opportunities for Asian-Americans to interact and socialize with one another. Although there exist many specific Asian nationality groups on campus, there is no one organization that encompasses these and brings them together. With the support and encouragement of many of our friends, we founded the Asian-American Association.[24]

FIG. 3.1 Members of the Asian American Association at a fall picnic, from the 1993 *Illio*. (Photo courtesy of Illini Media/*Illio*.)

Despite the acknowledgment of and awareness of the Alliance, there was no direct connection between the Alliance and AAA, although they even shared the same acronym. Rather, AAA had a more direct lineage to its parallel student organization at Michigan, and Chou recalled crafting UIUC's group's constitution and bylaws from Michigan's model.[25]

During its first semester, AAA hosted a picnic and a spring tango dance. Over the next few years the organization hosted other social activities, such as dances, sports outings (bowling, ice skating), cooking lessons, picnics, and a fashion show[26] (see fig. 3.1).

AAA's early years had a social focus. Chou recalled, "AAA was very small when we first started; we weren't even sure that it would continue. So at that point we were doing more social things to attract groups of Asian Americans together and to network from there. And I think it really took off after that when people started to raise other Asian American issues. But in the first year we didn't have any of that. Ours was really just about social networking."[27] Still, this social networking formed an important basis on which to build a new Asian American student community at UIUC, one that had the new challenge of transcending more diverse ethnic lines than the Asian American Alliance had had to navigate. As AAA grew, its diversity also grew. By 1991, five years after its founding, AAA had around 370 members, representing Chinese,

Taiwanese, Korean, Filipino, Vietnamese, Thai, Japanese, and South Asian (Indian) American backgrounds, reflecting the greater diversity of post-1965 Asian American communities.[28]

Emerging Asian American Racial Awareness

Political, cultural, and educational issues began to emerge within AAA by the late 1980s. In March 1988, AAA president Eugene Hsu spoke on a university panel discussion about racism. According to AAA's tenth anniversary packet, "Eugene stated, 'the "model-minority" image is misleading.' He continued by saying that Asian-Americans' incomes are just as diverse as any other minority group."[29] In addition, in the spring of 1989, AAA coordinated important awareness activities, including an Asian Awareness Day and the first annual Midwest Asian American Students Conference.

This change reflected a new development for the organization. Jody Lin, president of AAA, described this shift away from social events in 1989: "AAA quickly gained a reputation for holding great dances and exciting sporting events, but in the areas of Asian-American awareness and culture, there were few events, if any, of which to speak. Last year, however, in response to a rise in racial incidents on college campuses across the nation, [the] Asian-American Association took steps to expand Asian awareness on campus and to sponsor more events dealing with Asian culture and Asian-American perspective."[30] Announcements and articles in AAA newsletters reflected this shift in focus around this time, with an increase in articles related to anti-Asian racism, pressures of the model minority myth, and intergenerational and intercultural conflict between Asian immigrant parents and their U.S.-born children.

Jody Lin's mention of the rise of racial incidents referred to a growing awareness and documentation of anti-Asian violence in the 1980s. The most infamous of these attacks was the 1982 beating death of Chinese American Vincent Chin in Detroit. Two White automobile factory workers, Ronald Ebens and Michael Nitz, accosted Chin, called him a Jap, and blamed him for the unemployment of Detroit's autoworkers, referring to the backlash over Japan's auto imports during the city's economic recession. A fight ensued, with Ebens and Nitz beating and killing Chin with a baseball bat. Ultimately the men were sentenced to three years' probation and fined $3,780.[31] These unjust sentences mobilized a pan–Asian American movement and new organization, American Citizens for Justice (ACJ). As awareness of Chin's murder grew, Asian American coalitions in New York, Los Angeles, San Francisco, and Chicago began to speak out about anti-Asian violence in their communities. The ACJ pushed for a civil rights investigation, and in November 1983 a federal grand jury indicted Ebens and Nitz for violating Chin's civil rights; the following June a jury found Ebens guilty. However, due to legal errors, the case was retried in 1987 in Cincinnati, where a jury found Ebens not guilty. Vincent Chin has become an important figure and symbol of anti-Asian violence and represents the ways that Asian American groups are racially targeted during times of economic or military crisis, as they are presumed to be foreign and disloyal despite generations of citizenship in the United States.

Though most high profile, Chin's murder was not an isolated case. Other incidents of anti-Asian violence occurred in the 1980s and 1990s. Anti-Japanese sentiment rose in 1989 when the Mitsubishi Estate Company of Tokyo purchased stock in Rockefeller Center, with newspaper columnists complaining of a Japanese takeover. Helen Zia notes that these feelings were reflected in a rise of anti-Asian incidents; in a two-week period in December of 1989, at least nine Asian Americans were attacked in New York City.[32] In 1987 in New Jersey, a hate group calling itself the Dotbusters formed, and a rash of assaults and vandalism occurred against South Asian Americans.[33] Also in January 1989 in Stockton, California, Patrick Purdy opened fire on Cleveland Elementary School, which was 70 percent Asian American, killing five Southeast Asian American children and wounding thirty others.[34] Subsequent investigation discovered that Purdy resented Asians, and a racial motive was probably the cause of the attack. The rise of violence led to the founding of the Committee against Anti-Asian Violence in New York in 1986.

Attacks and racial harassment also occurred against Asian American college students. In December 1987, a group of eight Asian American students at the University of Connecticut were spit upon and racially harassed by White students on a bus on the way to and during a Christmas dance.[35] In 1989, Chinese American Jim Ming Hai Loo, a student in Raleigh, North Carolina, was killed by two White brothers, Lloyd and Robert Piche, who hurled racial slurs at Loo and blamed him for the death of U.S. soldiers in Vietnam.

The story of Vincent Chin and the 1988 documentary film profiling the case, titled *Who Killed Vincent Chin?*, profoundly affected Asian American student leaders. The film was shown at UIUC in May 1989, December 1990, December 1991, and December 1997. Student leaders described the significance of the film in raising awareness about anti-Asian racism. Ho Chie Tsai (BS, electrical engineering, 1994) recalled, "When we viewed the *Who Killed Vincent Chin?* documentary, that was the defining moment for me. When I walked out after the film was over, I realized that as a community, we really had to do something bigger and better."[36] Likewise, Karin Wang (BS, finance, 1992) described the impact of the documentary on her own personal and professional development: "I know I became much more interested in the political issues after we did a showing of *Who Killed Vincent Chin?* For me, the Vincent Chin case was part of the transformation process, about wanting to go to law school. When

I saw that video, I was astounded that something like that had happened, and that I didn't know about it, and even worse, that the perpetrators, who really didn't deny that they committed the crime, walked away."[37]

In light of the disturbing rise in anti-Asian racism and violence, AAA president Jody Lin, along with other student leaders, steered the young organization into a more educational role. By fall of 1990, Lin articulated the goals of AAA in its newsletter. He acknowledged AAA's social aspect but also emphasized the need for greater awareness and coalition building, writing, "This year, there are several general goals we would like to accomplish: 1) involve the members more in the planning and execution of programs, 2) maintain our solid reputation as a fun, social club, 3) provide even more awareness and culture programs, and 4) reach out to organizations of our ethnic groups through various programs."[38] That year a new position in AAA was created called "special projects chair," as well as an "awareness chair" in 1991 to expand AAA beyond a social group.

As special project and awareness chairs, respectively, Ho Chie Tsai (BS, electrical engineering, 1994) and Jessica Chen (BS, chemical engineering, 1994) took it upon themselves to learn more about Asian American studies (AAS). Hungry for AAS course material, Tsai decided to take a class in Asian American history at UCLA during the summer of 1991. Tsai recalled his excitement: "I'll never forget the feeling of walking through the 'stacks' of the AAS department. I couldn't believe how many resources were archived there! I was completely in awe that there were so many professors and graduate teaching assistants in the department. I'm quite sure I fell into the bright-eyed timid student category—a country mouse lost in awe of the bright lights, big city. I absorbed the experience. I knew there were lessons to be taken home to Champaign-Urbana."[39] The next summer, Tsai worked with Chen to gather resources from UCLA. "Our plan would be to try to learn what we could, but more importantly, 'research' their AAS program and bring back resources and syllabi."[40] These efforts were part of AAA's goal to gather resources in the absence of AAS courses on campus.

The Growth of Asian American Student Organizations

The late 1980s and early 1990s were a time when Asian ethnic and other Asian American organizations, along with AAA, began to develop and re-form at UIUC. There was the Philippine Student Association (PSA, with roots in the 1940s, reorganized in 1985 to focus on undergraduate student members), the Korean Undergraduate Students Association (KUSA, established in 1979 and changed its name to the Korean American Students Association, or KASA, in 1995), the Vietnamese Student Association (VSA, established 1983), the Indian Student Association (ISA, registered as a group in 1987, with roots from the

1940s), and the Taiwanese American Students Club (TASC, established in 1991).[41] Because of the proliferation of Asian ethnic organizations, building community across ethnic lines was a challenge in the late 1980s. Though AAA had a diverse ethnic membership, it tended to be East Asian (Chinese and Taiwanese American). Alumni recalled that a sense of competition infused the groups, even over visibility as the best social organization. Each organization had its own focus and mission.

A move toward making connections across ethnic lines was new, as new pan–Asian American organizations at UIUC beyond AAA began to articulate a larger Asian American awareness in the 1990s. These student organizations began working together to sponsor events and advocate for Asian American issues. This coalition building was difficult at times but was critical to raising awareness, in particular challenging the model minority myth and pushing for resources—namely, an Asian American cultural center as a university student affairs unit and an AAS program under academic affairs. Such resources were denied; students felt that this was because the administration did not recognize Asian American students as minorities.

While the establishment of AAA signaled an important first step in community building in this period, the increasing needs and interests of Asian American students led to the rise of additional pan–Asian American organizations. One such organization was the Asian Council, formed in the spring of 1990 by Ramesh Subramani (BS, chemical engineering, 1991). Subramani was a member of AAA as well as the Indian Student Association (ISA) and was interested in building better working relations among the different Asian American ethnic groups. The Asian Council was also more of an advocacy organization, compared to AAA. In an effort to serve as an umbrella group for Asian American organizations, the Asian Council's mission was "1. Provide a medium through which the Asian (American) groups on campus can communicate and cooperate to address Asian (American) issues and 2. To support Asian (American) programming."[42] Group membership was not gained by individuals but was composed of a council of presidents and vice presidents of the Asian American student organizations, in particular AAA, PSA, KUSA, ISA, and the Hong Kong Students Association (HKSA).

Working together was critical to mobilizing support for the advancement of Asian American issues on campus. The Asian Council coordinated and sponsored several programs in the 1990–1991 academic year that pushed for the inclusion of Asian Americans in minority programs, including Asian American involvement in a minority organization fair in September 1990 coordinated by the Office of Minority Student Affairs, and organizing an independent career conference in November 1990 to encourage employers to see Asian Americans as possible minority employees. The Asian Council also planned UIUC's first Asian American Awareness Month in March 1991, which would

ASIAN AWARENESS MONTH 1991

Date	Org	Event
3/1-3	AAA	**Midwest Asian American Students Conference** @ Illini Union. For more info, contact Karin Wang @ 367-8618
3/2	AAA	**Dance** 9pm-12:30am @ Illini Union Ballroom
3/2	ISA	**Open Gym** 1pm-4pm @ Huff Gym
3/6	HKSA	**Potluck Dinner** For more info, contact Alice Djung @ 384-5159
3/7	ISA	**"The Gulf War's Effect on India & India's Middle East Policy": Speaker Steve Cohen** 7pm @ 261 Illini Union
3/7-9 3/7 3/8 3/9	IUB	**International Fair** Exhibits 4pm-8pm Film Festival 6:30pm Exhibits 12pm-8pm Performances 8pm Exhibits 12pm-4pm Activities 12pm-4pm
3/9	PSA	**Formal: "It Had to Be You"** 7pm @ Chancellor Hotel Interested? Call Marianne Bantog @ 367-0110
3/14	ISA	**News Track Of India Today** (video) 7pm @ 263 Illini Union
3/15	IUB	**Asian Variety Show: "Far East Fanfare"** 8pm @ Illini Union Ballroom
3/15-16	AAA	**"The Last Emperor"** 8pm @ Lincoln Hall Theater Cosponsored with IUB Films Committee
3/16	HKSA	**Asian Olympics** 1pm-5pm @ IMPE Ice Cream Social to follow afterwards
3/16	ISA	**Catered Indian Dinner** 2pm-5pm @ YMCA For more info, contact Sweta Katwala @ 359-6621
3/16	KUSA	**Annual Talent Show** 7pm-10pm @ 112 Gregory
3/17	AC	**Taste of Asia & Games of Asia** 2pm-5pm @ YMCA

This calendar sponsored by Asian Council: Asian American Association, Hong Kong Student Association, Indian Student Association, Korean Undergraduate Student Association, & Philippine Student Association.

13

FIG. 3.2 Flyer for the first Asian American Awareness Month at UIUC, March 1991. (Photo courtesy of the UIUC Asian American Cultural Center.)

become an annual recognition each spring.[43] The month featured dances, an Asian variety show at the Illini Union, film showings, dinners, lectures, and sports events[44] (see fig. 3.2).

For Asian American students who sought a more focused space to fight racism and injustice, the Asian-Pacific American Coalition to Combat Oppression, Racism, and Discrimination (ACCORD) fit the bill. ACCORD was a student organization with a specific agenda: working together to fight racism against Asian and Pacific Americans (especially combating the model minority myth); supporting other Asian Pacific American (APA) social, cultural, and political groups; examining Asian American history; acting on APA political issues; opposing all forms of oppression (racism, classism, sexism, heterosexism); and promoting understanding within the APA community and with other communities of color.[45] Formed in the spring of 1991, ACCORD members clearly identified as people of color and as Asian Americans who had a racialized minority experience. They stated, "We do not tolerate the assumption that Asian-Americans and Pacific-Americans are 'honorary Whites.'"[46] Thus, ACCORD provided an alternative space from which to tackle Asian American political issues head on, especially as racial incidents increased on campus in the 1990s.

Racial Hostility on Campus

As noted earlier, campuses nationwide were hostile to non-White students in the late 1980s and early 1990s. Philip Altbach notes there were over 200 racial clashes on college campuses between 1986 and 1988.[47] Another figure noted that from fall 1986 to December 1988, at least one incident of ethnic violence was reported at 250 colleges and universities.[48] Oftentimes the incidents were altercations between White and Black students that involved racial epithets, racist threats posted through flyers and mailings, or racist caricatures. On many campuses, students protested these events and demanded an institutional response, including improved recruitment, retention, and hiring of minority faculty, staff, and students, as well as a more diverse curriculum that included ethnic studies.[49]

Mirroring national trends, incidents of anti-Asian graffiti and racist name-calling were commonplace in the late 1980s and early 1990s at UIUC. For instance, in the spring 1988 semester, anti-Asian graffiti was scrawled in the men's bathroom of Gregory Hall. After it was erased, more racist words and images appeared the next day.[50] Anti-Asian racism also occurred in the surrounding community, such as local radio station WZNF's morning show that featured a racist caricature, Chef Wang. In a caricatured Asian accent, the buffoonish Chef Wang read ingredients of a recipe and callers tried to guess the mystery dish. Chef Wang asked, "Whu-u-u-ud is misseryfoo?" (What is mystery food?)[51] While the radio station denied any racist intent, AAA leaders circulated a petition protesting the racist character in May 1991, with plans to send the petition to the Federal Communications Commission and local authorities.

ACCORD was visible on campus in raising awareness of anti-Asian sentiment. The student group held a rally with other antiracist student organizations in response to the fiftieth anniversary observance of Japan's bombing of Pearl Harbor. On 6 December 1991, it sponsored a rally titled "Beyond Barbed Wire: Asian Americans Speaking Out against Racism—The Legacy of World War II: From Internment Camps to Vincent Chin."[52] In a press release, the group explained that the reason for the rally was that media coverage of the fiftieth anniversary of Pearl Harbor omitted the voices and histories of Japanese Americans—those who served in the military during World War II and those who were incarcerated in internment camps despite their U.S. citizenship. In addition, ACCORD pointed out the connection between this history and the present backlash against Asia's economic development.[53] UIUC student MariCarmen Moreno was quoted in the *Daily Illini* as pointing out the persistence of anti-Asian racism: "People have to realize Asians are put in a rough position. . . . (Americans) have to understand that (Asian Americans) do face racism, that they're not 'Whitewashed' as a lot of people might think." She added, "I think it's about time that Asian- and Pacific-Americans bring this out to the public and out to the campus. Racism is an issue that affects all people of color. . . . This is the start of something big."[54]

Name calling, harassment, and intimidation were common experiences for Asian Americans at UIUC in the early 1990s. Student Chris Oei described some of these incidents in an ACCORD newsletter in 1991:

> Twice on this campus so far, I've been called "Charlie" with a fake Chinese accent by groups of White students driving by. Once, they pretended not to see me and stopped just before hitting me. . . . When I ask my Asian friends if they've ever been called racially derogatory names, half of them answer yes. Many of the Asian women I talked to said that they have been subjected to sexual harassment in a racially derogatory manner from the men on this campus. Campus isn't a safe place for Asian Americans. . . . At the AAA booth at the Illini Union one day, a woman walked up and told the Asian student in the booth to go back to her own country. She believed that Asians are a privileged minority that doesn't pay taxes. . . . As Asians, we are all blamed for unemployment. As students, we are looked upon as antisocial. People think of us as workaholics who break the grading curve in our classes. We are not well-liked.[55]

ACCORD initiated an effort to collect data on anti-Asian harassment at UIUC and in the larger community, soliciting information about incidents in its 1991 newsletters.[56] The purpose of the data collection was explained in an incident report form: "Your response to this form will 1) help to validate the common experience of people of Asian/Pacific ancestry and 2) provide data to show the need for resources and services addressing the concerns of Asian/Pacific Americans."[57] In addition, AAA sent out a survey to members in fall 1990 and published some findings in its February 1991 newsletter. One question read, "My discrimination experiences include . . . ," with these findings: 45 percent "names"; 38 percent "taunts"; 12 percent "none"; 2 percent "fights"; 2 percent "physical abuse"; and 1 percent "other/being stereotyped."[58]

UIUC fraternities were also sites of racial incidents that sparked protest on campus by students of color. In the spring of 1988, on a visit to the University of Wisconsin campus, new pledge members of the UIUC Acacia fraternity disrupted several university classes with staged fights, stink bombs, and in one instance, an attack on a professor. At least two of the disrupted classes were African studies courses, and an investigation ensued regarding racial motivations.[59] In another instance in the spring of 1992, five minority male students claimed they were de-pledged from the Pi Kappa Alpha (the Pikes) fraternity based on race; this included Brian Thomas (African American and White), John Acosta (Filipino American), Salem Muribi (Lebanese American), John Nikkah (Iranian American), and Michael Stuart (Filipino American).[60] Students of color discussed the persistence of racism on campus revealed through these two incidents. In the case of Pi Kappa Alpha, AAA president Karin Wang held that the incident proved racism existed in the Greek system. She remarked, "It was interesting that two of the pledges were Asian-Americans. . . . It's important that people know that racism isn't just happening to African-Americans— it happens to Asian-Americans and anyone who is not Caucasian."[61]

Spring 1992 also saw a Greek racial incident against an Asian American student. On 5 March 1992, Alpha Tau Omega (ATO) fraternity members shouted racial epithets at Thai American student Ken Hriensaitong as he walked by the fraternity; Hriensaitong then challenged some members to a fight. Police charged fraternity member Christopher McPeek with assault and Hriensaitong with assault and unlawful use of a weapon (with the charges later dropped).[62] ACCORD led about thirty students outside of ATO on 26 March 1992 in protest, demanding an apology to Hriensaitong from the fraternity[63] (see fig. 3.3).

Asian American students at UIUC felt these incidents were not isolated cases. Just as they had been involved in documenting anti-Asian racism at UIUC, ACCORD members contextualized their ATO protest with a hostile campus climate, calling on administrators to respond in a press release:

> As Asian Americans of diverse ethnic and social backgrounds, we can attest that this is just one example of incidents that happen on our campus. Every day people of Asian Pacific descent are targets of racism, ranging from taunts and racial slurs to verbal and physical threats. Our community has no recourse for addressing these issues. We have no counselors and few academic staff to whom we can bring our needs and concerns. . . . WE CONDEMN ALL RACIST ACTIONS DIRECTED AT ASIANS AND ASIAN AMERICANS. WE CALL FOR AN END TO ALL FORMS OF ETHNIC INTIMIDATION AND HARASSMENT. WE CHALLENGE THE UNIVERSITY ADMINISTRATION TO ACT AND MAKE THIS CAMPUS A SAFE PLACE FOR ASIANS, ASIAN AMERICANS, AND ALL PEOPLE OF COLOR.[64]

FIG. 3.3 The Asian-Pacific American Coalition to Combat Oppression, Racism, and Discrimination (ACCORD) leading a protest of ATO fraternity, 26 March 1992. (Source: *The Daily Illini*; photographer, Dale Hensel. Photo courtesy of Illini Media/ *The Daily Illini*.)

Thus, the protesters challenged the stereotypes of Asian Americans as model minorities who did not experience racism or, at the very least, did not complain when they did.

Asian American Coalition Building

Asian American coalition building on campus in the early 1990s was a monumental task. Building a pan–Asian American movement is always a struggle given the vast diversity of the Asian American population. Within the field of Asian American studies, scholars have critiqued how the term "Asian American" has come to center East Asian Americans at the expense of South Asian Americans, Filipino Americans, and Southeast Asian Americans.[65] Asian American students at UIUC struggled to build a movement that included representation from all major Asian ethnic organizations. This shift to broaden their community was reflected in October 1991 when the AAA newsletter's name changed from *The Dynasty* to *Horizons*. The change was explained this way: "Since it was first published, the newsletter had been called *The Dynasty*. We felt, however, that this name reflected too much on Chinese or Japanese heritage rather than that of Asians overall. Many suggestions were brought forth, but, after much debate and discussion, *Horizons* was chosen since it best represents what we hope to reach. . . . The horizon represents the vastness and unity of the world. Asians and Asian Americans, as well as everyone across the world are all united by this line. No matter where you are or what you believe, you will see the same horizon."[66]

Yet as AAA leaders moved toward greater inclusion, they did not do so flaw-lessly.[67] Despite these persistent challenges (those that would always accompany gains made, revealing that coalition building is not an idealized, smooth pro-cess), strides were still being made. Several administrators witnessed the change in political activism as students of different Asian ethnicities began to commu-nicate with each other. Clarence Shelley, founding director of the Special Edu-cational Opportunities Program, reminisced, "Their working in coalition across ethnicities made a big difference in their productivity. Earlier efforts were much less successful because it seemed that historical national animosities made some groups unwilling or unable to work with other groups. Asian American student leaders came to believe that if they worked in coalition, they would accomplish more—a strategy that worked almost immediately."[68]

Pan-Asian coalition building was a new development for Asian American students at UIUC. The creation of a student office space in the Illini Union facilitated this cooperation. In April 1992, a new student organization complex opened in the student union, housing fifty-four organizations in cubicles and offices on the second floor. As a result, Asian American organizations such as AAA, ISA, KUSA, PSA, the Taiwanese American Students Club (TASC), and the Vietnamese Student Association (VSA) had offices, and the common space created opportunities for members to talk with each other.[69] Richard Chang, sophomore in Liberal Arts and Sciences (LAS) and AAA member, noted, "Before groups were scattered all over the place, while now it's more centralized. It's more convenient if you need to talk to someone from another group."[70] Bill Riley, dean of students from 1986 to 2008, also attributed the student complex as a significant facilitator of Asian American students working together: "When we restructured as a campus the second floor south of the Illini Union and cre-ated the student organization's complex and allowed each organization to have a cubicle at the beginning, and we put them all in there, and then the Asian American student groups started growing and talking to each other, that was a significant time in my mind when they came together. They saw each other, they met together, and every day there was so much traffic and stuff going on. . . . It was like a programming center."[71] These coalitions would continue to grow through the mid-1990s, to great benefit for the Asian American movement.

Asian American Student Movements in Midwestern Context: The 1980s and 1990s

Asian American college students have a long history of working together across their respective campuses. As Asian students experienced in the 1920s and Asian American students experienced in the 1970s, networking across cam-puses through conferences helped students build community, share informa-tion, and hone a critique of racism on campus.[72] On the East Coast, Asian

American students at Yale University met in April 1977 to create the Inter-Collegiate Liaison Committee (ICLC); at a conference at Princeton in March 1978, the East Coast Asian Student Union (ECASU) was formed. Simultaneously, Asian American students on the West Coast formed the Asian Pacific Student Union in April 1978.[73] Around this time, a Midwest Asian Pacific American Student Association Network (MAPASAN) was established as well; each network sought to improve communication across campuses and advance Asian American student interests.[74]

The formation of AAA was directly influenced by Asian American students at the University of Michigan. Asian American student networking across Midwestern campuses began to develop through the late 1980s and early 1990s. The idea to create a Midwestern Asian American Students (MAAS) network was inspired by the existing networks ECASU and the Asian Pacific Student Union. Patricia Chou Lin (BA, sociology, 1991) was involved in AAA and coordinated the first MAAS conference. She recalled, "We saw the opportunity to create a Midwest network similar to the East and West Coast networks. We believed a conference would more easily bring Asian Pacific American students together to create necessary connections."[75]

Asian American students at UIUC began working with others in the Midwest to coordinate the first annual MAAS conference, which was held at UIUC in April 1989, with the title "The Asian Connection." About fifty students from five colleges attended.[76] According to a 1993 conference booklet, "The largest accomplishment of MAAS '89, other than to educate the students who attended [on Asian American issues], was that it was the beginning of network-building by five large schools—University of Illinois, Indiana University, University of Michigan, Purdue University, and Washington University."[77] AAA sponsored the MAAS conference at UIUC annually until 1996 (see fig. 3.4).

The second MAAS conference, held on 6–8 April 1990, revolved around the theme "Bridging the Gap: Asians Headed for the Future" and featured panels and workshops on leadership challenges and professionalization, as well as cultural ceremonies, sports events, a fashion show, and a formal dance.[78] The conference directory listed attendees from UIUC, Northwestern University, Miami University (Ohio), Michigan State University, Purdue University, Washington University, Ohio State University, and Wright State University (Ohio), with an estimated 150 participants.[79]

As UIUC's Asian American students were coordinating MAAS, other students were having similar conversations on the need to network in the region, articulating a specific Midwestern Asian American identity. In October 1989, members from six schools (Miami, Michigan State, Oberlin College, Ohio State, Purdue, and the University of Michigan) met in Granville, Ohio, to discuss the need for a regional organization to coordinate such efforts.[80]

FIG. 3.4 Cover of a Midwest Asian American Students (MAAS) conference program held at UIUC in 1993. (Photo courtesy of the UIUC Asian American Cultural Center.)

The Midwest Asian American Students Union (MAASU) was officially formed on 27 June 1990 with Charles Chang as the statutory agent. MAASU elected its interim officers at a conference jointly held with Purdue University that fall.

Charles Chang's family immigrated to the United States from Seoul, South Korea, in 1970, when Chang was six years old. He grew up Granville, where his was the first Asian family in town. Growing up in a small, predominantly White town without a Korean or Asian American community to support him, Chang recalled the racial issues that emerged for him:

> I think since getting off the plane, I've always been somewhat aware of the race issue. At the beginning I was getting into a lot of fights because, you know, they made fun of me, mostly of the way I talked because I couldn't speak English when I first got here. So I think race is always something that had been in the back of my mind, something I'd been trying to cope with understanding. And then later in high school I started to go through what a lot of kids go through—identity issues, trying to get who I was, as someone who was different from most of the other kids that I saw who were White. . . . Plus, not only that, I think I was trying to understand what it meant to be Korean because there were a few other Korean families in other towns I knew, but in terms of culture, I didn't really understand Korean culture either.[81]

In 1984 Chang enrolled at Ohio State University and became involved in the Asian American Association, a similar type of organization as the AAAs at Illinois and Michigan. Chang was president of the organization from 1987 to 1988 and was involved in pushing for Asian American resources on campus, including heading a campaign for a full-time student affairs staff position for Asian American students. As he grew in his leadership, Chang began to hear of similar Midwestern Asian American student organizations that held conferences at Oberlin, Michigan State, the University of Michigan, and UIUC. He recalled, "Around 1988 I started to realize that around the Midwest there were various other student groups, and I think they were probably all kind of in the same boat, starting to find that there are other student groups . . . isolated in these universities with no Asian communities. For some of us, we felt the need to reach out to each other, to feel stronger, to feel like we're not so small, isolated, and to support each other, while we're doing the work that we're trying to do."[82] Seeing this presence and new growth on campuses made Chang realize that the time was ripe to start to organize Asian American students in the Midwest. He stated, "I envisioned what MAASU would want to do, to bring these student organizations together to feel some solidarity and make them feel like they're not as isolated as they were. And another thing I was thinking was that politically, because they were so small, if we worked together and united, we would have more political clout together than alone."[83]

Information about the newly formed MAASU was made available at UIUC's third MAAS conference, held 1–3 March 1991. That year's conference's listed purposes were to "1. Educate the university community on current and vital Asian American issues; 2. Serve as a basis for forming a support network of Asian American student organizations across the Midwest area. Also, to serve as a means for Asian American faculty and staff on this campus to network with their peers on other campuses."[84] Continuing its consistent annual growth, the 1991 conference hosted 230 students, as well as faculty and staff, from eighteen colleges. The conference also kicked off the very first Asian American Awareness Month coordinated by the Asian Council. MAASU held its April 1991 conference at Michigan, and the year after, on 3–5 April 1992, MAASU held its conference jointly with UIUC's MAAS, which it would do again in March 1995. An estimated 400 students attended, representing over twenty colleges in the Midwest.[85]

MAASU brought Asian American students together to build a larger base of support, which was critical for those feeling geographically isolated from large populations of Asian Americans.[86] MAASU encouraged them to think of larger Asian American issues. For instance, Jeremy Bautista (BA, history, 1996) recalled the impact MAASU had on him; before then he had grown up in a predominantly White suburb in Chicago and had denied his Filipino heritage: "It just really woke me up. And I said, 'Wow! People are wrestling with similar family struggles as me, people are facing the same questions as I am, like with my whole disownment of being Filipino.' I really had a big identity crisis on my hands. . . . I definitely was encouraged to ask those hard identity questions now because here are 399 other people asking the same kind of thing! So I felt like that was good; that really pushed me to getting more involved on campus for Asian American awareness."[87]

Patricia Chou Lin also believed that MAAS and MAASU helped shape AAA's future direction. She said, "Many began to recognize there were commonalities Asian Pacific American students shared both across Asian cultures and beyond our university. One such example was the model minority image and related experiences and challenges. Coming together across Midwest universities raised the level of awareness, which led towards a mindset of working for a common goal. I believe this created the platform for the cultural center and other areas of continued progress for Asian Pacific Americans at the University of Illinois."[88]

In addition, networking with other Asian American students in the Midwest made UIUC students aware of what resources their campus lacked. Karin Wang recalled how much she had learned through the Midwest network that included Big Ten schools and also smaller colleges: "I think especially as we started to network across campuses, there was a lot I learned from the Midwest students. . . . We would see, 'Oh, Michigan has Asian American studies professors and classes. Why don't we have that?' And so we started to also push and say, 'Doesn't the U of I want to be like these other schools? Aren't we just as good as Michigan?'"[89] Thus, the start of networking across the Midwest raised not only personal awareness but a larger vision for what could and should exist at UIUC for Asian American students.

Administrative Responses to Asian American Students

With the rise in the number of Asian American student organizations at UIUC and a growing regional awareness of Asian American student needs, administrators began to take notice in the late 1980s and early 1990s. In 1988 vice chancellor for student affairs Stan Levy sent a copy of an article from the *New York Times* featuring Asian American issues along with a memo to several student affairs staff, including dean of students Bill Riley and associate vice chancellor Clarence Shelley. He wrote, "I am enclosing for your information an article which appeared recently in the *New York Times*. It is relevant to our experience, though it clearly has not been a large item on our agenda. We have focused our minority efforts on Blacks and Latinos, and have paid little-to-no attention to the Asian-American dilemma. I find the enclosed persuasive and sufficiently provocative. It may be time to begin to develop another focus of attention."[90] The article from July 10 discussed the pressures from the model minority myth that Asian American students felt at UC Berkeley; Asian American students who did not meet the expectations of the model minority myth were overlooked and underserved. Asian Americans were diverse, and more-recent immigrants needed assistance with financial aid and linguistic adjustment. The pressures to succeed also resulted in psychological stressors.[91]

There were also some key reports being written at the time informing UIUC administrators of Asian American experiences. In December 1989, Athena Tapales, a student intern in the Office of the Vice Chancellor for Student Affairs, submitted an eleven-page report to Levy about Asian Pacific Islanders (APIs). The report provided information on historical and contemporary issues facing Americans of Chinese, Filipino, Indian, Indochinese (Vietnamese), Japanese, and Korean descent. In particular, Tapales pointed out specific stressors facing Asian American students at UIUC. Asian American students faced academic pressure from their parents as well as from model minority myth expectations, and they also hesitated in employing counseling services due to cultural stigma. Moreover, they encountered acculturation stress as they negotiated between U.S. society and their immigrant parents' cultures, and they encountered discrimination as a racial minority. Tapales recommended development in three areas—providing curricula that included Asian American cultures, hiring of staff who understood the API experience, and supporting Asian American campus programs such as an Asian American Awareness Week (which did not yet exist). She highlighted successful programs housed under multi-ethnic and Asian American centers at Michigan State University and Ohio State University, which hired counselors and administrators to assist Asian American students. She argued, "Asian Americans should also be addressed as a minority on this campus. There seems to be a stigma on this University regarding APIs. Since they do not exhibit academic problems and experience overt discrimination, the University has not placed them under the minority category. However, in order to address the problems Asian American students face, they need to be acknowledged as a minority that needs support."[92]

Shortly thereafter, on 24 January 1990, Levy created an Asian American Task Force (AATF) comprised of student affairs staff to "review the needs of and issues faced by Asian American students and to report recommendations/ feedback to the Vice Chancellor for Student Affairs."[93] The AATF met through the spring 1990 semester, gathering information from other Big Ten institutions about their Asian American resources. They also met periodically with groups of Asian American students to assess their concerns and communicated with two interns at the counseling center who were working on an Asian American–needs survey instrument as part of the center's own efforts to reach diverse student populations.

Based on their conversations with students, the AATF reported on Asian American issues at UIUC. With a desire for greater cultural awareness, students desired staff support, Asian American programming, Asian American studies courses, support groups, and greater representation in mainstream programs on campus, such as through the Illini Union Board.[94] The AATF also noted that students desired an Asian American cultural center, which would provide a centralized meeting space for them to come together, learn about each others' cultures, and coordinate programs, as La Casa Cultural Latina did for Latinx students. The AATF mentioned that two existing institutional offices, the Office of Minority Student Affairs and the Office of International Student Affairs, were ultimately insufficient in supporting Asian American students.[95]

In addition, the AATF articulated feelings among Asian American students of not being viewed as a valid minority by administrators and by other students of color: "The Asian American students feel rejected by other minorities because of their 'super minority' image. They would like to co-sponsor programs with other minority student organizations because they feel the need to be supportive, but are reluctant because of perceived rejection. . . . Asian American students feel excluded from Minority Student Affairs. They do not have a 'home' such as the African-American, Latino and International students."[96] These developments revealed the rising awareness of and advocacy by student affairs administrators for Asian American students' needs, which included an Asian American cultural center and AAS courses.

Asian American students at UIUC in the late 1980s and early 1990s were frustrated with their invisibility in campus life. As they were not underrepresented, the university did not recognize them as a minority population in need of services such as programming support, counseling aid, or an inclusive curriculum, even while it included Asian American numbers in minority reports. Asian

American students were surprised to learn that they were not minorities when they came to UIUC. Ho Chie Tsai wrote in retrospect about one of the things he learned as a student: "When I was a freshman at the University of Illinois, I once walked into a minority fair and found that I wasn't considered a minority. How embarrassing."[97]

This is not to say that OMSA's academic-focused support services were not critical to serving underrepresented populations such as African American and Latinx students. However, because no other office provided support for Asian Americans and because taking on this task for OMSA would have required not only a significant increase in resources but also a shift in its mission, Asian American students had no place to go. While needing programming support rather than academic assistance, as the AATF pointed out, Asian American students were an invisible group, pushed out by discourses that focused on underrepresentation and by a model minority narrative that masked their continued struggles.

Jody Lin (BS, bioengineering, 1991) expressed his frustration with this situation. In a letter to the *Daily Illini*, he critiqued the campus's recent issue of *In Print* magazine that focused on issues of prejudice but had ignored Asian American experiences. He challenged this invisibility of Asian Americans in minority student discussions this way: "The typical view of Asians is that we are a "model minority"—all smart, successful, overachieving, science-oriented people—and this perception is simply not true. . . . As minorities on this campus, Asian-Americans have support needs too, but because of the perception that Asian-Americans are so successful, these needs are rarely recognized and addressed. . . . Asian-Americans may be labeled as a 'model minority,' but a 'forgotten minority' may be a more appropriate label."[98]

Asian American overrepresentation and the model minority sense of Asian American success worked against the recognition of Asian Americans as minorities. In response, Asian American students not only challenged their exclusion from minority categories but also articulated where this exclusion left them—Asian Americans were in a racial purgatory at UIUC because it was unclear where they fit. Vivian Chow, a junior majoring in commerce, said, "The problem is Asians are not a part of the majority, yet we are not considered a minority on this campus." In addition, Asian American needs, which did not fit a measure of underrepresentation or a Black-White model, got short shrift. Chow said, "People think because we have different needs, we have no needs at all."[99]

The late 1980s ushered in a new era of Asian American student activism at UIUC. A new cohort of second-generation Asian American students (a post-1965 generation) began to come together. Building a pan–Asian American movement was not easy in those early years, given the community's diversity. Yet gains were beginning to be made, and new Asian American organizations came to life on campus and across the Midwest. As Asian American students began to work together, they began to question university minority policies that focused on African Americans and Latinxs and overlooked Asian American student needs on a racially inhospitable campus. Activism for institutional resources such as Asian American awareness programs, counselors, staff, and two key units—an Asian American studies program and an Asian American cultural center—continued through the 1990s within a larger context of student activism at UIUC.

4

We Are Minorities

The Fight for Asian American
Studies and Student Services,
1992–1996

In the 1990s, Asian American student leaders challenged the University of Illinois at Urbana-Champaign (UIUC)'s double standard of counting Asian Americans in minority and diversity reports without providing them minority student services. As they were not considered minorities, they did not receive institutional support. In a forty-two-page proposal for an Asian American cultural center at UIUC, students argued that Illinois state law defined them as minorities. They wrote,

> We feel it is time for the University of Illinois at Urbana-Champaign to join
> the multicultural society of the United States by recognizing Asian Pacific
> Americans as a minority group. It is not only the proper thing to do, but it is
> also the law. We are not just a statistic to be used whenever the University needs
> to brag about its minority population. Under the Board of Education Act #205
> Section 9.16, Asian Pacific Americans are considered a minority in all Illinois
> Institutions of Higher Education. Thus special programs funding and financial
> aid must also be given to Asian Pacific Americans at the University of Illinois
> at Urbana-Champaign.[1]

Students repeatedly asserted that they were minorities and contested the model minority myth, a focus on parity, and a Black-White racial paradigm as they pushed for two key resources—an Asian American studies program and an Asian American cultural center. UIUC's African American studies program and African American cultural center were established in 1969, and its Latinx culture center, La Casa Cultural Latina, was established in 1974. However, there were no parallel resources for Asian American or Native American students, and an academic Latinx studies program did not exist in the early 1990s.

Asian American student activism at UIUC in the 1990s took place in a politically charged racial context. The early 1990s were a time of activism by African Americans, Latinxs, Asian Americans, American Indians, women, and the lesbian, gay, bisexual, and transgender community nationwide.[2] These students fought for ethnic studies classes, financial aid, and discrimination protections. Following national trends, in Urbana-Champaign, Native American, Latinx, African American, and Asian American issues also gained visibility. The local newspaper, the *Champaign-Urbana News-Gazette,* attributed the rise of these movements to the demographic growth in minority students on campus. In addition, college students had learned lessons from the civil rights movement of the 1960s.[3]

Even more significant in the 1990s was that activists emphasized that racism was not just an African American concern. Latinx students challenged UIUC administrators' neglect, arguing, in a similar vein to that of Asian American students, that they were overlooked in a minority model that focused on African Americans. A movement protesting the university's mascot, Chief Illiniwek, also emerged, and a small group of Native American students began to build coalitions to retire the Chief. Asian American activism and university responses took shape in this larger political context, expanding administrators' attention beyond African American students.

Latinx and Native American Students at UIUC in the 1990s

Latinx students struggled to be heard in UIUC minority programs that had focused on African American students since the early 1970s. Because of their activism, administrators established positions for a Latinx recruiter and Educational Opportunities Program (EOP) counselor and created La Casa Cultural Latina. Yet these resources were unstable; La Casa had a string of directors through the 1980s, with no director staying longer than three years until the mid-1980s. The lack of Latinx administrators was a key issue for students. In 1989 there were only two full-time Latinx administrators on campus, and students wanted three additional Latinx staff: a dean, and one administrator each in La Casa and the Office of Minority Student Affairs (OMSA).[4]

FIG. 4.1. Chief Illiniwek performing at a UIUC football game, from the 1991 *Illio*.
(Photo courtesy of Illini Media/*Illio*.)

Latinx students were also upset with bureaucratic changes in La Casa. In
the fall of 1988, La Casa (along with the Afro-American Cultural Program) was
moved under the aegis of OMSA.[5] In the fall of 1990, the position of associate
director of OMSA was created to supervise La Casa and help administer programs. Students felt that the change created a bureaucratic buffer between La
Casa's director and OMSA's director. La Raza, a new student organization, submitted a petition signed by 160 students contesting this change and La Casa's
paltry budget.[6] In the spring of 1991, students objected when an assistant director position was created for La Casa, which OMSA oversaw with no input
from La Casa's director.[7] They met with vice chancellor for student affairs Stan
Levy and chancellor Morton Weir, urging for the removal of La Casa's new
assistant director, whom they believed was undermining La Casa's recruitment
programs, and they protested OMSA's control over La Casa's hiring process.

Just as Latinx students were advocating for resources and autonomy, a new
movement for Native American concerns emerged at UIUC. A key issue of contention for students of color was Chief Illiniwek. From 1926 until 2007, Chief
Illiniwek represented the University of Illinois as the school symbol. Created
by UIUC student Lester Leutwiler, the Chief performed at university football
events, and as football's popularity rose after World War II, the Chief's performances evolved. In 1952, student Bill Hug began to incorporate acrobatics
such as split leaps into the Chief's dance (see fig. 4.1).

By the 1980s, the Chief logo (his head with headdress) was being printed
on university merchandise ranging from T-shirts and caps to toilet paper, uri-
nal screens, and trash cans.[8] For its supporters, the Chief evoked the imagery

of courage, freedom, and individualism and represented university tradition. However, for its detractors, the Chief represented an inauthentic and offensive racist mascot that signaled a hostile campus climate not only for Native American students but for all students of color. Native American and Alaskan Native student numbers had always been low at UIUC, never reaching over 100 students from 1968 to 2008 and ranging from 0.1 to 0.4 percent of the undergraduate student enrollment.[9] By the late 1980s, the question of the Chief began to gain momentum. In 1988, UIUC's art department recruited three Native American master's students from the School of American Indian Arts in Santa Fe.[10] One of these students was Charlene Teters, a member of the Spokane Nation. Teters created the student organization Native Americans for Progress, protested the Chief, and became involved in a movement to remove him as the university mascot.

In September 1990, a university civil rights group, the Coalition for a New Tradition, composed of students and community members, held a march for Native American awareness and submitted a petition signed by 350 people in support of the elimination of Chief Illiniwek; the inclusion of Native Americans in the curriculum; the creation of a Native American studies program and Native American cultural center; improved efforts for the recruitment and retention of Native American students, faculty, and staff; and the return of university-owned Native American artifacts to the Native American community.[11] Despite the group's efforts, in October the board of trustees voted to retain the Chief.

The anti-Chief movement forged on, as a multiracial coalition attested that the Chief negatively affected all racial minority groups. As Teters articulated about the Chief, "It's not only a Native American issue. It is an issue of racism. Anyone who is anti-racist must address this."[12] As these students pushed for Native American resources, they also supported the appeal for an Asian American cultural center in the 1990s.

Building Coalitions among Students of Color

Just as Asian American students were starting to build a pan-Asian coalition, the early 1990s signaled a time when students of color began working together for campus resources. These collaborations signified a collective challenge to racism. For instance, in the spring of 1991, a coalition of students of color (seventeen African Americans and two Latinxs) ran for positions in the Student Government Association (SGA), the official student voice of the university, on a slate called Vision.[13] The Vision slate won a number of positions, including student-trustee candidate, ten of the fifteen elected assembly members, and five of eight Student Organization Resource Fee Board positions. One student described Vision's victory this way: "People of color, Vision's constituency, are a very united community and they are much more interested in change than the typical White apathetic voter. . . . For once, people of color will not be in the minority."[14]

Osvaldo Morera, graduate student in psychology, commented on this movement and what it portended in his *Daily Illini* column. He described how on 14 October 1991, more than 250 African American, Latinx, and Native American students protested the lives lost through the legacy of Columbus (subsequent protests of Columbus Day included Asian Americans in 1992).[15] These students presented a list of demands to the administration that included creating a Latina/o studies program and a Native American studies program and cultural center, as well as enhancing the Afro-American studies program and cultural center.[16] In addition, Morera described the increasing activism of Asian American students and the involvement of Palestinian students in the rally. He noted that previous efforts by the university were aimed at dividing these groups from working together, but that this tactic would no longer work. He wrote, "The University has fallen considerably short in terms of numbers of ethnic students, ethnic faculty and ethnic research programs. Instead of addressing the problems, the University masks them and hopes they will disappear. The University has a time bomb ticking, and my word of warning is very simple: Watch out."[17]

A growing number of campus programs and events focused on collaboration across racial groups. On 9 April 1992, a panel of students of color discussed how to relieve tensions and build better coalitions between Asian Americans and African Americans.[18] Latinx students' demands were also tied to the needs of other students of color. At a rally on 1 May, senior Jason Ferreira described how the barriers to La Casa's growth would be repeated for other groups. He stated, "What's happened to La Casa will happen to the African-American cultural center . . . and there will never be an Asian-American or Native American cultural center, and you can bet if we don't get in gear, that racist mascot will never be gone."[19]

Despite these gains, building coalitions across communities of color was not easy, especially for Asian Americans. The discourse on campus that Asian American students were model minorities was hard to ignore, including by other students of color. Some Asian American students, especially those involved in the Asian-Pacific American Coalition to Combat Oppression, Racism, and Discrimination (ACCORD), tried to work in coalition with other groups representing students of color, and women of color had made significant strides to work together through the Young Women's Christian Association (YWCA) on campus.[20] Yet alliances were difficult to build, as Asian Americans were not seen as immediate allies by other students of color. Some ACCORD alumni recollected the challenges to building the coalition. Rhoda Gutierrez (BS, psychology, 1993) recalled, "The Asian American students were not really welcomed. We actually had to really negotiate our space there. . . . It was like we [Asian Americans] had economic privilege and we had, to a certain extent, been accepted within mainstream social spheres. So it wasn't like we were facing 'racism' or discrimination. . . . At times it was difficult to get in a word edgewise because there was so much hostility against us even trying to be part of this coalition."[21] It was not presumed that Asian American students experienced racism and discrimination because they were model minorities. These tensions would persist, even as fragile coalitions were built.

Latinx Students' Sit-ins: Spring 1992

As these issues were brewing, Latinx students continued to push for their needs. Chancellor Weir formed an independent three-person commission in 1992 to investigate Latinx students' demands, setting a deadline of 27 April for a response. After several meetings and delays, students felt it was time to take action. On 29 April they held a sit-in at the Office of Minority Student Affairs; university police dragged out nine Latinx students who had refused to leave, and students charged police with brutality and excessive force.[22] The sit-in fell on the same date as the news of the acquittal of Los Angeles police officers in the beating of Rodney King, sparking the Los Angeles riots. This coincidence seemed to confirm an institutional response of police force toward people of color. The unjust verdict in the Rodney King case fueled rallies and marches as well as sporadic incidents of violence in Urbana-Champaign in May 1992.[23]

On 1 May, Latinx students held a rally on the campus quad, attracting over 200 people. They sought the removal of La Casa's assistant director and La Casa from OMSA oversight and the creation of a Latinx student council to oversee the cultural center. Four days later, on Cinco de Mayo, a multiracial coalition of 120 students staged an eight-hour sit-in at the Henry Administration Building.[24] Their demands included increasing recruitment and retention of Latinx students, faculty, and staff; removing Chief Illiniwek and creating a Native American cultural center; and creating an academic Latina/o studies program.[25] In an attempt to break up the sit-in, police from UIUC, Urbana, and Champaign, along with state troopers, forcibly removed sixty students and arrested three for aggravated battery, resisting arrest, and obstructing justice.[26] There was also a rash of fires in campus buildings that night, with some officials suspecting a connection to the protests (see fig. 4.2).

Some Asian American students, particularly those in ACCORD, were involved in the sit-in and publicly supported Latinx students. Miya Yoshitani, an ACCORD member, stated to the *Daily Illini*, "Asian-Americans stand in solidarity with the Latino and Latina community fighting for their cultural center and for self-determination."[27] Neena Hemmady, another ACCORD member, affirmed, "For myself and the other Asian groups, I'd like to say we

FIG. 4.2 Police remove protestors from the Henry Administration Building, 5 May 1992. (Source: *The Daily Illini*; photographer, Mark Cowan. Photo courtesy of Illini Media/*The Daily Illini*.)

stand in complete solidarity with our Latina/o brothers. We (Asians) are in the midst of struggling for our own cultural center. The university always is trying to impose its view on how the ethnic groups should run their own affairs."[28]

UIUC had not seen such large-scale protest in some time. Paul Doebel, director of campus security, described the 5 May sit-in as the "most significant protest" since the antiwar demonstrations of the 1970s.[29] It was crucial for administrators to respond in a meaningful way. The university commission assigned by Chancellor Weir to investigate the Latinx students' demands presented its findings on 8 May; it found that the university had not provided enough commitment or sensitivity to Latinx students' needs.[30] It recommended stabilizing La Casa's budget, moving La Casa out of OMSA, and giving a new physical space to La Casa. In response, Weir formed an executive committee to work with students; some changes included stabilizing La Casa's budget, adding $30,000 in funding, and having La Casa report to a different unit than OMSA.[31]

University trustees and Illinois state senators were concerned by the protest, the report, and with students' charges of police brutality. State senators Miguel del Valle and Alice Palmer called for UIUC to drop disciplinary actions against protestors and arrested students and met with Chancellor Weir to express their concerns. Del Valle also commended the broad-based racial coalition that made the efforts possible. He stated, "Participating in the demonstration were a coalition of students which included Latina/os, African Americans, Caucasians, and Asians. I truly have not seen such an impressive coalition of diverse ethnic and economic backgrounds since the 1960s."[32] Legislators introduced a resolution calling for the university to conduct an investigation of Latinx concerns.[33]

On 14 October 1992, an Illinois State Senate subcommittee held a six-and-a-half-hour hearing in the Illini Union regarding Latinx students and other students of color, led by Senators del Valle and Palmer. During the hearing, Weir and UIUC president Stanley Ikenberry testified. Latinx, Asian American, and Native American students also described a hostile campus climate for minorities and the excessive police force used in ejecting student protestors in May.[34] Students worked on achieving amnesty for those arrested and pushed for a Latina/o studies program and improved retention efforts of students and faculty. Del Valle and Palmer stated they would investigate student disciplinary procedures and police oversight at UIUC.

ACCORD members gathered data to be included in the state subcommittee hearings to shed light on the racism faced by Asian American students. Students testified that Asian Americans were not model minorities and that anti-Asian harassment and violence on campus existed and included racial assaults, threatening phone calls to Asian American student activists, and racist comments hurled at Asian Americans to "go back to Asia." They stated, "The administration must actively seek to meet the needs and address the issues and interest of Asian/Pacific American students concerning the culture center, studies program with Asian/Pacific American faculty whose primary research interest is on Asian/Pacific Americans, counseling facilities, recruitment and retention by ethnicity, and office to handle anti-Asian/Pacific harassment and violence."[35] Students also pushed for the creation of a full-time staff person for Asian Pacific American (APA) student services.

Neena Hemmady (BS, civil engineering, 1994) recalled the significance of working on the data for the hearing: "We were collecting data, putting together a case of what it meant to be an Asian person in the higher education system of Illinois. We felt that there was discrimination and that it was difficult and challenging. There were things like the model minority myth that we had to challenge ourselves on, not to mention Asian Americans who didn't fit the myth and had to face severe economic challenges! . . . The gist of what we gave to the Illinois Board of Higher Education was: there was anti-Asian discrimination and it was very real. And that to me was also a big deal because it was us being very visible."[36] The testimony by ACCORD members was endorsed by Asian American student organizations including the Asian American Association (AAA), the Asian American Artists Collective, BARKADA: Philippine Support Group, the Hong Kong Students Association (HKSA), the Indian Student Association (ISA), the Indonesian Student Association, the Philippine

Student Association (PSA), Shakti (the YWCA Asian/Pacific American Women's Support Group), the Singapore Student Association, the Taiwanese American Students Club (TASC), the Vietnamese Student Association (VSA), and Wavemakers, an Asian American women's group.

Shaping a Different Kind of Activism for Asian American Students

But just as some ACCORD members were actively compiling data and testifying in the State Senate hearings, other Asian Americans avoided involvement. Some AAA leaders such as Jessica Chen (BS, chemical engineering, 1994) expressed frustration with Asian American students who were apathetic or feared getting involved in politics. She wrote in the November 1992 AAA newsletter, "It is thoroughly embarrassing to see the patheticness [sic] of the Asian American community. At the Senate hearings, the other three minority groups were well represented and displayed unity within themselves. Yet, just a handful (literally) of Asian Americans were present. . . . There is no excuse for the ignorance displayed by Asian Americans on campus when it comes to the issues we face. . . . If we can spend half an hour getting ready for a three-hour dance with 500 people attending, we can spend one hour at an Awareness meeting." She concluded: "Please don't let the Asian American community be humiliated again. . . . If as minorities we are expecting to accomplish anything on this campus, it will have to be done in coalition with the other minority groups on campus, where the strength in numbers lie [sic]."[37]

As Chen's letter revealed, while groups such as ACCORD took on a pointed political approach and were involved in larger coalitions among students of color on campus, many others were not involved or shied away. In response, Asian American student organization leaders took on the challenges of eliciting a wider investment by their members cautiously and strategically.

While there are many forms activism can take on, protests, rallies, marches, and sit-ins represent effective and visible ways to press for change, such as used by Latinx students and their supporters in May 1992. However, these forms of activism were not always plausible options for many Asian American students at UIUC. Several leaders were aware that the likelihood of gaining a large Asian American constituency to protest and take over administration buildings for resources was unlikely. Ho Chie Tsai (BS, electrical engineering, 1994) recalled the trepidation that other students felt about protesting. In appealing to a wider community of support for Asian American issues, he knew this: "I had to figure out a way that could be palatable. We talked about the 1992 sit-ins a lot. I think when the incidents actually peaked, it scared a lot of the Asian American students. Because even though they supported it, in their minds, they were probably thinking, we can't do it the same way, there's no way we could fight our fight the way they did."[38]

Part of the reason for this caution for Asian American students was cultural pressure from immigrant parents and a tacit comfort with being involved primarily in social activities. In the 1970s, Asian American Alliance founders also were mindful in appealing to a broad range of Asian American students, ultimately deciding not to name itself the Asian American Political Alliance. In the late 1980s many Asian ethnic and Asian American organizations had greater success with social events such as parties and fashion shows. Tsai said of his peers, "They were the new second-generation immigrants coming of age, whose parents came post-1965. A lot of them had grown up in the suburbs of Chicago, usually as a minority in their high school at the time . . . and I think the general attitude was just try to fit in, just do the regular things that everyone else does. You know, it wasn't cool to be different or identify as Asian American or think about identity. . . . 'Being political' and 'making waves' were not part of most people's natural tendency at that time."[39]

As newer organizations such as AAA, the Asian Council, and ACCORD sought to push a larger political and educational agenda, mobilizing support among reticent Asian American students posed a challenge. AAA leaders in particular strategically pushed for resources while trying not to alienate more-conservative Asian American students (potential supporters), all the while making pointed political statements. Thus, part of the approach of these leaders involved working tirelessly to build an educational element into the social events where Asian American students more readily convened. Jody Lin (BS, bioengineering, 1991), AAA president from 1989 to 1991, recalled using strategies that were less confrontational and more social, noting, "Social events were a way of bringing people of different ethnicities together. I think we always recognized that the social element was (and always would be) the main draw. But if we could inject some education or some awareness into those activities, and if that branched out into other directions, we were very happy about that."[40] Ho Chie Tsai also recalled the ways that AAA sought to infuse some educational content about Asian American issues into social events. At a dance party, an information board would outline the issues, or a fundraiser could raise funds for Asian American books. He stated, "We made it our mission that every dance had to have some other greater purpose attached to it."[41]

Even while emphasizing different tactics, Asian American student leaders were intent on building on the momentum of student activism on campus that took on more visible forms by Latinx students, and they called for unity in raising awareness of their needs. In a letter to Asian American student organization officers, Peter Ko, AAA external vice president, wrote of the need for unity to secure resources: "It is clear that only together can our voice be heard and the University recognize us and our need for an Asian [American] Studies curriculum, an Asian American cultural center, and minority support services. Only together can we make the U of I campus more culturally aware. After a year in which we've seen both the African American and the Latina/o Americans really come together for a cause, it is now time for the Asian Americans to show some unity."[42]

Asian American students would employ a variety of strategies as they pressed for university resources aside from outward protest that included petitions, proposals, awareness programs, and legal strategies, all of which challenged the model minority myth, the notion that Asian Americans were not a minority because they were not underrepresented, and a university focus on African American students. These strategies demonstrate various forms of activism (not limited to sit-ins and protest marches), contradicting the stereotype of a passive Asian American model minority.

Asian American Unity Building for Resources

While the Asian Council and ACCORD had faded by 1992, other pan–Asian American organizations were forming and began working together to raise awareness. One such group was the Asian American Artists Collective, founded in the spring of 1992. The Collective was a group of students who published *Monsoon,* a biannual journal of Asian American art and literature, and who coordinated art exhibits, poetry readings, and performances. The Collective's objectives revealed a political aim to break the silence surrounding Asian American experiences: "Asian Americans are the invisible minority and our voices have been historically silenced. The Collective aims to lift that veil of silence. We use creative expression to provide a forum for the diversity of voices among Americans of Asian descent. The commonalities of our experiences, our identities and our lives are the issues addressed by the Collective. The Asian American Artists Collective is about people who give a shit."[43]

Asian American alumni also began coming together in support of UIUC students. An Asian American Alumni Association was created in February 1993. One of its objectives was to "support development of Asian American needs on campus i.e. Asian American studies curriculum, Cultural Center."[44]

By the fall of 1992, Ho Chie Tsai, then copresident of AAA, was also beginning to think of building a larger Asian American coalition. He recalled his effort to connect with every Asian American organization on campus and established the Coalition of Asian Pacific American Organizations with the intent to build bridges among APA student groups through a new form: "There was no (real) educational, political or cultural (APA) organization at the time. . . . We realized what we needed was an organization that covered (all) the needs of the Asian American (APA) community."[45] This group was renamed the Asian Pacific American Coalition (APAC) in the spring of 1993, and it registered as a student organization that fall.

According to APAC's charter, ratified 29 April 1994, the group's functions were to strengthen and maintain unity among its member organizations, to promote awareness of APA issues and concerns, and to advocate for APA issues to the university.[46] APAC was established by the major undergraduate APA organizations at the time: AAA, the Asian American Artists Collective, HKSA, ISA, the Illini Union Board Asian American Programming Committee, the Korean Undergraduate Students Association (KUSA), PSA, Shakti (an Asian women's support group), TASC, and VSA.[47] Like the Asian Council, APAC did not recruit individual members; rather, membership consisted of two representatives from each of these organizations, along with elected co-directors. As a new and lasting coalition (APAC was still in existence at UIUC as of 2021), the group became the voice of Asian American advocacy. By the 1994 Midwest Asian American Students (MAAS) conference, the issues of an Asian American cultural center, an Asian American studies program, and recognition of Asian Americans as a minority group were listed as top issues for APAC.[48]

While building pan–Asian American unity is always a challenge, given the vast diversity of that category, it is important to note that in the early to mid-1990s, Asian American students at UIUC were successful because they had a unifying vision and because they built relationships across organizational lines. The effort to unite groups was symbolized in the creation of a shared T-shirt for Asian American organizations, which featured the same design on the back and the member organization's individual design on the front. During the 1992–1993 school year, the shirt's design was a drawing of people putting together a puzzle that became a map of Asian countries. Underneath the image read, "Unity thru Diversity."[49] Ho Chie Tsai recalled, "The idea was, if we could agree on a common T-shirt design, maybe as a symbol to our members, it would show that we were working very closely together but still keeping in mind that every group needed a unique identity. You would have your own lapel, and that would be your unique lapel. But on the back, it would all be the same"[50] (see fig. 4.3).

The annual MAAS conference at UIUC was also a site of Asian American coalition building. In 1993 the fifth annual MAAS conference, titled "Empowerment through Unity: Working Together as an Asian American Community," reflected this effort, as it was the first MAAS conference to be co-sponsored by AAA and ISA. This collaboration "was a result of a conscious effort to establish better communication and relations between the two groups and to draw in Southern Asians/Asian Americans into the larger Asian American community."[51] Conference co-coordinator Sonia Desai said, "South Asians and East Asians never really worked together before. There's always been a

FIG. 4.3 Shared T-shirt design used by Asian American student organizations, spring 1993. (Photo courtesy of the UIUC Asian American Cultural Center.)

separation."[52] Workshops examined issues of community building, with titles such as "Exploring the Different Ethnicities of Asian Americans," "Southern Asian American–Eastern Asian American Relations," and "Finding the Common Ground," and there were other workshops on leadership building, renouncing anti-Asian violence, and campus activism.[53]

The sixth annual MAAS conference, with the theme "Envision a New Horizon," was cosponsored by AAA, ISA, and PSA, demonstrating the growing pan–Asian American coalition. Workshops featured topics such as networking, leadership development, coalition building, political activism, Asian American identity, and Asian American arts and culture.[54] The conference booklet also featured a number of articles and essays on political issues facing Asian Americans, as well as cultural topics on Korean, Taiwanese, Indian, and Filipino American experiences.

Previously, animosity between organizations had been rife. Ho Chie Tsai remarked on the change as he was graduating in a letter to incoming freshmen: "There was a time when AAA and all the other Asian American student organizations each stood alone. . . . Interaction between the organizations was minimal. Competition was the mindset. As a result, it was not uncommon to find personal conflicts between officers of different organizations. A coalition of Asian American student groups was not even a possibility. . . . Today, the Asian American student organizations are actively working together to achieve common goals and to attain recognition for the entire Asian American community."[55] The new coalitions that grew in the 1990s enabled Asian American students to more effectively unite around gaining institutional resources and ensuring their experiences were seen and heard.

The Push for an Asian American Cultural Center

As Asian American students began working together, they presented a petition for an Asian American cultural center to Chancellor Weir in December 1992, signed by several hundred students, faculty, and staff.[56] Organizations such as AAA had helped distribute the petition at their social and cultural events and at MAAS conferences. The cultural center was an issue that united the Asian American organizations. Ho Chie Tsai (BS, electrical engineering, 1994) recalled, "We started collecting all those signatures, and AAA essentially became active collecting signatures and showing unity. . . . The petition took off at that point, and we were essentially collecting names everywhere we went."[57]

The following Asian American student organizations formally signed their support to the petition: AAA, the Asian American Artists Collective, BARKADA (a Philippine support group), HKSA, ISA, the Illini Union Board Asian American Programming Committee, KUSA, PSA, TASC, and VSA. The petition outlined the main reasons for an Asian American cultural center:

1 To support resources for Asian/Pacific American students by providing resources on Asian American issues, peer tutoring and counseling services, a centralized meeting space;
2 To fight racism against Asian/Pacific Americans by correcting stereotypes and disseminating information about the Asian American experience;
3 To support coalition building and unity in the APA community;
4 To serve as a link between APAs and other students of color by providing space for dialogue and support;
5 To educate the university and local community about the history and issues of Asian/Pacific Americans.[58]

The cultural center would provide a safe space for Asian American students in a racially inhospitable climate. At the time, Ho Chie Tsai described the continued racialization of Asian Americans in this way: "We need a cultural center as a social support system to service Asian-American needs because the campus is not such a comfortable place sometimes with the racist activities going on every day."[59]

In a memo dated 27 January 1993, Weir, now the outgoing chancellor, explained to students that cultural centers at UIUC were established for African American and Latinx students to assist them in their academic performance and adjustment on campus, evidenced by statistical parity. He wrote, "The situation with Asian/Pacific Americans is different. Students such as yourselves are not under-represented on the campus in terms of the population of the State of Illinois and there appears to be no comparable lag between predictors and performance in college. In addition, there are many Asian faculty members to provide role models, which is another concern of African-American and Latina/o students."[60] But, Weir conceded, "I am sure there are problems that an Asian/Pacific American faces while matriculating at Urbana-Champaign. There may well be a need for some special services and some additional curricular development." Weir recommended the creation of a task force to further explore the idea and encouraged students to raise the issue with the new chancellor.

Student leaders met with vice chancellor for student affairs Stan Levy in January 1993 and began gathering data on resources needed for a cultural center and building a large support base for the idea that included faculty and staff. In May 1993, leaders met with the new chancellor, Michael Aiken, but they received no official plan on the issue.[61]

Student leaders pushed forward. Richard Chang (BA, history, 1994) was instrumental in drafting a proposal for an Asian American cultural center, articulating new arguments inspired by conversations with national Asian American leaders. During the MAAS 1993 conference, Chang met with keynote speaker Paul Bock, who advised him on some important possible strategies.

Bock, a professor emeritus in the Department of Hydrology and Water Resources at the University of Connecticut (UConn), was an important advocate for Asian American students. In response to the racial harassment of Asian American students attending a dance on 3 December 1987 and to the university's poor handling of the event (with administrators interrogating Asian American students and protecting the perpetrators), Asian American students and supporters such as Bock began advocating for improved resources, including an Asian American cultural center, Asian American studies courses, and counselors trained in multicultural issues.[62] Bock also went on a hunger strike on the campus commons to raise awareness of Asian American issues. Bock had founded the UConn Asian Faculty Association and was faculty advisor to UConn's Asian American Students Association.

In April 1990, Bock filed a complaint with the U.S. Education Department's Office of Civil Rights regarding a Connecticut tax-supported 1986 Minority

Advancement Plan (MAP), which provided funds to public colleges to recruit students and faculty considered to be underrepresented as measured by state population statistics. In UConn's case, the MAP did not include Asian American and Native Americans because they were not underrepresented on that basis.[63] Bock's complaint charged that the MAP discriminated against Native Americans and Asian Americans; furthermore, no Asian American or Native American had ever been a member of the Connecticut Board of Governors for Higher Education or on any policy-making committee.[64]

The complaint criticized the notion of parity as the single measure for disadvantaged status. It read, "There may be some growing awareness that the definition for 'parity' based *solely* on numbers of a population produces unfairness for certain situations, particularly for small minorities such as Native-Americans and Asian-Americans. A person who is disadvantaged (say a recent Asian immigrant with poor educational background and English proficiency) should have equal access to affirmative action even though UConn Asian-Americans representing 3 percent of the student population is a number greater than the 0.6 percent parity for Connecticut."[65]

In 1993 the Office of Civil Rights ruled that MAP's exclusion of Asian Americans and Native Americans violated Title VI of the Civil Rights Act, which barred public institutions receiving federal funds from racial and ethnic discrimination.[66] Citing the precedent of the U.S. Supreme Court case *Hazelwood School District v. United States* (1977), the Office of Civil Rights held that the proper comparison for racial discrimination should be a comparison of actual staff demographics with those in the relevant labor market: "Under the rationale of this and numerous other cases, the Board should have used relevant student and labor market data, rather than general population data, to determine which racial and ethnic groups were under-represented in the Connecticut higher education system."[67] In addition, the Connecticut plan did not examine underrepresentation in particular institutions. Because it relied on these general measures, the MAP in effect excluded Asian Americans and Native Americans, even though they were underrepresented at a number of specific universities in the state. As a result, the Connecticut Board of Governors for Higher Education submitted a voluntary action plan and agreed not to use statewide population statistics as a benchmark for inclusion in the program, looking to other measures such as high school student data and labor market data. The board also agreed to include Native Americans and Asian Americans in the MAP.[68]

As the 1993 MAAS keynote speaker, Bock inspired Chang to investigate the existence of Illinois state laws that defined Asian Americans as a minority group. Doing so would be the smoking gun and proof that the university was unfairly denying services to Asian American students. Students Jeremy Bautista and Mark Harang found an Illinois state statute, ILCS 205/9.16, that defined Asian Americans as underrepresented minorities in higher education, which formed the basis for a new legal argument for Asian American resources.[69]

In May 1994, students submitted a forty-two-page proposal for an Asian Pacific American cultural center to administrators, written with the assistance of Chang (then a graduating senior), APAC, and La Casa Cultural Latina. Building off goals articulated in the 1992 December petition and in discussions among students, the proposal included a mission statement, budget figures, staff job descriptions, programming guidelines, recommendations for the formation of an Asian American studies program under the cultural center, and a timetable. The proposal was endorsed by APAC as well as the African American Cultural Center, La Casa Cultural Latina, and several faculty and university staff.

The proposal began with a strong criticism of current campus resources for APA students: "It is the consensus of the Asian Pacific American community at the University of Illinois at Urbana-Champaign that the existing curriculum, support services, and general campus policies are insensitive to the needs of Asian Pacific Americans. We feel that this promotes an atmosphere that is hostile or at best indifferent to the problems Asian Pacific Americans face."[70] The proposal asserted further that by denying APAs minority services, the campus was supporting the model minority myth, the presumption that all APA students were thriving. The students called for a correction of this type of "institutionalized racism."

The proposal also put forth legal claims. First, it cited the successful lawsuit filed by Bock at the University of Connecticut, where denying Asian Americans inclusion in minority programs based on overrepresentation arguments was deemed to be selective discrimination in violation of Title VI of the 1964 Civil Rights Act. Second, the proposal argued that UIUC must reach its commitment to equal opportunity and the board of trustees' own resolution "to foster programs within the law which will ameliorate or eliminate, where possible, the effects of historic societal discrimination."[71] Finally, the proposal stated that the Board of Education Act Number 205, Section 9.16, defined Asian Pacific Americans as "a minority in all Illinois Institutions of Higher Education." Thus, establishing a cultural center to serve this population would meet the state law's requirement. The authors argued, "The University of Illinois must make a commitment to provide services and funding to its largest minority population."[72]

Despite the continued push by students, as of the fall of 1994, the issue of the cultural center remained unresolved. Still, Clarence Shelley, associate vice chancellor at the time, recalled the importance of the forty-two-page proposal drafted by students, which he called "unassailable." Administrators often referred to the detailed student proposal to clarify the structures of and need for a center over the years. Shelley believed that faculty and administrators who supported the students' proposals often learned more than the students did during the process. He said, "The students' efforts helped a great deal in making the case for the center."[73]

Despite the lack of movement toward a cultural center in response to the proposal, some programming funds were granted to students. In September 1994, chancellor Michael Aiken, provost Larry Faulkner, interim vice chancellor for student affairs Patricia Askew, and dean of students Bill Riley met with student leaders to inform them of a new $30,000 fund established for Asian American student programming.[74] The administrators informed the students that "the purpose of these funds was to enable APA students to bring to this campus programs, activities, and events that they felt were appropriate, necessary, and desirable to celebrate and share their diverse ethnic and cultural heritage with the rest of the campus."[75] The funds were coordinated by a newly established Asian Pacific American Resource Board (APARB).

Despite the gain, students worried that accepting the money would signal appeasement. But according to Vida Gosrisirikul (BS, broadcast journalism 1994; JD, 1997), the student consensus was to take the money and use it to continue to push for a studies program and a cultural center, funding activist programs and speakers.[76] Reshma Saujani, sophomore in Liberal Arts and Sciences (LAS), was quoted in the *Daily Illini* commenting on what the funding signified: "I think Asian-Americans have been put on the back burner for too long and the University is recognizing this by giving us this money. But this money is in no way, shape or form going to stop our plight for a cultural center. It is still one of the major issues."[77]

In addition, a *Daily Illini* editorial on 29 November 1994 forewarned the meaning of this money. The editorial, titled "Asian Americans Should Be Wary," presented the funds as an opportunity for Asian American students to continue to demonstrate the need for a cultural center. If well used, the money could help administrators see that "Asian Americans are the ignored minority on this campus."[78] The editorial wondered if the money were a test to see how it would be spent. Concluding words showed that the campaign for a cultural center and studies program was far from over: "Hopefully, the University designated the stipend because they realize that the cultural center situation is far from resolved. Hopefully, this is just a step in [the] process, not the end of increasing awareness of Asian Americans."[79]

Legal Strategies for Asian American Minority Recognition

The granting of $30,000 was not the end to the issue, and students continued to advocate for resources. As identified in the cultural center proposal, student leaders continued to investigate the possibilities of a lawsuit against UIUC. State law ILCS 205/9.16 articulated that public institutions of higher education must develop strategies to increase the participation of minorities, of which Asians ("a person having origins in any of the original people of the Far East, Southeast Asia, the Indian Subcontinent or the Pacific Islands") were included.[80] The statute also outlined the role of the Board of Higher Education in requiring public institutions of higher education to determine compliance with the section, assess programs targeted to increase participation of these groups, and mandate information to determine compliance.

This state law fueled a heated point of contention—the university's situational claiming of Asian Americans as minorities. Students believed that UIUC was counting Asian Americans as minority students in federal reports but was not considering them minorities in need and providing them services. Students also believed that UIUC's counting them as minorities in reports such as to the Illinois Board of Higher Education garnered funding for minority programs—funds that did not trickle back down to Asian American students. For instance, in 1992 Anna Hui, senior in LAS and copresident of AAA argued, "The University uses minority student statistics on campus to get state and federal funding for minority programs, but that money never comes down to us."[81] Hui also articulated that Asian American students wanted to use the federal and state funding that the Office of Minority Student Affairs received, in part for including Asian American numbers in their reports. She said, "I think the University needs to re-evaluate the double standard on paper [of Asian Americans] as not being a minority."[82]

The money issue is unclear. In 1993 Chancellor Weir said the university did not receive state or federal funding for students of color.[83] In oral history interviews, administrators reiterated that while the university was obligated to report minority student numbers, these numerical counts were not likely tied to funding. Regardless, the paradox of being included in counting minority numbers, which yielded the positive effect of making the university appear diverse, but not providing services for Asian American students was troubling. And being acknowledged as a minority was critically associated with acquiring university resources.

Toward this end, students considered a lawsuit against the university. In response to the legal statutes mentioned in the 1994 proposal, UIUC administrators drafted several responses. In July 1994, Linda Bair of the Office of Affirmative Action explained the inclusion of Asian/Pacific Islanders (APIs) in Illinois Board of Higher Education (IBHE) reports on underrepresented students and staff—namely, APIs were included in IBHE reports, but such reports focused on groups such as Blacks and Hispanics, who were the most severely underrepresented at the graduate and undergraduate levels compared to their state figures. For instance, Blacks were 14.8 percent of the state and 7 percent of undergraduate enrollment; Hispanics were 7.9 percent of the state and 5.3 percent of undergraduates. In contrast, Asian Americans were 2.5 percent of the state and 11.9 percent of undergraduates.[84]

In August 1994, UIUC legal counsel also informed the administration that while state law ILCS 205/9.16 defined Asian Americans as minorities, Asian Americans had equivalent retention rates as nonminority (White) students. Furthermore, "the University has full discretion as to what specific actions the University takes." Legally, students' claims seemed thin. Counsel wrote, "State law is silent with respect to any language that provides an enforcement mechanism. State law defines the under-represented groups and provides specific reporting requirements. However, the mandates of State law end with those reporting requirements. That means that State law is silent in terms of any penalties or remedies for noncompliance. There is no private right of action created by this law which would give Asian American students a basis to sue if they are dissatisfied with the University's recruitment and retention efforts, including the lack of a cultural center."[85] The legal claim that state law mandated the university to establish minority programs such as an Asian American cultural center did not hold weight. Counsel concluded that UIUC would not be legally at risk for not establishing an APA cultural center.

It is unclear if these responses were shared with students. What is clear is that students continued to explore the options of a lawsuit in the 1994–1995 academic year, aided by the Asian American Pacific Islander Law Students Association (AAPILSA) at UIUC. AAPILSA discussed providing legal help if the case went to trial, in conjunction with undergraduate APAC students.[86] In particular, Melissa Choo, a third-year law student, drafted a memo analyzing possible legal arguments.

Choo's memo stated that UIUC had denied numerous support services to Asian American students that were available to other minorities. She outlined several legal arguments available to students: violation of Illinois statute 205/9.16 (a statute that clearly included Asian Americans); violation of Title VI of the Civil Rights Act of 1964 (that the university knowingly decided to deprive Asian American students of minority funding and support services, creating a disparate impact); violation of Title VI regulations issued by the Department of Health, Education, and Welfare (by denying services to Asian American students given to other minority students); and a constitutional claim under the equal protection clause of the Fourteenth Amendment (the university denied APA students a cultural center while funding other groups' centers). In relation to this last claim, Choo wrote, "This refusal is a decision based on the University philosophy that Asian Americans are not a 'minority' on campus. However, since Asian Americans are minorities under both federal and state law, they are entitled to the same protections as other minorities. Therefore, the actions that stem from the University philosophy above constitute violations of the equal protection clause."[87] Choo contested the university's claims of Asian American overrepresentation, citing the 1993 Office of Civil Rights ruling (the complaint filed by Paul Bock) that underrepresentation be determined not on census figures but on other measures, such as the student applicant pool.

Asian American students began preparing paperwork for a lawsuit in the Circuit Court of Cook County, Illinois, and a draft suit listed Vida Gosrisiri-kul, Todd Zoltan, and APAC as plaintiffs against the IBHE, the University of Illinois Board of Trustees, chancellor Michael Aiken, and university president James Stukel.[88] Though the lawsuit was not ultimately submitted, Asian American students were employing a critical new legal strategy and discourse that challenged UIUC policies that did not consider them a minority in need.

The Push for Asian American Studies

Students desired both Asian American academic and student support services. Within the cultural center proposal, students recommended that an Asian American studies program be housed in the center. In the early 1990s, UIUC faculty and staff began to join with students to advocate for the program. This movement took place in a national context of growth in the field of Asian American studies (AAS).

According to Mitchell Chang, AAS programs proliferated in the 1990s across the country. Several key factors influenced the trend: the nationwide rise of Asian American enrollments in higher education, that these students were beneficiaries of the civil rights movement and expected to be able to take ethnic studies courses, the growth of the field of AAS, the presence of other ethnic studies programs and services for African American and Latinx students, and a rising awareness of diversity in the academy.[89]

The field also began to grow outside of California, as evidenced by Peter Kiang's announcement at the 1987 Association for Asian American Studies Conference of a new wave of AAS programs on the East Coast.[90] On 13–15 September 1991, Cornell's AAS program hosted a symposium titled "East of California: New Perspectives in Asian American Studies" that brought together representatives from several colleges and universities to discuss the prospects and needs for Asian American studies. Those seeking to build AAS programs east of California faced different intellectual challenges; Gary Okihiro cited Steve Sumida and Gail Nomura from the University of Michigan who observed that "Asian Americanists east of California do not have the luxury of assuming the necessity for Asian American Studies, and instead must summon intellectual and pedagogical justifications other than the demographic reasons cited in California."[91]

Clark Cunningham, professor of anthropology, and Yuki Llewellyn, assistant dean of students and director of registered organizations, gathered requested data for the Cornell symposium, and Cunningham represented UIUC at the meeting. Nine identified issues were included in the UIUC report. Among them were that Asian American students reported not feeling that they had enough understanding or knowledge about their cultures and desired course offerings and programming, such as through an Asian American studies curriculum and a cultural center.

In particular, Cunningham and Llewellyn noted that Asian American students were not considered to be minorities on campus and hence were not eligible for "special services, educational opportunities, funding in scholarships, grants, or job opportunities." They continued: "Students are concerned that Asians and Asian Americans are perceived to be the 'model minority' in terms of their success in academics, ability to assimilate into White society, and the advantages of an upper middle class family incomes when in actuality, there are Asian American students who desperately need the kind of assistance given by the university to African American and Latina/o students. Since Asian/Pacific Islander students are demographically listed as minorities, the assistance and services given to minorities should be extended to them."[92]

Back on campus, Cunningham appealed to administrators for the need for an AAS program. Unlike the 1970s, there was now a critical mass of faculty on campus willing to help the effort. Cunningham wrote a memo to Peter Schran, director of the Center for East Asian and Pacific Studies, updating him on the Cornell symposium, suggesting the important role that UIUC could play in the field of AAS, and pointing to a growing movement on campus of students and faculty in support of it. He wrote, "Given the fact that Illinois is fifth ranked in the nation in its Asian American population, and that it leads all other Midwestern states in that regard (and in fact all non-coastal states in the nation) we believe that Asian American studies—in which some creative scholarly work is being done—should be developed now."[93]

Cunningham began to connect with other UIUC faculty and staff interested in offering courses on Asian American issues, with a larger vision. Cunningham's role as a tenured professor was pivotal. The role of multiple faculty was one advantage that had not existed before. In the 1970s, an early AAS class was offered, but in general there were few faculty who lent support to the Asian American Alliance, thus stunting progress for a full-fledged academic curriculum. Jody Lin (BS, bioengineering, 1991) did not recall assistance or leadership from faculty on Asian American issues in the 1980s either: "There were very few Asian American faculty around, let alone Asian American faculty that supported Asian American student activism. There were certainly Asian professors—but none that took an interest in Asian American issues."[94] By the

1990s, Cunningham and Llewellyn began working to gather information on faculty who had research, teaching, or service interests in working with Asian American students.

In 1992 Cunningham offered the first AAS course since the 1970s under Sociology/Anthropology 296C called "Asian American Experiences." The course was structured around readings and guest speakers, and students spoke of it as pivotal. Vida Gosrisirikul remembered, "Students were voraciously hungry for Asian American studies courses."[95] Other UIUC faculty teaching AAS courses included Nancy Abelmann (anthropology and East Asian languages and cultures), who taught a course on the Korean diaspora; Pallassana Balgopal (social work), who taught a class on Asian families in America; and Rajeshwari Pandharipande (religious studies), who taught on Hinduism in America. Slowly, course offerings began to increase. Cunningham and Llewellyn also requested curricular materials and guidance from AAS scholars across the nation. Peter Kiang, director of AAS at the University of Massachusetts Boston, visited UIUC in February 1991 to give a talk, and in sending materials to Cunningham, he commented on how impressed he was "with the interest and commitment to Asian American Studies expressed by students and staff."[96]

The role that tenured professors played in building an academic unit such as an AAS program was invaluable. While student affairs administrators could provide support, they did not have the same leverage. Bill Riley, dean of students from 1986 to 2008, articulated, "Student affairs is not an academic program. We can stand outside the gate all day and argue about what the needs are to make this a better place. But we at times don't get very far unless we can demonstrate that we've got faculty support that are saying that too, and we've got student support too."[97]

During this time, some students pointed to the legacies of the Asian American Alliance's efforts to push for an AAS program in 1973. Though not connected to the Alliance organizationally or through personal networks, some students researched Asian American student life at UIUC and educated others about this history. In expressing praise for Cunningham's course in 1992, Linus Huang (MS, computer science, 1993) put this gain in perspective in the Asian American Artists Collective newsletter: "While we can rejoice that Anthropology 296C exists at all, it would do well to remember that the Alliance's 1973 effort did not last very long; we are certainly not groundbreakers where Asian American Studies at the U of I is concerned, and it is testimony to the severity of the situation that few are even aware of this fact. Asian American students must assume responsibility for sustaining and developing Asian American Studies at the U of I."[98] That issue of the Collective's newsletter also contained the text of the 1973 Alliance proposal for an Asian American studies program, reminding students of the long struggle for AAS at UIUC that preceded them and needed to be sustained.[99]

Students were also taking it upon themselves to teach each other. Richard Chang (BA, history, 1994), who had been instrumental in crafting the proposal for the cultural center, had taken Cunningham's course and passed on the information he had learned. Chang offered a course on Asian American issues in the fall of 1993 through the Communiversity program of the university's Young Men's Christian Association (YMCA).[100] Chang encouraged other students to learn Asian American history, pointing out the huge lapses in UIUC curricula that overlooked Asian contributions to U.S. history. This gap fueled Asian stereotypes such as foreignness and the model minority myth. Chang wrote, "Just make sure you understand what kind of education you are getting. Be aware of what you are and are not learning." He advertised his Communiversity course, Cunningham's course, and AAA as resources for information. Of AAA, he wrote, "We are not just a social organization. We also try to provide you with the education that the University does not provide: your history and your heritage."[101] Similarly, APAC copresidents Reshma Saujani and Mark Harang described this need in the *Daily Illini* in 1991, pointing out the lack of an AAS curriculum, distinguishing it from Asian studies, and calling for a centralized location for Asian American resources in the library, as there was an Asian library but no centralized Asian American library. Saujani said, "We feel like if the University will not get the information out, it is our duty to educate the students and ourselves about issues concerning Asian American students."[102]

Despite the fact that UIUC had a renowned, world-class library, its Asian American resources left much to be desired. Some students applied to APARB for money to purchase resources for an Asian American library in a residence hall in 1994 but were denied due to funding guidelines. As Asian American students had been wanting better, more centralized Asian American resources in the library, AAA began raising money for Asian American materials. From fundraiser monies, they purchased a small collection of books and gathered articles and resources (such as Asian American studies course syllabi from UCLA) and housed them in the AAA office in the student union. These materials were available for anyone to borrow. Eventually they were donated to the UIUC library, with a sticker placed on the inside of books that read "Gift of the Association of Asian Pacific Organizations," the precursor organization to APAC. Ho Chie Tsai described the significance of these efforts for a library system that lacked Asian American materials: "There were plenty of Asian studies texts, and scattered educational texts or works by Asian American authors in the main library, but no collection impressive enough to note. In some respects, we wanted to make a subtle statement that the university wasn't doing enough for the APA community, and here we were, poor students, trying to raise money to buy resources that we felt were important in teaching our own history to ourselves."[103] Thus, Asian American students took on great efforts to teach each other and build collections in the absence of institutionalized resources.

Students elsewhere in Illinois were also pushing for Asian American resources in the 1990s. At Northwestern University in Evanston, Asian American students comprised 20 percent of student enrollment, and they believed the university was discriminating against them by denying them an Asian American studies program.[104] In 1991 a pan–Asian American student organization formed at Northwestern, the Asian American Advisory Board, which identified the lack of resources on campus. This organization submitted a proposal to the administration for a permanent staff position in student affairs specializing in Asian American issues, but it was rejected in the fall of 1992.[105] Asian American studies courses also were desired, and just like at UIUC, students began teaching themselves AAS through student-organized seminars starting in the spring of 1992. After numerous meetings with administrators, the Advisory Board presented a 200-page proposal for an Asian American studies program in February 1995; the proposal included syllabi and program descriptions as well as a projected timeline. The Advisory Board also submitted a petition of 1,200 signatures from faculty and students supporting the proposal.

Feeling frustrated after four years of advocacy, the Advisory Board took action. On 12 April 1995, more than 150 students and supporters marched on Northwestern's campus in support of Asian American studies. Seventeen students began a hunger strike, vowing to hold out until administrators provided a commitment to establish a program.[106] Within a week, ten remained on the hunger strike. The demands included a short-term plan to hire visiting lecturers, tenure-track faculty, and a permanent director for the program in the next four years. The Northwestern strike encouraged similar protests at Stanford, Princeton, and Columbia. Students at Stanford began a hunger fast in support of Northwestern students; students staged a sit-in in the president's office at Princeton calling for an ethnic studies center; and students at Columbia created an ad hoc committee for Asian American studies. A Princeton student affirmed, "It's been on our minds, and hearing what (NU strikers) have done helped add fuel to the fire."[107]

The hunger strike lasted nineteen days, ending without a university commitment for a program. Yet the administration agreed to offer a minimum of four AAS courses for the 1995–1996 year and committed to having the Curricular Policies Committee address the issue.[108] In May 1996, Northwestern's faculty of arts and sciences approved a plan for an Asian American studies program.

Asian American students at UIUC were aware of what was going on upstate, with leaders expressing similar frustration with the limited AAS course offerings at UIUC and making plans to draft a resolution in support of Northwestern's hunger strike.[109] And as news spread, *Daily Illini* columnist Stacey Jackson drew parallels between the struggles at Northwestern and UIUC for Asian American resources: "It's too bad that officials at a certain university three hours south of Northwestern don't recognize the needs of Asian Americans, either. Asian American groups here on campus have been calling for a cultural center for a long time. The University has responded by gift-wrapping an ambiguous answer in red tape. Beware, administration: A cultural center is needed."[110]

When UIUC students led a teach-in to discuss AAS on campus on 20 January 1996, they invited Northwestern students to participate. Titled "Look at Our Roots: Asian American Studies 101," the daylong event featured speakers on the academic discipline of AAS and on student movements for AAS across campuses. The *Daily Illini* described the reasons for the teach-in as given by Mary Despe, a senior communications major and organizer of the event: "Despe said she wanted the University to reflect the push for Asian American Studies programs at schools such as Northwestern and Princeton universities, where students conducted hunger strikes and sit-ins to demonstrate their commitment to Asian American Studies."[111] Thus, UIUC students' struggles were taking place in a larger context of student activism for resources such as Asian American studies programs.

Asian American Student Organization Programs

As the teach-in, cultural center proposal, and library collection development exemplified, Asian American students took on enormous amounts of work on their own to educate UIUC administrators and students about Asian American issues. In particular, they created programs, including an annual new Asian American student orientation called "Asiantation" and an activist conference called "Unseen Unheard."

Student leaders were concerned about the lack of orientation programs for Asian American students. OMSA offered a supplemental orientation primarily for new African American and Latinx students. In April 1994, Vida Gosrisirikul wrote a memo to dean of students Bill Riley proposing such an event for incoming Asian American freshmen for fall 1994. She described the conversations that APAC members were having on orientation needs, frustrated that they were excluded from the university's minority student orientation: "APA students are confused about which services are available to them. The confusion stems from the University's definition of a minority as a group that is under-represented and has retention problems. This definition is obviously different from how APAs consider the term minority." She continued, explaining how this confusion harmed students: "If APAs are not a minority, and if

APAs are not part of the White majority, what is their status? This confusion only makes the transition to college life more difficult. We would like to be given the same opportunity to reach out to incoming APA students as the Latina/o and African American organizations have. One way to help new APA students is through an APA Freshman Orientation, which would provide them with the resources and information to adjust and succeed at the campus environment."[112]

Gosrisirikul proposed a welcome event and an informational resource booklet that would be sent to APA freshmen their first week on campus. She also reiterated the necessity of the welcome event to support Asian American students who continued to face an inhospitable racial climate: "As an institution of education the University has the resources to implement this booklet and program, and the University should try to foster a healthy environment. APA students have reported more than fifty incidents involving racial slurs on this campus. The US government also reports that violence against Asians is rising. These circumstances make the implementation of an APA Freshman Orientation an even bigger priority."[113]

The Office of the Dean of Students supported the orientation event and booklet in the fall of 1994. More than 100 students attended the program, and 1,500 booklets were distributed.[114] In the booklet, Yuki Llewellyn, director of registered student organizations and assistant dean of students, included a welcoming letter, describing the movements on campus for Asian American student needs and for building cross-organizational unity. She told students, "You are invited to be part of this movement to let the campus know that Asian American students have unmet needs and that there is unity among Asian Americans. Working together you can make an important contribution toward improving the overall climate of this campus."[115]

In the fall of 1995, the orientation was funded by APARB and given the new name of "Asiantation," in contrast to "orientation." An anonymous poem opened the informational booklet, a poem that has opened almost every succeeding year's booklet, which articulated that the term "Asian" was not "Oriental." "Oriental" connoted a submissive, quiet, model minority; it was a "White man's word."[116] Gosrisirikul, Asiantation chairperson, described the importance of Asiantation and of bringing the APA community together: "I have increasingly come to understand how important words are. That's why we chose Asiantation as the theme of this year's orientation. We thought it would be eye-catching; that it would spark some curiosity; and most of all we thought it would emphasize that 'Asian is NOT Oriental.' The term 'Asian American' or 'Asian Pacific American' however, is a term of empowerment, of Asian people assuming control of the way they are viewed." She continued, expressing the importance of a large APA community coming together: "Unity will be important in dispelling these stereotypes, and giving ourselves a voice in mainstream

America. . . . I want to highlight the UNITY formed among the numerous APA organizations at the U of I in order to bring you Asiantation."[117]

Asiantation has continued at UIUC every year since 1994—with student leaders claiming it to be the "first orientation of its kind in the US that is directed specifically towards Asian Pacific American students" and that APA students on different campuses have been inspired to create their own Asiantation programs.[118] In creating Asiantation, Asian American student leaders continued to push the minority discourse at UIUC, challenging the notion that just because they were not underrepresented, they were not struggling with racial or cultural issues. Information about Asiantation in the *Daily Illini* read, "Asian Americans are not considered a minority on campus because there are proportionally more of them enrolled here than there are Asian Americans in the state of Illinois. These numbers, however, do not mean that Asian American students do not have their own unique issues to deal with. It also does not mean that Asian American students do not need or want their own chance to help new students to adjust to campus life. This need for Asian Pacific American students is the drive behind Asiantation."[119]

Just like with Asiantation, students created the annual student activism conference Unseen Unheard, in 1996. The name was a reference to how Asian Americans were unseen and unheard on campus. In the second conference's booklet, codirectors John Fiorelli and Snehal Patel wrote, "The title of this event implies, the Asian Pacific American Community has often been looked upon as the silent, 'model' minority; the group that won't rock the boat or cause commotion. Often thought of as a group that will 'turn the other cheek,' we have chosen not to support this ridiculous stereotype through our increasing involvement in community and political issues that affect our incredibly diverse community. However, the Asian Pacific American community must not only deal with being 'Unseen, Unheard,' but also 'Misseen, Misheard.'"[120]

The annual conference highlighted the overlooked experiences of Asian Americans. Its mission was threefold: "to dispel misunderstanding, ignorance, and apathy through education; to break through silence by facilitating discussion; and to develop and promote leadership, cooperation, and activism in the APA community."[121] The conference included workshops on topics such as discrimination, anti-Asian stereotypes, ethnic studies, Asian American feminism, identity, Asian American history, the model minority myth, and politics. Its booklet described the conference intent this way:

This conference provides a place where APA students can empower themselves and others to rip off the blindfolds that have traditionally made APAs invisible to others, that we can see ourselves and others not through the lens of a Western education, but through the lens of a multi-faceted, multi-dimensional model of society. This conference provides a place where we as APA students can rip the cotton from our ears and others' ears, so our screams, our protests, our voices of reason and passion, the voices of our community, our mothers, our fathers and children, can be heard. . . . By making our issues and concerns **SEEN and HEARD**, we begin to change the powers that be into empowerment within our own communities.[122]

Programs such as Asiantation, Unseen Unheard, and the MAAS conferences were completely planned and run by students. And they not only educated Asian American students but the entire university community as well. The programs were impressive and thought-provoking. Patricia Askew, vice chancellor for student affairs from 1995 to 2005, recalled, "I used to just be amazed that they could pull off that [MAAS/MAASU] conference where they had students come from all over the Midwest! I mean the amount of work that went into that! And Asiantation got better every year, and it just blew me away. The booklet and their timing was right. They got those students in there at the right time to introduce them, while they were freshmen. They made it fun and interesting."[123] Thus, Asian American programming was a critical form of activism and part of a larger movement of petitions, protests, proposals, and legal strategies to educate the university about Asian American student needs.

The 1990s were a ripe time for political activism at UIUC. Asian American students continued to build coalitions and create student organizations beyond the founding of the Asian American Association in the mid-1980s, responding to larger educational and political issues in the face of racial hostility. The importance of building Asian American unity during this time cannot be overemphasized. In 1993, PSA president Maria Gutierrez explained the significance of APAC in an interview in the *Daily Illini*: "The purpose of the [APAC] coalition is to provide one common voice that represents all Asian-Americans, and to give us, as Asian-Americans, more power and influence in University programming. We've seen a severe under-representation among Asian-American issues on this campus considering that we do comprise 11 percent of this University, which is more than any other minority student population. Although we are different, our diversity makes us powerful. We are all, of course, Americans, and our Asian-American experience is the thing that makes us unique and on that point alone we should unite."[124]

The 1990s were also a time when other students of color began to work together, finding commonalities in their struggle for resources such as cultural centers, studies programs, and the elimination of the Chief Illiniwek mascot. While Asian Americans found themselves on somewhat tenuous ground in joining these larger coalitions with students of color, Asian American voices were heard in the larger conversations surrounding the 1992 sit-ins and their aftermath. In particular, ACCORD members who testified at the subcommittee hearings after the 1992 sit-ins expressed the racial hostility they experienced, advocated for resources, and fully rejected the model minority myth.

Asian American student leaders also formulated a variety of activist strategies, considering the diversity of the Asian American student community and a hesitance for confrontational politics that made headlines in 1992. Through petitions, proposals, student programs, and legal strategies, these student leaders continued to push their demands for an Asian American studies program and Asian American cultural center, as well as a recognition by the university of their minority experiences, this time with a new group of faculty and administrative allies. Through their continued efforts, they educated UIUC about the need for campus resources and that Asian Americans were minorities despite their statistical overrepresentation. Their efforts would ultimately lead to the establishment of an Asian American studies program and Asian American cultural center at UIUC.

5

Seeing and Hearing Asian
American Students

By 1996, Asian American student efforts at the University of Illinois at Urbana-Champaign (UIUC) had achieved some tangible gains—programming dollars through the Asian Pacific American Resource Board (APARB), a growing Asian American studies (AAS) curriculum, and Asian American student-led programs. However, without a cultural center, official Asian American studies program, or similar institutional support, students remained dissatisfied. The situation fueled the push to establish a staff position designated to work with Asian American students in the dean of students office. Susan Maul, director of the Illini Union, original member of the Asian American Task Force, and APARB member, wrote to vice chancellor for student affairs Patricia Askew on 2 May 1995 explaining this need: "Even when a decision was made to provide $30,000 funding to the Asian American students, I believed that a staff person was what they needed and wanted the most. . . . Although there are all kinds of staff members within Student Affairs available to help them with programming, designating one staff member to work with them would certainly indicate that the University is supportive of the Asian American population on campus and recognizes that they have special needs."[1]

Askew reiterated this need to chancellor Michael Aiken on 22 December. In a memo, she requested the establishment of an assistant dean position to help Asian American students with programming and support. She described her conversations: "Students like Jeremy Bautista express a sincere need to have a dean or advisor to turn to when they are coping with stressful situations—someone who understands the Asian-Pacific American culture, the parental expectations, the model minority stereotype, and so forth. After listening to Jeremy relate some of the problems he faced, and describe the void he felt in not finding a professional staff member who understood him culturally, I am convinced of the need to establish this new Assistant Dean position."[2] As a result, a new position of assistant dean of students for Asian Pacific American (APA) affairs was established and hired for fall of 1996 to advise students and to serve as a liaison to other university administrators.[3]

The Establishment of an Asian American Studies Program

While this new staff position was an important and significant resource, it did not end the struggle. Asian American student leaders continued to view these resources as only partial steps within a larger movement. Though they now had funding and a staff position, they still did not have an Asian American studies program or a cultural center. Students reminded each other of the larger goal, such as in the September 1996 Asian Pacific American Coalition (APAC) newsletter, where members described the situation to new students. While African American and Latinx students had cultural centers, ethnic studies programs, and minority student status, Asian American students had none, despite years of struggle. Even with the addition of an assistant dean position, they wrote, "But we still don't have a studies program or a cultural center. Things can change, but only if you want it to. Get your ass in gear. APA student activism can't exist without you. Everything that's happened so far is because of us. Students. Get involved."[4]

Around this time, advances for a cultural center stalled, but the academic side began to flourish. Given some progress made for Asian American studies, students shifted their focus on the curriculum and its potential impact for all students. The campus student newspaper the *Daily Illini* quoted Jeremy Bautista of APAC: "We've decided to focus on the studies program because, the more you know, either as an Asian American or not, the more information you'll have to make an accurate decision on problems facing the Asian American community."[5]

In the spring of 1996, Asian American students submitted a list of AAS demands to administrators, which included a program director, physical office space, clerical and graduate assistant staff, a cross-listing of all AAS books in the library system, and additional AAS books and journal subscriptions. They also demanded that at least five classes a semester be taught with at least 50 percent AAS content in a variety of disciplines, including English, history, political science, anthropology, sociology, education, community health, religious studies, music, and fine and applied arts.[6]

Asian American student leaders and faculty met with UIUC administrators, in particular associate provost David Liu, to discuss the establishment of an Asian American studies program. During a meeting in June 1996, Liu suggested forming an ad hoc committee and requested a listing of faculty who might be interested in being involved. At the meeting he also committed to working with students and faculty on the issue.[7] By the fall of 1996 the ad hoc committee was established, consisting of approximately fifteen faculty members and three students.[8] The committee investigated ways to establish a program, explored how to institutionalize AAS courses and an academic minor, and met with the campus's directors of African American studies and Latina/o studies. The committee also invited national AAS scholars to campus.

By October of 1996, UIUC announced that the College of Liberal Arts and Sciences would set aside two faculty positions in AAS. One hire was made in the field of Asian American political science. Despite this progress, committee members were frustrated over their limited input in hiring decisions. By April 1997, ad hoc committee member Vida Gosrisirikul (BS, broadcast journalism, 1994; JD, 1997) expressed her impatience on the slow progress for AAS in an email to students: "There is NO APA Studies Program at the U of I. There have been a few classes here and there such as Prof. Balgopal's Asian American Families and another course Asian American Experiences, but NO formal APA Studies Program. Many other University campuses have APA studies, namely UCLA (and many other UC schools), U of Wisconsin, Cornell, etc. but U of I has NOT done enough towards establishing a program here." She also urged students to attend a meeting with invited speaker Don Nakanishi from UCLA. She wrote, "We need to show the University that we will NOT be ignored. This proposal is only the most recent in a long struggle for APA Studies. Unless, we show them that we care about this issue the University will continue to do . . . NOTHING!!!!!! PLEASE DO SOMETHING!!!!"[9]

Despite a slow start and some confusion over the new hires, the committee was reorganized in the fall of 1997 and headed by George Yu, who was the director of the Center for East Asian and Pacific Studies. The committee was renamed the Asian American Studies Committee and was given six faculty lines, with the charge to transform itself into an Asian American studies program in three years. According to Yu, the committee was given $1 million to build the program, money that funded faculty and staff salaries, facilities, programming, and operations.[10] UIUC's creation of six faculty lines received national news within the field of Asian American studies.[11] Finally, after almost twenty-five years since the Asian American Alliance's proposal and after decades of activism, an Asian American studies program would become a reality at UIUC.

Due to their long-standing efforts, UIUC students, faculty, and administrators had laid a strong foundation for an Asian American studies program.

Between 1997 and 2000, the Asian American Studies Committee filled six faculty lines. In 2000, the committee became the Asian American Studies Program under the College of Liberal Arts and Sciences. In 2012 the program became the Asian American Studies Department and in 2019 had twenty-five faculty and an undergraduate major and minor, along with a graduate minor.[12]

The Establishment of an Asian American Cultural Center

Even with the accomplishment of establishing the Asian American studies program, the push for the Asian American cultural center continued. Making an argument for support services for such a high-achieving population (in the aggregate) was still a challenge, but students persisted in their efforts. Gains in Asian American student affairs resources had been made through the early 1990s, such as the $30,000 in funding for Asian American programs and an Asian American staff position in the dean of students office. In 1998, a full-time counselor was hired by the counseling center with a specialty working with Asian American students. Despite these new resources, an Asian American cultural center remained elusive. In April 1997, Asian American students sponsored a cultural center day consisting of workshops and activities. Joline Robertson, external vice president of the Asian American Association (AAA), believed that "persistence will eventually overcome" and that a cultural center would one day be a reality at UIUC.[13]

A new cohort of student leaders took on the cultural center battle in the late 1990s and also worked to ensure the success of the new AAS program. In doing so, they continued to argue that Asian Americans had a minority experience despite being statistically overrepresented. Persistence was key to the eventual creation of an Asian American cultural center, along with the continued help of allies in the administration. In 2001 Nancy Cantor was appointed UIUC chancellor. Cantor had been provost and executive vice president for academic affairs at the University of Michigan when students filed court cases against the university's use of affirmative action in undergraduate (*Gratz v. Bollinger*) and law school (*Grutter v. Bollinger*) admissions, heard by the U.S. Supreme Court in 2003. During those cases, Cantor was a champion of diversity and defended affirmative action.[14]

In October 2002, Chancellor Cantor and Vice Chancellor Askew appointed an ad hoc committee on Asian Pacific American campus life. They charged the committee to assess the personal, social, and academic needs of Asian American students. The committee conducted a large-scale online survey to assess Asian American students' needs and perceptions of the quality of academic and extracurricular life at UIUC. Students reported rates of racial discrimination on campus and dissatisfaction with the university's performance in meeting Asian American student needs. In a final report, the committee submitted nine

FIG. 5.1 Ground breaking for the Asian American Cultural Center, 13 October 2004. (Photo courtesy of the UIUC Asian American Cultural Center.)

recommendations, the top one being the creation of an APA cultural center. Other recommendations included disaggregating APA student data, hiring more APA staff, expanding Asian American studies and library resources, improving interracial relations, and redeveloping an Asian American alumni network.[15]

Advances continued, and in August 2003, provost Richard Herman announced the approval of an Asian American cultural center, which held its grand opening on 9 September 2005 at 1210 West Nevada Street in Urbana, a center that was physically connected to the Asian American studies program building. At the celebration, Betty Jang, then president of the Asian American Alumni Network, reflected on the long journey to that day, remarking, "I ask the University with a smile, 'What took you so long?'"[16] (see figs. 5.1, 5.2, and 5.3).

Building Asian American Community

UIUC's minority programs, starting with the Special Educational Opportunities Program, focused on African American students. Latinx students challenged this focus in the 1970s through the 1990s, arguing they too were minorities with specific needs. Asian American students, following a different argument outside of underrepresentation, added to this challenge of what it meant to be a minority on campus. In addition, students of color began to work together in the 1990s, seeing their commonalities and need for resources at a predominantly White institution.

FIG. 5.2 Ribbon cutting for the opening of the UIUC Asian American Cultural Center, 9 September 2005. (Photo courtesy of the UIUC Asian American Cultural Center.)

FIG. 5.3 Buildings of the Asian American Studies Program (front) and Asian American Cultural Center (back) at UIUC, 2010. The Asian American Cultural Center is physically connected to the Asian American Studies Program building. (Photo courtesy of the UIUC Asian American Cultural Center.)

Beginning in the 1970s, Asian American students challenged UIUC minority policies and programs that excluded them based on the model minority myth, statistical measures of parity, and a Black-White racial model. These students and their allies relentlessly argued that Asian Americans were minorities and had educational needs that would be served with resources such as an Asian American studies program and an Asian American cultural center.

This history of Asian American activism at Illinois reveals several important insights into understanding Asian American student experiences, beyond the model minority facade. The first is the salience of an Asian American racial identity. Race has always imbued the experiences of Asian and Asian American students since their first appearance on college campuses in the early twentieth century. As seen in the 1970s through the 1990s, Asian American students of different ethnic backgrounds shared a common racial experience and sought ways to build a larger community to address their needs at Illinois. In the 1970s, when numbers were small, Asian American students (primarily Chinese and Japanese Americans) sought each other out, either through high school networks or by approaching each other at orientation events or in dormitories. A shared racial identity was obvious to Asian American Alliance members who protested the Vietnam War along racial lines and desired academic courses that reflected their histories and experiences.

In the late 1980s and early 1990s, a new and more diverse Asian American community came together at UIUC, the children of post-1965 Asian immigrants. While their numbers were larger than those from the 1970s, these students still sought each other out, initially for social support and then gradually to discuss educational needs and respond to anti-Asian incidents on campus and in the community. With a growing awareness of Asian American issues, these students began to critique the university's framing of minority issues along statistical representation and a Black-White model, contesting the university's convenient counting of them as minorities to appear diverse but in denying them minority services.

While a pan-Asian identity was salient for many, there were also challenges in building a larger community to gain resources. In the 1980s and 1990s, a more diverse Asian American community emerged, forming pan-Asian organizations such as the AAA, the Asian Council, the Asian-Pacific American Coalition to Combat Oppression, Racism, and Discrimination (ACCORD), and APAC. However, these groups also faced challenges of building bridges across ethnic lines, with organizations competing with each other for popularity and membership. Changes began to take place due to shared organization space in the Illini Union and through personal efforts by key student leaders, who joined multiple organizations and emphasized shared interests. For instance, Jeremy Bautista (BA, history, 1996) worked to build bridges; at one point he had leadership positions in both AAA and the Philippine Student Association (PSA). He recalled, "My situation of being in good relationships with both sides—I think that helped in the development of APAC, because a lot of us did that. I think Ho Chie [Tsai] at one time was a member of every organization that he could be. I wasn't the only one who did that, to try to build good cohesiveness. . . . It didn't matter what group you belonged to; we didn't fractionalize over style differences. And so building this coalition, it was literally on the backs of people's relationships and friendships, the unifying vision of certain members."[17] The importance of building personal relationships is evidenced by the fact that today many of these Asian American alumni remain steadfast friends.

Because of the sheer size and diversity the Asian American community encompasses, building coalitions is always a challenge and an imperfect process. At times, some groups marginalized others. Still, the 1990s were a unique time when these ethnic lines began to cross and a new momentum emerged among Asian American student leaders at UIUC who, now with the support of faculty and administrators, focused on their shared racial experiences, on personal friendships, and a focus on unity.

Not the Model Minority: Asian American Student Activism

The model minority myth supports the false view of Asian American students as quiet, politically passive, and indifferent. The historical record is clear that Asian American students have protested racial injustice through visible means such as demonstrations, sit-ins, and hunger strikes. At the same time, the concept of activism needs to be expanded beyond these forms to highlight the other ways Asian American students have taken action. Culturally, some Asian American students at Illinois had expressed a hesitancy to engage in confrontational political tactics, but they also strategically took on other approaches to build their movement. In the 1970s, the conscious decision not to name the Asian American Alliance a "political alliance" revealed an effort to attract members in a nonintimidating manner, even though it raised awareness about racial issues. Similarly, in the 1990s, there were barriers keeping student leaders from garnering widespread support for political activism. The backdrop of the Latinx sit-ins in 1992 spurred them to consider alternative strategies, as they were aware that many Asian American students would hesitate to take a confrontational route. Jeremy Bautista recalled some members of APAC articulating a specific strategy to build unity: "You have a system here; let's work within it. Because there's no reason why we couldn't because there are no rules against that. So you almost break them from the inside. And we looked at APAC building critical mass. That was the term I used a lot. We knew that we couldn't do it without a consensus. And that was built on people's shoulders."[18]

At the same time, while Asian American leaders focused on strategies that were collaborative and behind the scenes, they also balanced this cooperation with the potential to use more vocal protest. Asian American student leaders at UIUC admitted that culturally it would have been an uphill battle to garner a mass protest by Asian American students to the degree that had occurred before on campus. However, they were also aware that such tactics were effective. A *Daily Illini* article quoted Vida Gosrisirikul: "Gosrisirikul said that at other universities, APA students had protested for recognition. This was how both the African American Cultural Center and La Casa Cultural Latina were established on this campus. . . . 'We are willing to fight for what we think is right, but we are also prepared to discuss and compromise with the University,' Gosrisirikul said."[19]

Certainly, Asian American students benefited from the fallout of the 1992 sit-ins on campus led by Latinx students and their supporters. Latinx students created a campus context where administrators were determined to avoid a repeat of the volatile protests. The sit-in strategies had lasting effects for all students at Illinois, showing how student protest effectively pushed the university to respond to student needs. It is uncertain, given the prevalence of model minority rhetoric, if UIUC administrators were surprised at the activism of Asian Americans or if they sought to reward them for their tactics, which were not as confrontational as those of Latinx students. Perhaps Asian American students did not need to engage in these confrontational tactics because not doing so fit the racialized narrative of their model minority agreeableness.

Currently, the historical record does not provide evidence of these thoughts among students or administrators. Rather, it reveals the many forms of activism Asian American students strategically took. Activism takes many forms in the way it challenges an institution. In a post-1992 climate, it had become less necessary to engage in direct confrontation in order to gain visibility. At the same time, Asian American students were relentless over the years in their continued pressures through petitions, programs, proposals, and legal arguments, always returning to the rejection of the model minority myth, of the idea that Asian Americans had no needs, and of their exclusion from minority programs and services. These student leaders looked to African American and Latinx students as collaborators and inspirations for the services they had secured. Vida Gosrisirkul noted, "Because Asian American students had minimal experience with obtaining services at the university, we sought guidance from the directors of La Casa and the Black House and other organizations of color at U of I. We wanted to know how these institutions got their start. What struck us most was that these vital resources were not merely created by the university out of thin air; they were instituted as a direct result of student initiative and protest. We knew that we as students needed to mobilize if our voices were ever going to be heard."[20] Thus, Asian American students at UIUC were not passive model minorities; rather, they embraced different forms of activism, revealing the many ways they were change agents in shaping higher education's policies and services.

Racial Isolation in the Midwest

Race mattered to these students, as racial isolation is a challenge in middle America. Growing up in homogenously White communities leaves its impact on Asian Americans, who often come to college to find a larger Asian American community for the first time. Learning about Asian American history and experiences evokes a racial identity awakening for many, as it enables them to put into words the racial isolation they have felt. For example, Karin Wang (BS, finance, 1992), who grew up in predominantly White Midwestern areas (Fort Wayne, Indiana, and then Wheaton, Illinois), reflected on the role that organizations like AAA played for her. In such groups, she was shocked to find Asians of all ethnicities that shared her experiences, to whom she did not have to explain herself. She said her experiences in organizations like AAA were transformative:

> Because I grew up in these really White towns and suburbs, I always kind of struggled with the fact that I was different. In Indiana, for example, people constantly called me names, but oddly, they were people who were my friends. People would say "Chink" and things like that to me, but there was no consciousness that that was offensive. And my parents were immigrants and probably not that well integrated themselves, so it wasn't like they knew what to make of some of these things. . . . When I got involved in AAA, the political part of that identity became really crucial. Because I finally was able to articulate what I had been feeling for sixteen to eighteen years that I had never had words for.[21]

A distinct Asian American identity emerged for students who grew up in less diverse regions in the Midwest, testifying to the importance of supportive networks such as the Midwestern Asian American Students Union (MAASU). MAASU founder Charles Chang recalled that the isolation he experienced in the Midwest made him keenly aware of being a minority but that finding an Asian American community helped to empower students: "Some people grow up without a sense of feeling empowered that they can say whatever they want. If you're the one minority who has totally different opinions from everyone else, then you might be timid, . . . which is why I think some Asian Americans go to college and find a larger group of Asians that makes them feel more comfortable. They all of a sudden start feeling more empowered, able to talk about who they are and their experiences."[22] MAASU conferences provided an important educational space for students to learn about Asian American experiences, students who often represented universities that lacked such institutional resources and a critical understanding of Asian American student needs. This support network also energized students to push for AAS programs and cultural centers on their own campuses.[23]

Another aspect relevant to this history is the predominance of the Black-White racial model, which prevails in the Midwest. Recent studies have highlighted specific regional challenges facing Midwestern Asian American students, who make up smaller populations compared to the West and East Coasts. A Midwestern focus on underrepresented African American and Latinx students has erased Asian American students from diversity and equity discourse. Jeffrey K. Grim, Nue Lee, Samuel Museus, Vanessa S. Na, and Marie P. Ting interviewed Asian American students in the Midwest who described how administrators focused on statistical measures such as retention for Black and Latinx students "as a rationale for ignoring Asian Americans."[24] The untold stories of Asian American activism in the Midwest also keeps Asian American students from being able to see themselves as activists in their own right. This invisibility supports the need for greater documentation of activist histories in the Midwest.

Beyond Parity: Centering Race and Asian American Voices

Are Asian Americans minorities? Following traditional definitions based on the model minority myth, statistical parity, and the Black-White racial paradigm, Asian Americans are excluded from minority discussions. This erasure is evidenced in the changing terms used when describing minority students. For instance, James Anderson, dean of the College of Education and UIUC professor since 1974, discussed the evolution of terms used at UIUC and the ways that the term "minority" was conflated with "Black" and then teased out to differentiate Asian Americans from other groups: "I think at some point the university decided that the Asian American students, while classified as a minority population, were not an underrepresented population. So initially, we never used the word 'underrepresented'; it was just 'minority' or 'Black' students. . . . But I think at some point you got the evolution of the concept underrepresented minority. And I think underrepresented minority is a concept that was introduced in order to distinguish Black, Latino, and Native American students from Asian American students."[25] Thus, this shift from minority to underrepresented minority has become code to distinguish Asian Americans from other students of color. Likewise, Dana Takagi notes that starting in the 1990s, "as 'minority' has come to mean under-represented (based on parity) minority, Asian Americans have no figurative stance because they are neither White nor under-represented on the same terms as African Americans or Latinos, as broad groups."[26]

As at other schools, the focus on underrepresentation and academic needs has been and continues to be the focus for minority programs at UIUC. In the cases of the African American and Latinx cultural centers, university rationale emphasized the centers' positive effects on the retention and academic success of these students. However, that rationale did not apply to Asian American students. Clarence Shelley, founding director of the Special Educational Opportunities Program (SEOP), recalled, "We did not take a very careful look at the fact that these [Asian American] students were not using our counseling services as much. We did not examine their levels of comfortability in the residence halls, or their participation in student activities and services." He concluded, "I'm thoroughly convinced that because these students did so well academically that they [were presumed to not] really need a cultural center. It is so ironic in retrospect that their academic performances and lower levels of activism were used by many to justify not developing and encouraging the development and use of services."[27] As the understanding of minority student needs was equated with underrepresentation, model minority Asian American students were excluded from the discussion.

This is not to say that underrepresentation should not be a measure in identifying needs for minority groups. This is a crucial problem for certain populations, and generating a critical mass of students of color can improve campus climate. However, the assumption that parity means equity is flawed. For example, Sylvia Hurtado, Jeffrey Milem, Alma Clayton-Pedersen, and Walter Allen argue that campus climate is produced within larger institutional and environmental contexts such as government policies and sociohistorical forces that propel policy change. Furthermore, within an institution this framework highlights four interconnected dimensions in which to assess racial climate, of which statistical parity is just one: an institution's history, structural diversity (numerical representation in student body and faculty), psychological climate (student perceptions of group relations), and behavioral climate (how groups actually interact).[28] In addition, as Esther Chan points out, a reliance on structural diversity supports a color-blind assumption that numerical representation is enough, ignoring other factors that contribute to racial equity.[29] Basically, enrollment and retention numbers do not tell the entire story.

When examining the qualitative data of Asian American students' experiences with campus climate, issues of racial hostility and marginalization emerge. For instance, studies show that Asian American students continue to experience alienation on college campuses despite their statistical success and high achievement. They still continue to struggle with racial tensions, even when their numbers outpace state or national statistics, at the extreme end resulting in hate crimes and racial violence.[30] Parity does not equal complete integration, nor does it signal a group's shift from minority to majority status. The view of Asian Americans as untrustworthy foreigners persists, affecting campus climate.

Within a discourse of underrepresentation, Asian American students at UIUC had to push the minority discourse and craft different arguments—contending that overrepresentation did not mean that equity or full integration had been achieved and arguing that the whole campus would benefit from learning about Asian American experiences and histories. They testified to anti-Asian hostility at UIUC not captured by statistical measures of academic achievement that served as the standard for gauging minority need. They showed the limitations of the university's understanding of these nonacademic issues, and they challenged the arguments for underrepresentation and overrepresentation. Vida Gosrisirikul powerfully questioned the university's problematic rationale that did not recognize Asian Americans as a minority deserving of services, which conflicted with the reality of what Asian American students experienced at UIUC. She wrote,

> Being the largest group of people of color at the U of I does not mean that APA students do not have to deal with racist comments on this campus. It does not mean that APAs automatically do not require any of the services that other minorities on this campus receive. It does not mean that stereotypes such as that APAs are all well-off economically, do not exist here. . . . But the fact remains that numbers do not guarantee equitable treatment. Equitable treatment can only come through education—education of the campus community as a whole, and education of APAs themselves. A cultural house would serve as a center for that education, through organizing and providing programs, seminars, lecturers, films, etc. that would be open to all.[31]

The Asian American minority experience was a racial one, not one of statistical underrepresentation. As Paula Kim, codirector of APAC (BA, history and political science, 2001) wrote, "Many of us [Asian Americans] do face issues of discrimination and racism. But the University does little to acknowledge this. They say because we have high numbers and a higher retention rate than other groups, we must not have many problems. By not having resources available to us, the University is saying that we aren't really a minority. That implies that we have been successfully integrated into the majority, which at this school happens to be Caucasians. But we're not the same as Caucasians."[32]

Assuming Asian Americans do not struggle with underrepresentation belies the fact that some Asian American subgroups such as Southeast Asians and Pacific Islanders still struggle with educational access, retention, and poverty. It is critical to remember that once Asian American data is disaggregated, there are many ways in which Asian American groups still qualify for minority ser-vices along measures of underrepresentation. Asian Americans are a highly diverse group, and disaggregated data shows wide ranges of academic achieve-ment along ethnic and disciplinary lines.[33] Thus, despite charges of overrepre-sentation, underrepresentation still exists for Asian American subgroups and in some disciplines.

Additional studies also need to examine the role of socioeconomic status on educational access and adjustment; advocates pushing for disaggregation of Asian American data along ethnic or socioeconomic lines argue that doing so will also help to identify and address socioeconomic barriers. These acknowl-edgments led to the federal designation of "Asian American and Pacific Islander–Serving Institutions" in 2007, as part of the College Cost Reduction and Access Act. The now-named Asian American Native American Pacific Islander–Serving Institutions (AANAPISI) program funds instructional and support services at universities with at least 10 percent AANAPI students and at least 50 percent of the school's students receiving federal financial assistance. This legislation refutes the model minority myth, advocates for services for disadvantaged Asian American subgroups, and rejects the lumping of Asian Americans with White students.[34]

One of the limitations of this study is its focus on middle-class Asian Amer-ican student leaders. Karin Wang reflected:

We were not conscious at the time of how the model minority myth also plays down the disparities in the community, economically. I had no consciousness at the time of Vietnamese and Cambodian refugees, for example, since most Chinese, Korean, or Filipino Americans on campus had parents who came in the early 1970s, parents who might come with a higher level of education or some resources. They were not fleeing a war for the most part. So the Asian Americans I knew on campus I think were predominantly East Asian, and some were Indian, and most came from more-privileged suburban families. We all went to pretty good schools. More of us came from the suburbs than from Chinatown. So that was something I just wasn't aware of yet. At the time, when we talked about the model minority myth being detrimental, it was more about a fairly privileged group of Asian Americans not having access to the kind of university support for programming.[35]

The stories of Asian American leaders at UIUC are ones primarily of a middle-class population. Yet these students highlighted and centered race in their analysis as well as cultural conflict with immigrant parents that led to pressures and need for support.

These students' arguments that centered race over class are critical in challenging traditional minority discourse. A movement solely pushing to disaggregate Asian American data to reveal underrepresentation continues to reify a "minority equals underrepresented" argument. Asian American students at UIUC pushed that very discourse by highlighting the salience of race despite socioeconomic privilege, overrepresentation, and academic achievement. Just as early Asian foreign students' socioeconomic status did not shield them from anti-Asian sentiment, class privilege did not protect Asian American students from racism in the 1970s–1990s. Thus, despite certain socioeconomic privileges and high academic achievement that seemed to put Asian Americans in a position of comfort and adjustment, Asian American students continued to reject the model minority myth and critically redefine measures of minority experiences along racial (non-White) lines.

Bringing Asian Americans Back into Minority Discussions

As a non-White racial group, Asian American college students continue to face racism on campus. These instances are taking new forms, such as on social media, which can take on more blatantly racist forms given its anonymity. Yet these attacks maintain familiar forms that depict Asians as foreigners, Yellow Peril groups taking over campuses. Some examples include:

- March 2011: A White female student at UCLA posted a YouTube video of her complaining about the loud Asian students in the library, mimicking their Asian accents and stating, "The problem is these hordes of Asian people that UCLA accepts into our school every single year."[36]
- October 2015: Social media platform Yik Yak was found to propagate anti-Asian messages at the University of Iowa complaining of an Asian takeover and the campus feeling like a "Chinatown."[37]
- September 2018: A law tutor posted a Facebook rant about rich Asian students taking over Orange County, flooding colleges, driving expensive cars (poorly, of course), and being obsessed with money. She complained of Asians flooding schools like UC Irvine, her alma mater, with intentions to marry rich.[38]
- October 2018: Anti-Asian comments complaining of Asians "taking over" at Washington University in St. Louis occurred through a group chat, "Why are Asians invading our study room?"[39]

Social media provides a new venue to express the all-too-familiar racism that targets Asian American students as foreigners taking over universities and threatening White students. A research study showed that such incidents of anti-Asian racism on social media platforms negatively affected Asian

American students' sense of belonging with White students and with their predominantly White institutions.[40]

In addition, persistent racial tensions across the country have sparked a reenergized wave of community protest against oppression and violence, as evidenced in the Black Lives Matter movement protesting police brutality against African American communities. Asian Americans have been involved in supporting Black Lives Matter, recognizing that an unjust criminal justice system affects all people of color. However, Asian American allyship is not a given. The figure of Asian American police officer Tou Thao, who stood by as his colleague Derek Chauvin murdered George Floyd, stands as a stark reminder of how Asian Americans must interrogate their own complicity with anti-Black racism. In addition, Asian Americans are not automatically trusted as fellow people of color, allies against racism.[41]

Asian Americans face a tenuous racial positioning in a Black-White model, being pitted against African Americans as the model minority or the good minority, which hinders cross-racial coalition building. Similarly, some Asian Americans feel it is not their place to compare their oppressions, as police brutality affects Asian Americans at a much lower rate.[42] However, a narrow lens on Black-White racial issues limits our understanding of how racism functions in this country. Racial awareness must expand to consider how whiteness operates in the United States; the current rise in xenophobia affects Latinx communities, with President Trump's policies of building a border wall, separating families, and rescinding protections from Dreamers under the Deferred Action for Childhood Arrivals (DACA) policy. The racist trope of Asians as disloyal foreigners has also persisted during the global pandemic, as many Americans blame COVID-19 on China, referring to it in the racist terms "the Chinese virus" or "the kung flu," which has led to a rise of anti-Asian violence. Asian American students have been Zoombombed with racial slurs and verbally and physically assaulted. Anti-Asian comments posted on social media express fear of catching coronavirus from other Asian students. In May 2020, data collected at San Francisco State University documented over 1,200 such incidents. Another organization, STOP AAPI HATE, collected over 1,800 reports of pandemic harassment in forty-five states in the first several months of the pandemic; by March 2021, it reported 6,603 anti-Asian hate incidents.[43] The 16 March 2021 shootings in Atlanta, resulting in the tragic deaths of eight people, six of whom were Asian women, have raised awareness of anti-Asian violence, misogyny, and hatred in this country. Asian American students have cited the shootings as evidence for the need for Asian American studies curriculum and support centers on their campuses.[44] In this unprecedented time when global viruses of COVID-19 and racism run rampant, the rise in anti-Asian hate and violence cannot be denied.

Given the continued significance of racism in this country, university minority programs that have been defined along underrepresentation and have originated from a Black-White racial binary are limited in understanding Asian American student experiences. Asian Americans, in not fitting in the traditional underrepresented minority model, have been uncritically removed or excluded from minority programs and services. Asian American students at UIUC challenged the model minority myth, statistical measures of adjustment and success, and the limited Black-White racial model, pushing the minority discourse further and demonstrating that racial and cultural differences affected their experiences despite high rates of academic achievement and socioeconomic status. In this way they revealed different arenas of their racialization and marginalization and were able to establish services and programs to educate the whole university about their experiences. It is only by learning about these histories that one can push beyond parity alone and see how race operates on college campuses beyond Black and White, ensuring that Asian American students are ultimately seen and heard.

Appendix: List of Oral History Interviews

Alumni

1970s

Bing, Frank
Bishop, Cordell
Chan, Suzanne Lee
Chen, Bill
Eng, Ock
Harano, Ross
Hatten, Winnie Hong
Hirota, Patricia
Huang, Terence
Ikeda, Deborah (Shikami)
Joe, Teresa
Lee, Peter
Lee, Steve
Lee, Wanda (Kawahara)
Moy, Herman
Moy, Mary
Moy, Rose
Naddy, Terry

Nishimoto, Warren
Poy, Paul
Shimomura, Gary
Shintani, Terry
Ueno, Rumi
Wong, Albert
Wong, Paul
Yung, Ed

1980s–1990s

Ali, Anida Yoeu
Bautista, Jeremy
Chang, Charles
Chang, Richard W.
Chen, Jessica
Chou, Loretta
Gosrisirikul, Vida
Gutierrez, Rhoda
Hemmady, Neena
Honda, Gene
Kumaki, Bob
Lin, Jody
Lin, Patricia (Chou)

Qadeer, Umbreen
Subramani, Ramesh
Tsai, Ho Chie
Wang, Karin
Yamate, Sandra

Faculty and Administrators

Anderson, James D.
Askew, Patricia
Chih, David
Cunningham, Clark
Didos, Samira (Ritsma)
Engelgau, Gary
Jeffries, Michael
Levy, Stan
Llewellyn, Yukiko
Riley, Bill
Seals, Tom
Shelley, Clarence
Yu, George

Acknowledgments

This history of Asian American student activism, a project that began in my doctoral studies, could not have been completed without my mentors at the University of Illinois at Urbana-Champaign (UIUC): educational historians James Anderson, Christopher Span, Timothy Cain, and especially Yoon Pak, who has remained a steadfast mentor and friend for over twenty years. This history would not have come to fruition if it were not for Yoon's encouragement and reminder of the importance of documenting these student voices. I am also grateful to my colleagues Oiyan Poon, Mario Rios Perez, and Jon Hale, who all provided support and constructive feedback as I worked on the proposal and manuscript. Thank you to the reviewers and editors at Rutgers University Press, in particular Ben Justice and Lisa Banning for their encouragement and feedback through the publishing process. And special thanks to Joy Williamson-Lott, whose work on Black Power at the University of Illinois greatly informed my research, for writing the foreword.

This history belongs to the alumni, faculty, and administrators who shared their time, stories, and insights with me. In sum, I interviewed forty-four University of Illinois alumni and sixteen retired faculty and administrators. Special thanks to Mary Moy, who helps keep the Asian American Alliance alumni community connected, and to the 1990s cohort of leaders, especially Jeremy Bautista, Richard Chang, Vida Gosrisirikul, Ho Chie Tsai, and Karin Wang. Thank you to the staff at the Asian American Cultural Center and the Asian American Studies Program at UIUC for sharing archival material with me.

Personal thanks to my friends and supporters over the years: Kent Ono, Pia Sengsavanh, Ning Zulauf, Emily Wee, Tysza Gandha, and Laura Brenier Davies. Thanks finally to my family: my parents, my sister, my brother Danny S. Lee who helped design the cover art, and my husband, Jim, and our pets, who made writing in quarantine enjoyable and productive.

Notes

Preface

1 Yen Le Espiritu, *Asian American Panethnicity: Bridging Institutions and Identities* (Philadelphia: Temple University Press, 1992); William Wei, *The Asian American Movement* (Philadelphia: Temple University Press, 1993).
2 Similarly, I cite the terms "Latina/o" or "Hispanic" when so used in the archival record, but use the term "Latinx" in my own analysis.
3 Student Affairs Task Force, "Strategic Plan for Multicultural Programs and Services for Student Affairs at UIUC," 9 September 1991, p. 14, Record series 41/1/21, Box 12, Folder: Multicultural Programs, Strategic Plans, 1991, 1993–1994, 1996–1998, University of Illinois at Urbana-Champaign Archives.

Introduction

1 Lorelle L. Espinoza, Jonathan M. Turk, Morgan Taylor, and Hollie M. Chessman, *Race and Ethnicity in Higher Education: A Status Report* (Washington, DC: American Council on Education, 2019), https://www.equityinhighered.org/.
2 "Which Highly Selective Colleges Have the Highest and Lowest Percentages of Asian Undergraduates?" *Chronicle of Higher Education*, 9 September 2018, https://www.chronicle.com/article/Which-Highly-Selective/244470; Scott Jaschik, "The Numbers and the Arguments on Asian Admissions," *Inside Higher Ed*, 7 August 2017, https://www.insidehighered.com/admissions/article/2017/08/07/look-data-and-arguments-about-asian-americans-and-admissions-elite; Scott Jaschik, "Yale Is New Target over Alleged Anti-Asian Bias," *Inside Higher Ed*, 27 September 2018, https://www.insidehighered.com/admissions/article/2018/09/27/us-reveals-investigation-alleged-anti-asian-bias-yale.
3 While some Chinese American groups have vocally opposed race-conscious admissions, many scholars in the Asian American community support the consideration of race in holistic admissions review as beneficial for all students. For example, in 2018, 531 scholars with expertise in Asian Americans, racial equity, and admissions filed an amicus curiae brief in support of Harvard. Oiyan A. Poon, Liliana M. Garces, Janelle Wong, Megan Segoshi, David Silver, and Sarah

Harrington, "Confronting Misinformation through Social Science Research: SFFA v. Harvard," *Asian American Law Journal* 26 (2019): 4–12; Julie J. Park and Amy Liu, "Interest Convergence or Divergence? A Critical Race Analysis of Asian Americans, Meritocracy, and Critical Mass in the Affirmative Action Debate," *Journal of Higher Education* 85 (2014): 36–64; Michele S. Moses, Daryl J. Maeda, and Christina H. Paguyo, "Racial Politics, Resentment, and Affirmative Action: Asian Americans as 'Model' College Applicants," *Journal of Higher Education* 90 (2019): 1–26.

4 Keith Osajima, "Asian Americans as the Model Minority: An Analysis of the Popular Press Image in the 1960's and 1980's," in *Contemporary Asian America: A Multidisciplinary Reader*, ed. Min Zhou and James Gatewood (New York: New York University Press, 2000), 449–458; Frank Wu, *Yellow: Race in America beyond Black and White* (New York: Basic Books, 2002).

5 When I use the term "Asian Pacific American" (APA), it is only when quoting an original source that used that term.

6 National Commission on Asian American and Pacific Islander Research in Education, "The Relevance of Asian Americans and Pacific Islanders in the College Completion Agenda, 2011," http://care.gseis.ucla.edu/wp-content /uploads/2015/08/2011_CARE_Report.pdf; Samuel D. Museus, "Asian Americans and Pacific Islanders: A National Portrait of Growth, Diversity, and Inequality," in *The Misrepresented Minority: New Insights on Asian Americans and Pacific Islanders, and the Implications for Higher Education*, ed. Samuel D. Museus, Dina C. Maramba, and Robert T. Teranishi (Sterling, VA: Stylus, 2013), 11–41; Espinoza et al., *Race and Ethnicity in Higher Education*.

7 Claire Kim, "The Racial Triangulation of Asian Americans," *Politics and Society* 27 (1999): 105–138; OiYan Poon, Dian Squire, Corinne Kodama, Ajani Byrd, Jason Chan, Lester Manzano, Sara Furr, and Devita Bishundat, "A Critical Review of the Model Minority Myth in Selected Literature on Asian Americans and Pacific Islanders in Higher Education," *Review of Educational Research* 86 (2016): 469–502; Osajima, "Asian Americans as the Model Minority."

8 John David Skrentny, *The Ironies of Affirmative Action: Politics, Culture, and Justice in America* (Chicago: University of Chicago Press, 1996).

9 Dana Takagi, "Asian Americans and Diversity Talk: The Limits of the Numbers Game," in *Diversity in American Higher Education: Towards a More Comprehensive Approach*, ed. Lisa M. Stulberg and Sharon Lawner Weinberg (New York: Routledge, 2011), 160.

10 Paul Brest and Miranda Oshige, "Affirmative Action for Whom?" *Stanford Law Review* 47 (1995): 855–900.

11 Jean Yonemura Wing, "Beyond Black and White: The Model Minority Myth and the Invisibility of Asian American Students," *Urban Review* 39 (2007): 455–487; Robert Teranishi, *Asians in the Ivory Tower: Dilemmas of Racial Inequality in American Higher Education* (New York: Teachers College Press, 2010); Samuel D. Museus, Dina C. Maramba, and Robert T. Teranishi, introduction to *The Misrepresented Minority: New Insights on Asian Americans and Pacific Islanders, and the Implications for Higher Education*, ed. Samuel D. Museus, Dina C. Maramba, and Robert T. Teranishi (Sterling, VA: Stylus, 2013), 1–10.

12 Juliana Menasce Horowitz, Anna Brown, and Kiana Cox, "Race in America 2019," Pew Research Center, 9 April 2019, https://www.pewsocialtrends.org/2019 /04/09/race-in-america-2019/.

13 In the spring of 2020, due to the prevalence of COVID-19 (what President Trump called the "Chinese flu"), a rise in anti-Asian violence occurred nationwide. "Reports of Anti-Asian Assaults, Harassment, and Hate Crimes Rise as Coronavirus Spreads," Anti-Defamation League, 18 June 2020, https://www.adl.org/blog /reports-of-anti-asian-assaults-harassment-and-hate-crimes-rise-as-coronavirus -spreads. Another report documented almost 3,800 anti-Asian incidents from March 2020 to February 2021. "2020–2021 National Report," Stop AAPI Hate website, 1 June 2021, https://stopaapihate.org/2020-2021-national-report/.

14 Sucheng Chan, *Asian Americans: An Interpretive History* (Boston: Twayne Publishers, 1991).

15 Kim, "Racial Triangulation of Asian Americans."

16 Frank Wu, "Neither Black nor White: Asian Americans and Affirmative Action," *Third World Law Journal* 15 (1995): 239.

17 Yen Le Espiritu, *Asian American Panethnicity: Bridging Institutions and Identities* (Philadelphia: Temple University Press, 1992).

18 Asian Americans and Latinxs are highly visible in institutions of higher education; in 2000, Asian Americans made up 5.9 percent and Hispanics made up 8.9 percent of students enrolled in all institutions of higher education. William B. Harvey and Eugene L. Anderson, *Minorities in Higher Education: Twenty-first Annual Status Report: 2003–2004* (Washington, DC: American Council on Education, 2005).

19 Eileen O'Brien, *The Racial Middle: Latinos and Asian Americans Living beyond the Racial Divide* (New York: New York University Press, 2008); Robert S. Chang, "Toward an Asian American Legal Scholarship: Critical Race Theory, Post-Structuralism, and Narrative Space," *California Law Review* 8 (1993): 1241–1323; Robert S. Chang and Keith Aoki, "Centering the Immigrant in the Inter/national Imagination," *California Law Review* 85 (1998): 1395–1447; Margaret Chon, "On the Need for Asian American Narratives in Law: Ethnic Specimens, Native Informants, Storytelling and Silences," *UCLA Asian Pacific American Law Journal* 3 (1995): 4–32.

20 Museus, Maramba, and Teranishi, introduction to *Misrepresented Minority*; Samuel D. Museus, "A Critical Analysis of the Exclusion of Asian Americans from Higher Education Research and Discourse," in *Asian American Voices: Engaging, Empowering, Enabling,* ed. Liz Zhan (New York: National League for Nursing, 2009), 59–76.

21 Asian American Studies Department website, University of Illinois at Urbana-Champaign, accessed 29 May 2021, https://asianam.illinois.edu/directory/faculty; University of Illinois at Urbana-Champaign Course Catalog, Asian American Studies, http://catalog.illinois.edu; "Facilities," Asian American Cultural Center website, University of Illinois at Urbana-Champaign, accessed 10 October 2019, https://oiir.illinois.edu/aacc/about-aacc/facilities.

22 Jeffrey Grim, Nue L. Lee, Samuel D. Museus, Vanessa S. Na, and Marie P. Ting. "Asian American College Student Activism and Social Justice in Midwest Contexts," *New Directions for Higher Education* 185 (2019): 27–28; Elizabeth M. Hoeffel, Sonya Rastogi, Myoung Ouk Kim, and Hasan Shahid, *The Asian Population, 2010: Census 2010 Brief,* https://www.census.gov/prod/cen2010/briefs /c2010br-11.pdf.

23 Erika Lee, "Asian American Studies in the Midwest: New Questions, Approaches, and Communities," *Journal of Asian American Studies* 12 (2009): 252.

Chapter 1 The Historiography of Asian American College Students

1 John Thelin, *A History of American Higher Education* (Baltimore: Johns Hopkins University Press, 2004).

2 James D. Anderson, "Race in American Higher Education: Historical Perspectives on Current Conditions," in *The Racial Crisis in American Higher Education: Continuing Challenges for the Twenty-first Century*, rev. ed., ed. William A. Smith, Philip G. Altbach, and Kofi Lomotey (Albany: State University of New York Press, 2002), 4.

3 Eileen Tamura, "Asian Americans in the History of Education: An Historiographical Essay," *History of Education Quarterly* 41 (2001): 58–71.

4 Michael S. Hevel and Heidi A. Jaeckle, "Trends in the Historiography of American College Student Life," in *Rethinking Campus Life: New Perspectives on the History of College Students in the United States*, ed. Christine A. Ogren and Marc A. VanOverbeke (New York: Palgrave Macmillan, 2018), 19–20.

5 Luping Bu, *Making the World Like Us: Education, Cultural Expansion, and the American Century* (Westport, CT: Praeger, 2003); Stephanie Hinnershitz, *Race, Religion, and Civil Rights: Asian Students on the West Coast, 1900–1968* (New Brunswick, NJ: Rutgers University Press, 2015).

6 Ronald Takaki, *Strangers from a Different Shore: A History of Asian Americans* (Boston: Back Bay Books, 1998).

7 Daryl J. Maeda, *Chains of Babylon: The Rise of Asian America* (Minneapolis: University of Minnesota Press, 2009); Sucheng Chan, *Asian Americans: An Interpretive History* (Boston: Twayne Publishers, 1991).

8 Bu, *Making the World Like Us*.

9 Barbara M. Posadas and Roland Guyotte, "Unintentional Immigrants: Chicago's Filipino Foreign Students Become Settlers, 1900–1941," *Journal of American Ethnic History* 9 (1990): 26–48.

10 Hinnershitz, *Race, Religion, and Civil Rights*.

11 Sarah M. Griffith, *The Fight for Asian American Civil Rights: Liberal Protestant Activism, 1900–1950* (Urbana: University of Illinois Press, 2018).

12 Weili Ye, *Seeking Modernity in China's Name: Chinese Students in the United States, 1900–1927* (Stanford, CA: Stanford University Press, 2001), 83.

13 Hinnershitz, *Race, Religion, and Civil Rights*.

14 Poshek Fu, "Across the Pacific: The University of Illinois and China," in *The University of Illinois: Engine of Innovation*, ed. Frederick E. Hoxie (Urbana: University of Illinois Press, 2017).

15 Carol Huang, "The Soft Power of US Education and the Formation of a Chinese American Intellectual Community in Urbana-Champaign, 1905–1954," PhD diss., University of Illinois at Urbana-Champaign, 2001, 52.

16 Kathleen Andal, "The Filipino Pensionado Experience: Educational Opportunity at the University of Illinois at Urbana-Champaign, 1904–1925," master's thesis, University of Illinois at Urbana-Champaign, 2002, 2–3.

17 Record series 41/2/41, Box 6, Folder: Chinese Student Club; Record series 41/2/41, Box 11, Folder: Hawaii Club, 1953–60; Record series 41/2/41, Box 19, Folder: Philippine Association. Later clubs include the Hawaii Club (1953), Indian Student Association (1948), Korean Students Association (1956), and a Thai Student Association (1978). Record series 41/2/41, Box 11, Folder: Hawaii Club,

1953–60; Record series 41/2/41, Box 13, Folder: Indian Student Association 1948; Record series 41/2/41, Box 15, Folder: Korean Students Association; Record series 41/2/41, Box 25, Folder: Thai Student Association, University of Illinois at Urbana-Champaign Archives.

18 Fu, "Across the Pacific," 191; Huang, "Soft Power of US Education."

19 Gary Okihiro, *Storied Lives: Japanese American Students and World War II* (Seattle: University of Washington Press, 1999).

20 Allan Austin, *From Concentration Camp to Campus: Japanese American Students and World War II* (Urbana: University of Illinois Press, 2004), 1.

21 Okihiro, *Storied Lives.*

22 Okihiro, *Storied Lives*; Huang, "Soft Power of US Education."

23 This activist history also includes Asian American involvement in off-campus issues, such as in labor movements, housing issues, New Left organizations, and Chinatown communities. Daryl J. Maeda, *Rethinking the Asian American Movement* (New York: Routledge, 2011). I do not address these issues in this study, as the Midwestern locale of Urbana-Champaign is not situated in an urban area with a sizeable Asian American community, and the archival record shows that students focused primarily on on-campus issues.

24 William Wei, *The Asian American Movement* (Philadelphia: Temple University Press, 1993), 2.

25 Karen Umemoto, "'On Strike!' San Francisco State College Strikes, 1968–1969: The Role of Asian American Students," in *Contemporary Asian America: A Multidisciplinary Reader*, ed. Min Zhou and James Gatewood (New York: New York University Press, 2000), 49–79; Thai-Huy Nguyen and Marybeth Gasman, "Activism, Identity, and Service," *History of Education* 44 (2015): 339–354; Daryl J. Maeda, *Chains of Babylon: The Rise of Asian America.*

26 Terry H. Anderson, *The Movement and the Sixties: Protest in America from Greensboro to Wounded Knee* (New York: Oxford University Press, 1995).

27 Anderson, *Movement and the Sixties*, 164.

28 Wei, *Asian American Movement*, 38–39; Norman Nakamura, "The Nature of GI Racism," in *Roots: An Asian American Reader*, ed. Amy Tachiki, Eddie Wong, Franklin Odo, and Buck Wong (Los Angeles: Regents of the University of California, 1971), 24–27; Evelyn Yoshimura, "GI's and Asian Women," 28–29 in the same volume.

29 Charles Teddlie and John Freeman, "Twentieth Century Desegregation in U.S. Higher Education—A Review of Five Distinct Historical Eras," in *The Racial Crisis in American Higher Education: Continuing Challenges for the Twenty-first Century*, rev. ed., ed. William A. Smith, Philip G. Altbach and Kofi Lomotey (Albany: State University of New York Press, 2002), 77–99.

30 Beatriz Clewell and Bernice Anderson, "African Americans in Higher Education: An Issue of Access," *Humboldt Journal of Social Relations* 21 (1995): 66–67.

31 Terry Anderson, *The Pursuit of Fairness: A History of Affirmative Action* (Oxford: Oxford University Press, 2004), 99.

32 Joy Ann Williamson, *Black Power on Campus: The University of Illinois, 1965–1975* (Urbana: University of Illinois Press, 2003), 26.

33 John B. Williams, *Desegregating America's Colleges and Universities: Title VI Regulation of Higher Education* (New York: Teachers College Press, 1988), 5.

34 Anderson, *Pursuit of Fairness*, 125.

35 John David Skrentny, *The Ironies of Affirmative Action: Politics, Culture, and Justice in America* (Chicago: University of Chicago Press, 1996).

36 Sherry Gorelick, *City College and the Jewish Poor: Education in New York, 1880–1924* (New Brunswick, NJ: Rutgers University Press, 1981); Marcia Graham Synnott, *The Half-Opened Door: Discrimination and Admissions at Harvard, Yale, and Princeton, 1900–1970* (Westport, CT: Greenwood Press, 1979); Jerome Karabel, *The Chosen: The Hidden History of Admission and Exclusion at Harvard, Yale, and Princeton* (New York: Houghton Mifflin, 2005).

37 John Aubrey Douglass, "Anatomy of Conflict: The Making and Unmaking of Affirmative Action at the University of California," in *Color Lines: Affirmative Action, Immigration, and Civil Rights Options for America*, ed. John David Skrentny (Chicago: University of Chicago Press, 2001), 118–144.

38 Sharon S. Lee, "The De-minoritization of Asian Americans: A Historical Examination of the Representations of Asian Americans in Affirmative Action Admissions Policies at the University of California," *Asian American Law Journal* 15 (2008): 129–152.

39 Asian American Law Students' Association, "Report of the Boalt Hall Asian American Special Admissions Project," *Amerasia* 5 (1978): 24.

40 Asian American Law Students' Association, "Report of the Boalt Hall Asian American Special Admissions Project," 25.

41 Brief for Asian American Bar Association of the Greater Bay Area, as Amicus Curiae Supporting Petitioners, *Regents of the University of California v. Bakke*, 438 U.S. 265 (1976) (No. 76-811).

42 Brief for the United States of America, as Amicus Curiae Supporting Petitioners, *Regents of the University of California v. Bakke*, 438 U.S. 265 (1978) (No. 76-811), in *Bakke v. Regents of the University of California*, ed. Alfred A. Slocum (Dobbs Ferry, NY: Oceana Publications, 1978), 51.

43 Asian and Pacific American Federal Employee Council, *Government's Amicus Brief: The Bakke Case and Asian/Pacific Americans* (Washington, DC: ERIC Document Reproduction Service No. ED154057, 1977), 1, 7.

44 Douglass, "Anatomy of Conflict," 127.

45 Douglass, 128.

46 Douglass, 128.

47 Matt Grace, "Asians Suffer under Model-Minority Myth," *Daily Bruin*, 22 September 1997, http://dailybruin.com/news/1997/sep/22/asians-suffer-under-model-mino/, paragraph 57. Filipinos remained under affirmative action recruitment and retention programs until 1985 at UCLA and 1989 at UC Berkeley.

48 Ling-chi Wang, "Meritocracy and Diversity in Higher Education: Discrimination against Asian Americans in the Post-Bakke Era," *Urban Review* 20 (1988): 196.

49 Dana Takagi, *The Retreat from Race: Asian-American Admissions and Racial Politics* (New Brunswick, NJ: Rutgers University Press, 1992); Wang, "Meritocracy and Diversity in Higher Education."

50 Michael Scott-Blair, "Ethnic Imbalance Shifts at UC," *San Diego Union*, 1 December 1986, A1.

51 Scott-Blair, "Ethnic Imbalance Shifts," A37.

52 Takagi, *Retreat from Race*.

Chapter 2   Making Noise in the Background

1 Frank Bing (UICU alumnus), interview by Sharon S. Lee, 9 November 2008 and 8 February 2009 in Chicago.
2 Sucheng Chan, *Asian Americans: An Interpretive History* (Boston: Twayne Publishers, 1991); Ronald Takaki, *Strangers from a Different Shore: A History of Asian Americans* (Boston: Back Bay Books, 1998).
3 Huping Ling, *Chinese Chicago: Race, Transnational Migration, and Community since 1870* (Stanford, CA: Stanford University Press, 2012); Barbara M. Posadas and Roland Guyotte, "Unintentional Immigrants: Chicago's Filipino Foreign Students Become Settlers, 1900–1941," *Journal of American Ethnic History* 9 (1990): 26–48.
4 Susan Moy, "The Chinese in Chicago: The First One Hundred Years," in *Ethnic Chicago: A Multicultural Portrait*, ed. Melvin G. Holli and Peter d'A. Jones (Grand Rapids, MI: William B. Eerdmans Publishing Co., 1995), 379.
5 Adam McKeown, *Chinese Migrant Networks and Cultural Change: Peru, Chicago, Hawaii, 1900–1936* (Chicago: University of Chicago Press, 2001).
6 Moy, "Chinese in Chicago," 394–396.
7 Moy, 383–384.
8 Ling Arenson, "Beyond a Common Ethnicity and Culture: Chicagoland's Chinese American Community since 1945," in *Asian America: Forming New Communities, Expanding Boundaries*, ed. Huping Ling (New Brunswick, NJ: Rutgers University Press, 2009), 69.
9 Masako Osako, "Japanese Americans: Melting into the All-American Pot," in *Ethnic Chicago: A Multicultural Portrait*, ed. Holli and d'A. Jones (Grand Rapids, MI: William B. Eerdmans Publishing Co., 1995), 410, 423.
10 Charlotte Brooks, "In the Twilight Zone between Black and White: Japanese American Resettlement and Community in Chicago, 1942–1945," *Journal of American History* 84 (2000): 1644–1687; Jacalyn D. Harden, *Double Cross: Japanese Americans in Black and White Chicago* (Minneapolis: University of Minnesota Press, 2003).
11 Frank Cicero, *Creating the Land of Lincoln: The History and Constitution of Illinois, 1778–1870* (Urbana: University of Illinois Press, 2018); Elmer Gertz, "The Black Laws of Illinois," *Journal of the Illinois State Historical Society (1908–1984)* 56 (1963): 454–473.
12 Richard M. Breaux, "Nooses, Sheets, and Blackface: White Racial Anxiety and Black Student Presence at Six Midwest Flagship Universities, 1882–1937," in *Higher Education for African Americans before the Civil Rights Era, 1900–1964*, ed. Marybeth Gasman and Roger L. Geiger (New Brunswick, NJ: Transaction Publishers, 2012), 43–73.
13 Carrie Franke, "Injustice Sheltered: Race Relations at the University of Illinois at Urbana-Champaign, 1945–1962," PhD diss., University of Illinois at Urbana-Champaign, 1990.
14 Joy Ann Williamson, *Black Power on Campus: The University of Illinois, 1965–1975* (Urbana: University of Illinois Press, 2003).
15 Williamson, *Black Power on Campus*, 17.
16 ET Sanford, Director of Student Financial Aid to Staff Members, 18 October 1971, Record series 41/2/14, Box 4, Folder: SEOP, 1970–72, University of Illinois at Urbana-Champaign Archives.

17 Williamson, *Black Power on Campus*, 57.

18 "Educational Assistance Programs at the University of Illinois," Faculty letter from the Office of the President, University of Illinois, No. 171, 3 February 1969, p. 3, Record series 41/2/14, Box 1, Folder: Research, Background Materials, University of Illinois at Urbana-Champaign Archives.

19 Recommendation to the All-University Committee on Admissions Regarding the Admission of Disadvantaged Students to the Chicago Circle, Medical Center, and Urbana-Champaign Senates, 16 June 1968, Record series 41/2/14, p. 1, Box 3, Folder: SEOP Project 500 1 of 3, University of Illinois at Urbana-Champaign Archives.

20 Minority Fall Semester Enrollment, Urbana-Champaign Campus, 16 March 1972, Record series 41/2/14, Box 1, Folder: Admissions 71–72, University of Illinois at Urbana-Champaign Archives.

21 Joseph Smith, "Report on the Minority Student Programs Urbana-Champaign Campus," April 1977, p. 9, Record series 24/9/2, Box 5, Folder: Minority Student Programs—Reports, 1977, University of Illinois at Urbana-Champaign Archives.

22 Michael Jeffries, "Educational Opportunities Program Annual Report, 1981–82," 16 July 1982, p. 31, Record series 41/64/40, Box 2, Folder: Committee on Minority Student Affairs, University of Illinois at Urbana-Champaign Archives.

23 Clarence Shelley to Bob Evans, re: News Release on SEOP, 12 May 1971, Record series 41/2/14, Box 2, Folder: SEOP staff, 1970–72, University of Illinois at Urbana-Champaign Archives.

24 Special Educational Opportunities Program Brochure, no date, Record series 41/2/14, Box 6, Folder: SEOP info, booklets, 1972–74, University of Illinois at Urbana-Champaign Archives.

25 Williamson, *Black Power on Campus*, 66.

26 Diann F. Geronemus, "Perspective: Latin American and White Students in the Special Educational Opportunities Program," December 1970, p. 4, Record series 41/2/14, Box 2, Folder: Latin American Students—General Information, 1972, University of Illinois at Urbana-Champaign Archives.

27 Geronemus, "Perspective," 16–17.

28 Luis Esquilin to Barry Munitz, 27 October 1971, Record series 41/2/14, Box 6, Folder: Latina/o Students, 1971–1973, University of Illinois at Urbana-Champaign Archives.

29 Urban Hispanic Students Organization to Dean Hugh Satterlee, 28 February 1972, Record series 41/2/14, Box 3, Folder: Action on Hispanic Students, University of Illinois at Urbana-Champaign Archives.

30 Urban Hispanic Organization to Clarence Shelley, 3 May 1972, Record series 41/2/14, Box 3, Folder: Action on Hispanic Students, University of Illinois at Urbana-Champaign Archives.

31 Editorial, "Hispanics Left Out," *Daily Illini*, 29 September 1972.

32 Memorandum to the file, from Vice Chancellor Hugh Satterlee, Subject: Discussion with Chancellor JW Peltason, 9 January 1973, dated 17 January 1973, Record series 41/2/14, Box 3, Folder: Latina/o Student Affairs 1973–73, University of Illinois at Urbana-Champaign Archives.

33 Latina/o Cultural House Proposal Submitted to the University Administration via Vice Chancellor Hugh M. Satterlee, 23 April 1974, Record series 41/2/14, Box 6, Folder: Latina/o Students' Proposal; Recruitment; Student Status, 1974–1975, University of Illinois at Urbana-Champaign Archives.

34 Tom Frisbie, "Latina/os Arrested at Circle Campus," *Daily Illini*, 28 September 1973.

35 Hugh M. Satterlee to Chancellor JW Peltason, 29 April 1974, Record series 41/64/40, Box 2, Folder: Correspondence, 1974–76, University of Illinois at Urbana-Champaign Archives.

36 Robbye Hill, "Latina/o Student House Opens on Campus," *Daily Illini*, 14 September 1974.

37 "Summary of Progress Efforts Aimed at the Recruitment and Retention of Latina/o Students, 1974–75," Record series 41/64/40, Box 1, Folder: Bilingual/ Bicultural Programs, University of Illinois at Urbana-Champaign Archives.

38 Jacob Jennings Jr., Assistant Director Research and Governmental Relations, Illinois State Board of Higher Education, Special Support Services Programs at Selected Illinois Institutions of Higher Education, A Report, Section C: University of Illinois-Urbana Educational Opportunities Program (EOP), 1974, Record series 1/1/13, Box 1, Folder: IBHE State Board Meetings, July-November 1974, University of Illinois at Urbana-Champaign Archives.

39 University of Illinois at Urbana-Champaign Office of Equal Opportunity and Access, "Undergraduate Enrollment by Racial/Ethnic Category, University of Illinois at Urbana-Champaign, Fall 1967 to Fall 2008," http://oeoa.illinois.edu /Undergraduate%20Enrollment%20by%20Race.pdf.

40 City of Pekin website, "The History of the City of Pekin," accessed 15 October 2009, http://www.ci.pekin.il.us/history.asp.

41 James Loewen, *Sundown Towns: A Hidden Dimension of American Racism* (New York: New Press, 2005).

42 Various Pekin Chinks Clippings, Folder: Pekin Chinks, University of Illinois at Urbana-Champaign Asian American Cultural Center Archives.

43 "Big Stink over 'Chink,'" Folder: "Pekin Chinks," University of Illinois at Urbana-Champaign Asian American Cultural Center Archives; Rick Baker, "Delegation Still Pressuring to Rename Pekin 'Chinks,'" *Bloomington-Normal Pantagraph*, 8 October 1974.

44 Dan Mergens, "The Pekin Mascot Controversy: A Closer Look at Institutional Racism in a 'Sundown Town,'" senior thesis, Northern Illinois University, December 2007, Folder: Pekin Chinks, University of Illinois at Urbana-Champaign Asian American Cultural Center Archives; Loewen, *Sundown Towns*. Interestingly, James Loewen points out that the term "Dragons" is also a reference to the Ku Klux Klan.

45 Ross Harano (UIUC alumnus), interview by Sharon S. Lee, 4 November 2008 in Urbana, Illinois.

46 Harano interview.

47 Clarence Shelley (founding director of UIUC Special Educational Opportunities Program), interview by Sharon S. Lee, 22 March 2007 in Urbana, Illinois.

48 Rose Moy (UIUC alumnus), interview by Sharon S. Lee, 20 November 2008 in Chicago.

49 Moy interview.

50 William Wei, *The Asian American Movement* (Philadelphia: Temple University Press, 1993).

51 Paul Wong (former UIUC professor of sociology and Asian studies), phone interview by Sharon S. Lee, 3 October 2008.

52 Patricia Hirota (cofounder of Asian American Alliance), phone interview by Sharon S. Lee, 12 March 2009.
53 Patricia Hirota Wong, letter to the editor, *Daily Illini*, 19 January 1971.
54 Request for University Recognition of a New Undergraduate Student Organization Not Maintaining a House, Asian American Alliance, 24 January 1971, Record series 41/2/41, Box 3, Asian American Alliance, University of Illinois at Urbana-Champaign Archives.
55 Asian American Alliance Spring 71 Calendar, ca. 1971, Record series 41/68/157, Folder: Asian American Alliance, 1971, 1974, University of Illinois at Urbana-Champaign Archives.
56 Patricia Hirota Wong, letter to the editor, *Daily Illini*, 16 February 1971.
57 The *Daily Illini* listed meetings on March 17, March 28, May 2, and May 8 of that semester. *Daily Illini* Notices, 17 February 1971, 17 March 1971, 27 March 1971, 1 May 1971, 8 May 1971.
58 Warren Nishimoto (UIUC alumnus), phone interview by Sharon S. Lee, 23 March 2009.
59 Steve Lee (UIUC alumnus), phone interview by Sharon S. Lee, 4 April 2009.
60 Suzanne Lee Chan (UIUC alumnus), interview by Sharon S. Lee, 6 June 2009 in Fremont, California.
61 Herman Moy (UIUC alumnus), phone interview by Sharon S. Lee, 18 March 2009.
62 Wanda Kawahara Lee (UIUC alumnus), interview by Sharon S. Lee, 8 February 2009 in Chicago.
63 Paul Wong interview, 3 October 2008.
64 Patricia Hirota interview, 12 March 2009.
65 Asian American Alliance meeting notes, 17 March 1971, Record series 41/68/157, Folder: Asian American Alliance, 1971, 1974, University of Illinois at Urbana-Champaign Archives.
66 "Fellow Asian Americans" flyer, Asian American Alliance, 5 February 1971, Record series 41/6/840, Box 5, Folder: Asian American Alliance, University of Illinois at Urbana-Champaign Archives. Emphasis in original.
67 Paul Wong interview, 3 October 2008.
68 Roger Simon, "UI Students Protest War, US Marines," *Daily Illini*, 29 September 1969; Roger Simon, "10 Arrested during Sit-in: Action Taken at Draft Office; Two Burn Cards Near Union," *Daily Illini*, 17 October 1967; Roger Simon, "Protestors End Dow Visit: Company Cancels Recruiting after Massive Demonstration," *Daily Illini*, 26 October 1967; Roger Simon, "Reinstate Seven Students: Faculty Senate Committee Puts Students on Probation," *Daily Illini*, 12 December 1967.
69 Charles DeBenedetti and Charles Chatfield, *An American Ordeal: The Antiwar Movement of the Vietnam Era* (Syracuse, NY: Syracuse University Press, 1990), 112.
70 Barbara Roth, "Peaceful Marches Set for Coasts," *Daily Illini*, 17 April 1971.
71 Paul Wong, "The Emergence of the Asian-American Movement," *Bridge* 2 (1971): 36.
72 Asian American Alliance, meeting minutes, ca. April 1971, Record series 41/68/157, Folder: Asian American Alliance, 1971, 1974, University of Illinois at Urbana-Champaign Archives.
73 Warren Nishimoto interview, 23 March 2009.

74   G. Robert Hillman, "1,000 March in War Protest," *Daily Illini*, 6 May 1971.

75   Mary Dubin, "39 Arrested in Union," *Daily Illini,* 7 May 1971.

76   Paul Wong interview, 3 October 2008.

77   *Daily Illini*, 6 May 1971.

78   Wong, "Emergence of the Asian-American Movement," 36; emphasis in original. Thai-Huy Nguyen and Marybeth Gasman, "Activism, Identity, and Service: The Influence of the Asian American Movement on the Educational Experiences of College Students," *History of Education* 44 (2015): 339–354.

79   Asians and Asian Americans Come March With Us! Asian American Alliance Flyer, Wednesday, 5 May 1971, Record series 41/68/157, Folder: Asian American Alliance, 1971, 1974, University of Illinois at Urbana-Champaign Archives. Emphasis in original.

80   Terry Shintani (UIUC alumnus), phone interview by Sharon S. Lee, 13 August 2008.

81   Asian American Flyers, "The Asian American Alliance Presents Nisei: The Pride and the Shame," 4 March 1971, and "Hiroshima Nagasaki, Time of the Locust, Hunger in America," 20 April 1971, Record series 41/68/157, Folder: Asian American Alliance, 1971, 1974, University of Illinois at Urbana-Champaign Archives.

82   Asian American Alliance handout, "Suggested Discussion Topics," 8 May 1971, Record series 41/68/157, Folder: Asian American Alliance, 1971, 1974, University of Illinois at Urbana-Champaign Archives.

83   Herman Moy interview, 18 March 2009.

84   Rick Pope, "199 Courses Penetrate Many Areas," *Daily Illini*, 4 February 1972.

85   Asian American Alliance, Proposal for an Asian American Studies Program, 1 February 1973, Record series 41/6/840, Box 5, Asian American Alliance, University of Illinois at Urbana-Champaign Archives.

86   It is unclear at this point to whom the proposal was submitted and/or what the official response was.

87   Paul Wong interview, 3 October 2008.

88   Kathy Reinbolt, "Five Groups Get Money: UGSA Releases Funds," *Daily Illini*, 16 March 1971.

89   Patricia Hirota Wong, letter to the editor, *Daily Illini*, 18 May 1971.

90   Terry Shintani interview, 13 August 2008.

91   Ellen Ferber, "U of I Searches for Qualified Minority Students," *Daily Illini*, 10 November 1976.

92   Asian American Alliance handout, "Suggested Discussion Topics," 8 May 1971, Record series 41/68/157, Folder: Asian American Alliance, 1971, 1974, University of Illinois at Urbana-Champaign Archives.

93   Debbie Shikami Ikeda (UIUC alumnus), interview by Sharon S. Lee, 6 June 2009 in Fremont, California.

94   Frank Bing interview, 8 February 2009.

95   Clarence Shelley interview, 22 March 2007.

96   Steve Lee interview, 4 April 2009.

97   Debbie Shikami Ikeda interview, 6 June 2009.

98   Steve Lee interview, 4 April 2009.

99   Steve Lee interview, 4 April 2009.

100   Patricia Hirota interview, 12 March 2009.

101   Warren Nishimoto interview, 23 March 2009.

102 Wei, *Asian American Movement*, 30.
103 Rice Paper Collective, *Rice Paper*, vol. 1, no. 1, 1974, Folder: Midwest History, University of Illinois at Urbana-Champaign Asian American Cultural Center Archives.
104 Rice Paper Collective, *Rice Paper*, vol. 1, no. 1, 1974, p. 9.
105 Rice Paper Collective, *Rice Paper*, vol. 1, no. 2, winter 1975, Folder: Midwest History, University of Illinois at Urbana-Champaign Asian American Cultural Center Archives.
106 Steve Lee interview, 4 April 2009.
107 Stephen Lee, "University of Illinois—Asian American Alliance," position paper, 24 September 1974, Rice Paper Collective, *Rice Paper*, vol. 1, no. 2, winter 1975, p. 7, Folder: Midwest History, University of Illinois at Urbana-Champaign Asian American Cultural Center Archives.
108 Asian American Week Planning Committee, letter to the editor, *Daily Illini*, 16 February 1974.
109 Application for Registered Student Organization Status for period 1 July 1974 to 1 October 1975, for Asian American Alliance, 10 September 1974, Record series 41/2/41, Box 3, Asian American Alliance, University of Illinois at Urbana-Champaign Archives.

Chapter 3   We Are Not Model Minorities

1 Jody Lin and Karin Wang, "'Model Minority' Tag Hurts Asian-Americans," *Daily Illini,* 21 March 1991.
2 University of Illinois at Urbana-Champaign Office of Equal Opportunity and Access, "Undergraduate Enrollment by Racial/Ethnic Category, University of Illinois at Urbana-Champaign, Fall 1967 to Fall 2008," http://oeoa.illinois.edu/Undergraduate%20Enrollment%20by%20Race.pdf.
3 David Brand, "The New Whiz-Kids: Why Asian-Americans Are Doing So Well, and What It Costs Them," *Time*, 31 August 1987, 51.
4 Eugenia Escueta and Eileen O'Brien, "Asian Americans and Higher Education: Trends and Issues," *Research Briefs* 2 (1991): 1 (ERIC Document Reproduction Service No. ED381103).
5 Sucheng Chan and Ling-chi Wang, "Racism and the Model Minority: Asian-Americans in Higher Education," in *The Racial Crisis in American Higher Education*, ed. Philip G. Altbach and Kofi Lomotey (Albany: State University of New York Press, 1991), 53.
6 William Wei, *The Asian American Movement* (Philadelphia: Temple University Press, 1993).
7 Asian American Institute, *Asian American Compass: A Guide to Navigating the Community*, 3rd ed. (Chicago: Asian American Institute, 2006), 10.
8 Wei, *Asian American Movement*, 151.
9 Stanley R. Levy to Deans, Directors, and Department Heads, Subject: Office of Minority Student Affairs, 10 February 1988, Record series 41/1/6, Box 112, Folder: Minority Student Affairs, 1987–1988, University of Illinois at Urbana-Champaign Archives.
10 Office of Minority Student Affairs Program Description, 5 October 1987, Record series 41/1/6, Box 112, Folder: Minority Student Affairs, 1987–1988, University of Illinois at Urbana-Champaign Archives.

11 Elaine Copeland, Director of Minority Student Affairs Office to Executive Head
of Departments, Subject: Recruiting Minority Graduate Students, in April 1977
Report on the Minority Student Programs, Urbana-Champaign Campus,
4 April 1977, Record series 24/9/2, Box 5, Folder: Minority Student Programs and
Report, 1977, University of Illinois at Urbana-Champaign Archives; Minority
Student Affairs Office, Graduate College at University of Illinois at Urbana-
Champaign, "A Listing of Educational Grants for Minority Students from
Selected Foundations, Funds, and Individuals," Record series 41/1/6, Box 112,
Folder: Minority Student Affairs, 1987–1988, University of Illinois at Urbana-
Champaign Archives; Summary of Graduate College Efforts to Increase Enroll-
ment of Under-represented Minority Students at the University of Illinois,
Urbana-Champaign, Record series 41/1/6, Box 81, Folder: Report by the Ad-hoc
Committee on Minority Student Affairs, 1983, University of Illinois at Urbana-
Champaign Archives.
12 Public Act 85-283 (Senate Bill No. 1101) in *Laws of the State of Illinois Eighty-Fifth
Assembly 1987, Public Act 85-1 Thru Public Action 85-1009*, 1606–1607.
13 State of Illinois Board of Higher Education 1986 Report on Minority Participa-
tion in Illinois Higher Education, 8 July 1986, p. 1, Record series 41/1/6, Box 111,
Folder: Minority Retention IBHE, 1989–1990, University of Illinois at Urbana-
Champaign Archives.
14 State of Illinois Board of Higher Education, 1987 Report on Minority Student
Participation in Illinois Higher Education, Part A, p. 1, Record series 24/9/2, Box 6,
Folder: Allerton Conference: 1988—"The Role and Responsibility of the U of
I for the Education of Minorities," University of Illinois at Urbana-Champaign
Archives.
15 Sabrina L. Miller, "The 80s Mark Strides in Minority Enrollment," *Daily Illini*,
finals ed., 1989.
16 Institutional Plan to Improve the Participation and Success of Minority, Female,
and Disabled Students and Staff at the University of Illinois at Urbana-Champaign,
1990, p. 1, Record series 41/1/6, Box 111, Folder: Minority Retention IBHE,
1989–1990, University of Illinois at Urbana-Champaign Archives.
17 D. J. Wermers, Assistant Director, University Office of School and College
Relations, "Enrollment at the University of Illinois by Racial Ethnic Categories,
Fall Terms 1967–1975," Folder: Misc. Student Affairs Memos re: Asian Americans, University of Illinois at Urbana-Champaign Asian American Cultural
Center Archives.
18 Robin Gareiss, "Minorities: How Successful Are UI Recruitment and Retention
Efforts?" *Daily Illini*, 30 September 1986.
19 Institutional Plan to Improve the Participation and Success of Minority, Female,
and Disabled Students and Staff at the University of Illinois at Urbana-Champaign,
1990, p. 1, Record series 41/1/6, Box 111, Folder: Minority Retention IBHE,
1989–1990, University of Illinois at Urbana-Champaign Archives.
20 Lin and Wang, "'Model Minority' Tag Hurts Asian-Americans."
21 Constitution of the Asian-American Association, University of Illinois, 26 June
1986, Folder: AAA Archives, University of Illinois at Urbana-Champaign Asian
American Cultural Center Archives.
22 Loretta Chou (UIUC alumnus), phone interview by Sharon S. Lee, 17 June 2009.
23 "A Brief Overview of the Meeting," Asian-American Association Newsletter,
AAA News, April 1986, Issue #1, Champaign-Urbana, p. 1, Record series 41/2/40,

Box 10, Folder: Asian American Association Newsletters 1986–1998, University of Illinois at Urbana-Champaign Archives.

24 "How We Started," Asian-American Association Newsletter, AAA News, April 1986, Issue #1, Champaign-Urbana, p. 1, Record series 41/2/40, Box 10, Folder: Asian American Association Newsletters 1986–1998, University of Illinois at Urbana-Champaign Archives.

25 Loretta Chou interview, 17 June 2009.

26 "Remember When," AAA 10th anniversary commemorative packet, Folder: AAA Historical Resources, University of Illinois at Urbana-Champaign Asian American Cultural Center Archives.

27 Loretta Chou interview, 17 June 2009.

28 Midwest Asian American Students Conference 1991 Booklet, p. 12, Folder: MAAS/MAASU Early Programs, University of Illinois at Urbana-Champaign Asian American Cultural Center Archives.

29 "Remember When," AAA 10th anniversary commemorative packet.

30 Jody Lin, "Welcome," *The Dynasty*, Newsletter of the Asian-American Association 4, no. 1 (September 1989): p.1, Folder: AAA Newsletters, University of Illinois at Urbana-Champaign Asian American Cultural Center Archives.

31 Helen Zia, *Asian American Dreams: The Emergence of an American People* (New York: Farrar, Straus, and Giroux, 2000).

32 Zia, *Asian American Dreams*, 90.

33 United States Commission on Civil Rights, *Civil Rights Issues Facing Asian Americans in the 1990s* (Washington, DC: United States Commission on Civil Rights, February 1992).

34 Zia, *Asian American Dreams*, 91.

35 United States Commission on Civil Rights, *Civil Rights Issues Facing Asian Americans in the 1990s*, 41–44.

36 Ho Chie Tsai (UIUC alumnus), interview by Sharon S. Lee, 28 July 2008 in Manchester, Indiana.

37 Karin Wang (UIUC alumnus), phone interview by Sharon S. Lee, 8 September 2008.

38 Jody Lin, "Letter from Jody," *The Dynasty*, Newsletter of the Asian-American Association 5, no. 1 (September 1990): 1, Folder: AAA Historical Resources, University of Illinois at Urbana-Champaign Asian American Cultural Center Archives.

39 Ho Chie Tsai interview, 28 July 2008.

40 Ho Chie Tsai interview, 28 July 2008.

41 "About the Asian American Student Community at the U of I," *Perspectives: A Special Publication of the 1994 MAAS Conference*, pp. 39–41, Folder: MAAS/MAASU Early Programs, University of Illinois at Urbana-Champaign Asian American Cultural Center Archives.

42 "Asian Council News," *The Dynasty*, Newsletter of the Asian American Association 5, no. 3 (October 1990): 7, Folder: AAA Newsletters, University of Illinois at Urbana-Champaign Asian American Cultural Center Archives.

43 Asian Council Minutes, 17 September 1990, Folder: Asian Council, University of Illinois at Urbana-Champaign Asian American Cultural Center Archives.

44 Asian Awareness Month 1991 flyer, Folder: Asian American Awareness Month, 1991, 1995–1997, University of Illinois at Urbana-Champaign Asian American Cultural Center Archives.

45 Asian-Pacific American Student Alliance newsletter, vol. 1, no. 1, September 1991. Folder: ACCORD (Asian-Pacific American Coalition to Combat Oppression, Racism, and Discrimination), University of Illinois at Urbana-Champaign Asian American Cultural Center Archives.

46 Asian-Pacific American Coalition to Combat Oppression, Racism, and Discrimination (ACCORD) flyer, ca. 1991, Folder: ACCORD (Asian-Pacific American Coalition to Combat Oppression, Racism, and Discrimination), University of Illinois at Urbana-Champaign Asian American Cultural Center Archives.

47 Philip G. Altbach, "The Racial Dilemma in American Higher Education," in *The Racial Crisis in American Higher Education,* ed. Philip G. Altbach and Kofi Lomotey (Albany, NY: State University of New York Press, 1991), 7.

48 Alan Colón, "Race Relations on Campus: An Administrative Perspective," in *The Racial Crisis in American Higher Education,* ed. Philip G. Altbach and Kofi Lomotey (Albany, NY: State University of New York Press, 1991), 69.

49 Tony Vellela, *New Voices: Student Political Activism in the 80s and 90s* (Boston: South End Press, 1988).

50 Carol Loretz, "Internment of Japanese Not a Debt to Mark 'Paid,'" *Daily Illini,* 24 June 1988.

51 As described by Michael Walker, "UI Example Abets Community Racism," *Daily Illini,* 24 April 1991.

52 ACCORD ad, "Beyond Barbed Wire," *Daily Illini,* 5 December 1991.

53 "Press Release: Asian-Pacific-Americans Speak Out against Racism," ca. 1991, Folder: ACCORD (Asian-Pacific American Coalition to Combat Oppression, Racism, and Discrimination), University of Illinois at Urbana-Champaign Asian American Cultural Center Archives.

54 Anna Curry, "Demonstrators Protest Anti-Asian Attitudes," *Daily Illini,* 9 December 1991.

55 Chris Oei, "Racial Violence and You," Asian-Pacific American Coalition to Combat Oppression, Racism, and Discrimination (ACCORD) newsletter, vol. 1, no. 2, December 1991, Folder: ACCORD (Asian-Pacific American Coalition to Combat Oppression, Racism, and Discrimination), University of Illinois at Urbana-Champaign Asian American Cultural Center Archives.

56 "Anti-Asian and Anti-Pacific Peoples Alert!!!!!" Asian-Pacific American Student Alliance newsletter, vol. 1, no.1, September 1991, and Asian-Pacific American Coalition to Combat Oppression, Racism, and Discrimination (ACCORD) newsletter, vol. 1, no. 2, December 1991, Folder: ACCORD (Asian-Pacific American Coalition to Combat Oppression, Racism, and Discrimination), University of Illinois at Urbana-Champaign Asian American Cultural Center Archives.

57 "Asian/ Pacific Committee against Anti-Asian Harassment and Violence Incident Report Form," Folder: ACCORD (Asian-Pacific American Coalition to Combat Oppression, Racism, and Discrimination), University of Illinois at Urbana-Champaign Asian American Cultural Center Archives.

58 "AAA Survey Results," *The Dynasty: Newsletter of the Asian-American Association* 5, no. 6 (February 1991): 2. Folder: AAA Newsletters, University of Illinois at Urbana-Champaign Asian American Cultural Center Archives; *Horizons: Newsletter of the Asian American Association at the University of Illinois at Urbana-Champaign,* November 1992, Record series 41/2/41, Box 10, Folder: Asian American Association Newsletters 1986–1998, University of Illinois at

Urbana-Champaign Archives. Additional incidents of name calling and racial slurs were documented in the 1994 MAAS conference booklet. Katherine Chu, "What's Your Experience?" *Perspectives: A Special Publication of the 1994 MAAS Conference*, p. 43, Folder: MAAS/ MAASU Early Programs, University of Illinois at Urbana-Champaign Asian American Cultural Center Archives.

59 Catherine Spellman, "Acacia Pledges Cause Chaos on Trip: University, Federal Investigations Ensue," *Daily Illini*, 20 April 1988.

60 Suzy Frisch and Dorothy Puch, "Five Rejected Pledges Accuse Fraternity of Racism," *Daily Illini*, 30 April 1992.

61 Quoted in Cattleya Pinyo, "Students Blast Racism at UI," *Daily Illini*, 1 May 1992.

62 Elaine Richardson, "Protestors Confront Fraternity Members," *Daily Illini*, 27 March 1992.

63 Michael Gray, "Scuffle at UI Leads to Racism Protest," *Champaign Urbana News-Gazette*, 27 March 1992.

64 "For Immediate Release," ACCORD press release, ca. 1992, Folder: ACCORD (Asian-Pacific American Coalition to Combat Oppression, Racism, and Discrimination), University of Illinois at Urbana-Champaign Asian American Cultural Center Archives; emphasis in original.

65 Shilpa Davé, Pawan Dhingra, Sunaina Maira, Partha Mazumdar, Lavina Shankar, Jaideep Singh, and Rajini Srikanth, "De-Privileging Positions: Indian Americans, South Asian Americans, and the Politics of Asian American Studies," *Journal of Asian American Studies* 3, no. 1 (2000): 67–100; Lavina Shankar and Rajini Srikanth, eds., *A Part Yet Apart: South Asians in Asian America* (Philadelphia: Temple University Press, 1998); Joanne Rondilla, "The Filipino Question in Asia and the Pacific: Rethinking Regional Origins in Diaspora," in *Pacific Diaspora: Island Peoples in the United States and across the Pacific*, ed. Paul Spickard, Joanne Rondilla, and Debbie Hippolite Wright (Honolulu: University of Hawai'i Press, 2002), 56–68; Helen Toribio, "The Problematics of History and Location of Filipino American Studies within Asian American Studies," in *Asian American Studies after Critical Mass*, ed. Kent Ono (Malden, MA: Blackwell Publishing, 2005), 166–176; Aihwa Ong, *Buddha Is Hiding: Refugees, Citizenship, the New America* (Berkeley: University of California Press, 2003). These issues are also discussed for Asian American college student movements in Edmund Lee, "Unity Now, Sensitivity Later?" *A. Magazine*, April/May 1998, pp. 31–35.

66 *Horizons: The Newsletter of the Asian American Association* 1, no. 1 (October 1991): 1, Folder: AAA Historical Resources, University of Illinois at Urbana-Champaign Asian American Cultural Center Archives.

67 In December 1991, South Asian American students on campus critiqued an article the AAA published in the *Daily Illini* that still centered East Asian American experiences when discussing Asian American issues. Kiran Vasireddy and Sreenu Dandamudi, "See All Asian Racism," *Daily Illini*, 11 December 1991.

68 Clarence Shelley (founding director of University of Illinois at Urbana-Champaign Special Educational Opportunities Program), interview by Sharon S. Lee, 22 March 2007 in Urbana, Illinois.

69 Ho Chie Tsai, "The View from Here," reprinted in Unseen Unheard program booklet, 2006, University of Illinois Urbana-Champaign Asian American Cultural Center.

70 Quoted in Kerri Scholl, "Organization Complex Provides Vital Offices: More Student Groups Now Have Headquarters," *Daily Illini*, 14 April 1992.

71 Bill Riley (former UIUC dean of students), interview with Sharon S. Lee, 15 April 2009 in Urbana, Illinois.

72 Luping Bu, *Making the World Like Us: Education, Cultural Expansion, and the American Century* (Westport, CT: Praeger, 2003); Stephanie Hinnershitz, *Race, Religion, and Civil Rights: Asian Students on the West Coast, 1900–1968* (New Brunswick, NJ: Rutgers University Press, 2015); Sarah M. Griffith, *The Fight for Asian American Civil Rights: Liberal Protestant Activism, 1900–1950* (Urbana: University of Illinois Press, 2018).

73 East Coast Asian American Student Union History, accessed 23 July 2009, http://ecaasunational.org/site/?page_id=239.

74 It is unclear how MAPASAN was related to MAAS or MAASU. Wei, *Asian American Movement*, 153.

75 Patricia Chou Lin (UIUC alumnus), interview by Sharon S. Lee, 22 July 2008 in Naperville, Illinois.

76 Mark Allen, "Forum to Raise Awareness of Asian-American Culture," *Daily Illini*, 1 March 1991.

77 "MAAS History," MAAS 1993 conference booklet, "Empowerment through Unity," 9–11 April 1993, Folder: MAAS/MAASU Early Programs, University of Illinois at Urbana-Champaign Asian American Cultural Center Archives.

78 Bridging the Gap, Second Annual Midwest Asian-American Student Conference, University of Illinois Urbana-Champaign, 6–8 April 1990, Record series 41/2/40, Box 10, Folder: Asian American Association—Midwest Asian American Students Conference 1990–1993, University of Illinois at Urbana-Champaign Archives.

79 Third Annual Midwest Asian-American Students Conference, MAAS 1991, Folder: MAAS/MAASU Early Programs, University of Illinois at Urbana-Champaign Asian American Cultural Center Archives.

80 "About MAASU," Midwest Asian American Students Union website, accessed 20 July 2009, http://www.maasu.org/history.html.

81 Charles Chang (MAASU founder), phone interview by Sharon S. Lee, 8 October 2008.

82 Charles Chang interview, 8 October 2008.

83 Charles Chang interview, 8 October 2008.

84 Midwest Asian American Students (MAAS) Conference General Info, 1–3 March 1995, Record series 41/2/40, Box 10, Folder: Asian American Association-Midwest Asian American Students Conference 1990–1993, University of Illinois at Urbana-Champaign Archives.

85 As MAASU grew and MAAS faded out after 1996, UIUC remained active in the network, hosting the annual MAASU conference in February 2002 and March 2007. "MAAS History," MAAS 1993 conference booklet, "Empowerment through Unity," 9–11 April 1993, Folder: MAAS/MAASU Early Programs, University of Illinois at Urbana-Champaign Asian American Cultural Center Archives.

86 Corinne M. Kodama, OiYan A. Poon, Lester J. Manzano, and Ester U. Sihite, "Geographic Constructions of Race: The Midwest Asian American Students Union," *Journal of College Student Development* 58 (2017): 872–890.

87 Jeremy Bautista (UIUC alumnus), interview with Sharon S. Lee, 7 July 2007 in Chicago.

88 Patricia Chou Lin interview, 22 July 2008.

89 Karin Wang interview, 8 September 2008.

90   Stanley R. Levy to S. Eugene Barton, Gary B. North, William L. Riley, Clarence
     Shelley, and Hank R. Walter, Subject: Asian-American Students, 22 August 1988,
     Folder: Misc. Student Affairs Memos re: Asian Americans, University of Illinois
     at Urbana-Champaign Asian American Cultural Center Archives.
91   Richard Bernstein, "Asian Newcomers Hurt by Precursor's Success," *New York
     Times*, 10 July 1988.
92   Athena Tapales to Stanley R. Levy, Subject: Asian Pacific Islanders: Findings,
     8 December 1989, pp. 8–9, Folder: Asian American Task Force, University of
     Illinois at Urbana-Champaign Asian American Cultural Center Archives.
93   Asian-American Task Force Report, submitted by Susan Yung Maul, 14 May 1990,
     Folder: Asian American Task Force, University of Illinois at Urbana-Champaign
     Asian American Cultural Center Archives.
94   "Asian American Students at UIUC in 1997," Report by Yuki Llewellyn, Assistant
     Dean for Registered Organizations, UIUC, Folder: APARC, 1998–99, University
     of Illinois at Urbana-Champaign Asian American Cultural Center Archives;
     Asian American Programming Committee, Illini Union Board, Asiantation 1995
     Asian Pacific American New Student Orientation, University of Illinois at
     Urbana-Champaign Asian American Cultural Center.
95   Asian American Task Force to Stan Levy, re: Status of the Task Force, 27
     March 1990, p. 3, Folder: APA Faculty and Staff Development, University of
     Illinois at Urbana-Champaign Asian American Cultural Center Archives.
96   "Summary of Asian American Issues/Concerns and Program Recommendations,"
     Asian-American Task Force Report, Submitted by Susan Yung Maul, 14
     May 1990, p. 1, Folder: Asian American Task Force, University of Illinois at
     Urbana-Champaign Asian American Cultural Center Archives.
97   Asian American Alumni Association, Asiantation 1995 Asian Pacific American
     New Student Orientation, University of Illinois Urbana-Champaign, University
     of Illinois at Urbana-Champaign Asian American Cultural Center.
98   Jody Lin, "Asian-Americans Left Out," *Daily Illini*, 8 November 1990.
99   Quoted in Sharon Farlow, "Asian-American Students Seek a Place to Call Home,"
     Crossroads: The Multicultural Magazine of the Daily Illini, 23 March 1994.

Chapter 4   We Are Minorities

1   Richard W. Chang et al., "Proposal for an Asian Pacific American Cultural
    Center," 3 May 1994, p. 42, Folder: Asian American Cultural Center Proposals,
    University of Illinois at Urbana-Champaign Asian American Cultural Center
    Archives.
2   Robert A. Rhoads, *Freedom's Web: Student Activism in an Age of Cultural
    Diversity* (Baltimore: Johns Hopkins University Press, 1998).
3   Julie Wurth, "UI's Changing Complexion: With Campus Numbers on Rise,
    Minority Students Fight to Be Heard," *Champaign-Urbana News-Gazette*,
    10 May 1992.
4   Albert Vargas, "Caught in a Casa 22: Scarcity of Hispanic Administrators Leaves
    Latina/os in a Bind," *Daily Illini*, 25 July 1990.
5   La Carta newsletter, October 1988, Record series 41/64/840, Box 1, Folder:
    Newsletters, University of Illinois at Urbana-Champaign Archives.
6   Mona Blaber, "Latina/o Group Protests New Supervisor," *Daily Illini*, 3 October
    1990.

7   Osvaldo Morera, "La Casa's Problems Stem from Director's Lack of Influence," *Daily Illini*, 16 March 1991.

8   Carol Spindel, *Dancing at Halftime: Sports and the Controversy over American Indian Mascots* (New York: New York University, 2000), 137.

9   University of Illinois at Urbana-Champaign Office of Equal Opportunity and Access, "Undergraduate Enrollment by Racial/Ethnic Category, University of Illinois at Urbana-Champaign, Fall 1967 to Fall 2008," accessed 15 October 2009, http://oeoa.illinois.edu/Undergraduate%20Enrollment%20by%20Race.pdf.

10 Spindel, *Dancing at Halftime.*

11 Sridhar Chigurupati, "Anti-Chief Protestors Send Demands List to Ikenberry," *Daily Illini*, 17 September 1990.

12 Tara Burghart, "After Two Years, Chief Furor Still Rages," *Daily Illini*, 28 August 1991; "A Chronology of the Chief Illiniwek Issue, University of Illinois, accessed 24 September 2009, http://www.uillinois.edu/chief/Chronology.pdf.

13 Alyssa Tucker, "Candidates Reinforce Current Goals of Diversity," *Daily Illini*, 4 March 1991.

14 Greg Keller, "University Voters Choose Mitchell, Begovich as Reps," *Daily Illini*, 8 March 1991.

15 Elaine Richardson and Jenni Spinner, "Columbus Day Rally Celebrates Struggle," *Daily Illini*, 13 October 1992.

16 Osvaldo Morera, "UI Policies Stifle Progress of Multicultural Groups," *Daily Illini*, 4 November 1991.

17 Morera, "UI Policies Stifle Progress."

18 Kim Greuter, "People of Color Discuss Ways to Make Their Groups Closer," *Daily Illini*, 10 April 1992.

19 Elaine Richardson, "Latina/os Continue Protests," *Daily Illini*, 4 May 1992.

20 Jonathan Brown, "Students Discuss Issues of Multiculturalism," *Daily Illini*, 6 December 1991; Melita Marie Garza, "YWCA at Forefront of U of I Fight," *Chicago Tribune*, 14 May 1992.

21 Rhoda Gutierrez (UIUC alumnus), interview by Sharon S. Lee, 20 July 2008 in Chicago.

22 Elaine Richardson, "Latina/os Sit In at UI Building: La Casa Changes Demanded," *Daily Illini*, 30 April 1992; Julie Wurth, "Latina/o Students Not 'Giving Up' after Staging UI Sit-in," *Champaign-Urbana News-Gazette*, 30 April 1992.

23 J. Philip Bloomer, "Anger over Verdict Draws 1,000 to Late-Night UI Protest," *Champaign-Urbana News-Gazette*, 2 May 1992; Mike Monson, "Stay Cool, C-U Mayors and Clergy Urge: Interracial Rows on Friday Night Spark Concern," *Champaign-Urbana News-Gazette*, 3 May 1992.

24 Elaine Richardson, "Students Rally in UI Building; Three Arrested. La Casa Protest Leads Sit-in," *Daily Illini*, 6 May 1992; Julie Wurth and Chris Schultz, "UI Students Vow to Keep Up 'Struggle': Three Arrested in Protest; Rash of Fire Calls Made," *Champaign-Urbana News-Gazette*, 6 May 1992; Melita Marie Garza, "Cops Roust U of I Latina/o Protesters," *Chicago Tribune*, 6 May 1992. There are different estimates of the number of students that participated in the sit-in in the administration building. Estimates range from 100 to 150 students.

25 "Latina/o Student Demands and Solutions, Spring 1992," *La Carta Informativa: A Newsletter of La Casa Cultural Latina*, vol. 1, Spring 1992, Record series 41/64/840, Box 1, Folder: Newsletters, University of Illinois at Urbana-Champaign Archives.

26 Richardson, "Students Rally in UI Building"; Wurth and Schultz, "UI Students Vow to Keep Up 'Struggle'"; "Protest, Fires Hit U of I Campus," *Chicago Defender*, 7 May 1992.
27 Elaine Richardson, "Latina/os Continue Protests," *Daily Illini*, 4 May 1992.
28 Garza, "Cops Roust U of I Latina/o Protesters."
29 Melita Marie Garza, "Hispanic Concerns Surface at U of I," *Chicago Tribune*, 6 May 1992.
30 Elaine Richardson, "University Report Answers Latina/o Demands," *Daily Illini*, 12 June 1992.
31 Elaine Richardson, "Court, Committees Consider Latina/o Issues," *Daily Illini*, Welcome Back Edition, 17–23 August 1992; Julie Wurth, "Bitingly Critical, Panel Outlines Path to Progress," *Champaign-Urbana News-Gazette*, 9 May 1992.
32 Miguel del Valle, "U of I Students Protest," *Chicago Defender*, 2 June 1992.
33 Julie Wurth, "Lawmakers Seek Amnesty in UI Latina/o Protest," *Champaign-Urbana News-Gazette*, 23 May 1992.
34 "U of I Defends Action in Sit-ins: Minority Students Say Police Used Unnecessary Force," *Chicago Tribune*, 15 October 1992; Julie Wurth, "Legislators to Investigate UI Student Disciplinary Procedures," *Champaign-Urbana News-Gazette*, 15 October 1992.
35 "Senate Hearings—Testimony Given by Asian Pacific Americans," *Horizons: Newsletter of the Asian American Association at the University of Illinois at U/C*, November 1992, p. 5, Record Series 41/2/41, Box 10, Folder: Asian American Association Newsletters 1986–1998, University of Illinois at Urbana-Champaign Archives.
36 Neena Hemmady (UIUC alumnus), interview by Sharon S. Lee, 20 July 2008 in Chicago.
37 Jessica Chen, "AA = Asian Apathy," *Horizons: Asian American Association Collective Newsletter* (November 1992): 1, 9, Folder: AAA Historical Resources, University of Illinois at Urbana-Champaign Asian American Cultural Center Archives.
38 Ho Chie Tsai (UIUC alumnus), interview by Sharon S. Lee, 28 July 2008 in Manchester, Indiana.
39 Ho Chie Tsai interview, 28 July 2008.
40 Jody Lin (UIUC alumnus), interview with Sharon S. Lee, 20 August 2008 in La Grange, Illinois.
41 Ho Chie Tsai interview, 28 July 2008.
42 Peter Ko to Asian Organization Officers, 20 July 1992, Folder: AAA Meetings, Documents, University of Illinois at Urbana-Champaign Asian American Cultural Center Archives.
43 Asian American Artists Collective, Asiantation 1995 Asian Pacific American New Student Orientation, University of Illinois Urbana-Champaign, University of Illinois at Urbana-Champaign Asian American Cultural Center.
44 Asian American Alumni Association, Asiantation 1995 Asian Pacific American New Student Orientation, University of Illinois Urbana-Champaign, University of Illinois at Urbana-Champaign Asian American Cultural Center.
45 Quoted in Anita Banerji, "Getting Involved," academic paper for Journalism 380, University of Illinois at Urbana-Champaign, 30 April 1997, Folder: Asian American Cultural Center Activism, University of Illinois at Urbana-Champaign Asian American Cultural Center Archives.

46 Charter of the Asian-Pacific American Coalition, 20 April 1994, APAC Binder, University of Illinois at Urbana-Champaign Asian American Cultural Center Archives.

47 Charter of the Asian-Pacific American Coalition.

48 "About the Asian American Student Community at the U of I," *Perspectives: A Special Publication of the 1994 MAAS Conference*, p. 39, Folder: MAAS/ MAASU Early Programs, University of Illinois at Urbana-Champaign Asian American Cultural Center Archives. It is important to note that Asian American students wanted both an academic studies program and a cultural center and pushed for both as parallel developments.

49 "T-shirt Designs," *Asian American Artists Collective Newsletter* 1, no. 1 (November 1992): 3, Folder: AAA Historical Resources, University of Illinois at Urbana-Champaign Asian American Cultural Center Archives.

50 Ho Chie Tsai interview, 28 July 2008.

51 "MAAS 1993," MAAS 1993 conference booklet, "Empowerment through Unity," 9–11 April 1993, Folder: MAAS/ MAASU Early Programs, University of Illinois at Urbana-Champaign Asian American Cultural Center Archives.

52 Nallsra Luangkesorn, "Finding Common Ground in the Asian Pacific American Community," *Crossroads: The Multicultural Magazine of the Daily Illini,* 29 April 1993.

53 Workshop Schedule, MAAS 1993 Spring conference program, 1993, p. 5, Record series 41/2/40, Box 10, Folder: Asian American Association-Midwest Asian American Students Conference 1990–1993, University of Illinois at Urbana-Champaign Archives.

54 *Perspectives: A Special Publication of the 1994 MAAS Conference*, Folder: MAAS/ MAASU Early Programs, University of Illinois at Urbana-Champaign Asian American Cultural Center Archives.

55 Ho-chie Tsai, "The View from Here," reprinted in Unseen/Unheard program booklet, 2006, University of Illinois at Urbana-Champaign Asian American Cultural Center.

56 Sharon Farlow, "Asian-American Students Seek a Place to Call Home," *Crossroads: The Multicultural Magazine of the Daily Illini*, 23 March 1994; Matthew Goldfeder, "Asian-Americans Working for Cultural Center," *Daily Illini*, 26 January 1993. Sources conflict over the number of signers of the petition. Student documents and *Daily Illini* articles quote between 400 to 800 names on the petition.

57 Ho Chie Tsai interview, 28 July 2008.

58 Petition letter, Folder: Asian American Cultural Center Activism, University of Illinois at Urbana-Champaign Asian American Cultural Center Archives.

59 Michael Dizon, "UI Asian-Americans Request Cultural Center," *Daily Illini*, 17 November 1992.

60 Morton Weir to Rona Abello, Lena Choe, Jessica Chen, Anna Hui, and Ho Chie Tsai, 27 January 1993, Folder: Asian American Cultural Center Activism, University of Illinois at Urbana-Champaign Asian American Cultural Center Archives.

61 Leah Setzen, "Asian Center Still on Hold Despite Plea," *Daily Illini*, 31 August 1994.

62 David Morse, "Prejudicial Studies: One Astounding Lesson for the University of Connecticut," in *The Asian American Educational Experience: A Source Book for*

Teachers and Students, ed. Don T. Nakanishi and Tina Yamano Nishida (New York: Routledge, 1995), 339–357.

63 Scott Jaschik, "US Asked to Study Conn. Programs for Minority Groups," *Chronicle of Higher Education*, State Notes, 9 May 1990.

64 Discrimination Complaint Form, Complaint No. 01-90-2039, United States Department of Education Office for Civil Rights, Region I, Boston. Available through Freedom of Information Act.

65 "Racism at UConn, the Asian-American Experience," Testimony to UConn Ad Hoc Sub-Committee on Discriminatory Harassment, 6 February 1989, p. 8, Attachment 8 of Discrimination Complaint Form, Complaint No. 01-90-2039, United States Department of Education Office for Civil Rights, Region I, Boston. Emphasis in original.

66 Scott Jaschik, "Asian-Americans Pleased by US Ruling," *Chronicle of Higher Education*, 19 May 1993.

67 Ruling of Office for Civil Rights to Connecticut Board of Governors for Higher Education, Complaint Number 01-90-2039, 7 May 1993, United States Department of Education Office for Civil Rights, Region I, Boston.

68 Scott Jaschik, "Affirmative Action in Connecticut: US Says Plans Limited to Blacks and Hispanics Violated Federal Civil-Rights Law," *Chronicle of Higher Education* online, 5 October 1994, http://chronicle.com/che-data/articles.dir /articles-41.dir/issue-06.dir/06a03501.htm.

69 Richard W. Chang (UIUC alumnus), interview by Sharon S. Lee, 2 March 2007 in Urbana, Illinois.

70 Richard W. Chang et al., "Proposal for an Asian Pacific American Cultural Center," 3 May 1994, p. 2, Folder: Asian American Cultural Center Proposals, University of Illinois at Urbana-Champaign Asian American Cultural Center Archives.

71 Chang et al., "Proposal for an Asian Pacific American Cultural Center," 2.

72 Chang et al., "Proposal for an Asian Pacific American Cultural Center," 3.

73 Clarence Shelley (founding director of UIUC Special Educational Opportunities Program), interview by Sharon S. Lee, 22 March 2007 in Urbana, Illinois.

74 Yuki Llewellyn to Bill Riley, Re: Status Report on Asian Pacific American Resource Board (APARB), 15 December 1994, Folder: APARB, 1994–95, University of Illinois at Urbana-Champaign Asian American Cultural Center Archives.

75 Yuki Llewellyn to Bill Riley, Re: Preliminary Annual Report of Asian Pacific American Resource Board (APARB) for 1994–95, 19 May 1995, Folder: APARB, 1994–95, University of Illinois at Urbana-Champaign Asian American Cultural Center Archives.

76 Vida Gosrisirikul (UIUC alumnus), interview by Sharon S. Lee, 2 March 2007 in Urbana, Illinois.

77 Caroline Yu, "Asian-American Group Receives Funding from UI: APAC: $30,000 Granted for Asian-American Issues; Some Say It Might Be a Test for a Future Cultural Center," *Daily Illini*, 22 November 1994.

78 "Asian Americans Should Be Wary," *Daily Illini*, 29 November 1994.

79 "Asian Americans Should Be Wary."

80 Chapter 110: 1/1 to 805/2 in *West's Smith-Hurd Illinois Compiled Statutes Annotated*, higher education (St. Paul, MN: Thomson West, 2006), 115–116.

81   Michael Dizon, "UI Asian-Americans Request Cultural Center," *Daily Illini*, 17 November 1992.

82   Trey Gehrt, "Asian-American Cultural-Center Talks Begin," *Daily Illini*, 27 January 1993.

83   Gehrt, "Asian-American Cultural-Center Talks Begin."

84   Linda Bair, Office of Affirmative Action to Paul Riegel Office of the Chancellor, Re: Asian/ Pacific Islanders and the IBHE Report on Under-represented Students and Staff, 7 July 1994, Folder: APAC Lawsuit, University of Illinois at Urbana-Champaign Asian American Cultural Center Archives.

85   Renotta Young-Kelley, Office of University Counsel to Steve Veazie, re: Cultural Centers at UIUC, 17 August 1994, Folder: APAC Lawsuit, University of Illinois at Urbana-Champaign Asian American Cultural Center Archives, p. 2.

86   Ohn Park to Asian American Pacific Islander Law Students Association members Sangmoon Chang, Vida Gosrisirikul, Henry Lin, Chung Poon, and Christine Yang, 15 February 1995, Folder: APAC Lawsuit, University of Illinois at Urbana-Champaign Asian American Cultural Center Archives.

87   Melissa Choo, legal paper, ca. 1995, p. 24, Folder: APAC Lawsuit, University of Illinois at Urbana- Champaign Asian American Cultural Center Archives.

88   Complaint draft, Vida Gosrisirikul et al. v. Illinois State Board of Higher Education et al., undated, Folder: APAC Lawsuit, University of Illinois at Urbana-Champaign Asian American Cultural Center Archives.

89   Mitchell Chang, "Expansion and Its Discontents: The Formation of Asian American Studies Programs in the 1990s," *Journal of Asian American Studies* 2 (1999): 181–206.

90   Peter Kiang, "The New Wave: Developing Asian American Studies on the East Coast," in *Reflections on Shattered Windows: Promises and Prospects for Asian American Studies*, ed. Gary Okihiro, John M. Liu, Arthur A. Hansen, and Shirley Hune (Pullman: Washington State University Press, 1988), 43–50.

91   Gary Okhiro, "Introduction," in *East of California: New Perspectives in Asian American Studies*, ed. Gary Okihiro and Lee C. Lee (Ithaca, NY: Cornell University Asian American Studies Program, 1992), 3.

92   Clark Cunningham and Yuki Llewellyn, "University of Illinois at Urbana-Champaign," in *East of California: New Perspectives in Asian American Studies*, ed. Gary Okihiro and Lee C. Lee (Ithaca, NY: Cornell University Asian American Studies Program, 1992), 87.

93   Clark Cunningham to Peter Schran, 12 May 1992, Folder: Research/ Presentations, University of Illinois at Urbana-Champaign Asian American Cultural Center Archives.

94   Jody Lin interview, 20 August 2008.

95   Vida Gosrisirikul interview, 2 March 2007.

96   Peter Kiang to Clark Cunningham, 27 February 1991, Folder: AASC History, Memos, University of Illinois at Urbana-Champaign Asian American Studies Program Files.

97   Bill Riley (former UIUC dean of students), interview with Sharon S. Lee, 15 April 2009 in Urbana, Illinois.

98   *Asian American Artists Collective Newsletter* 1, no. 1 (November 1992): 10, Folder: AAA Historical Resources, University of Illinois at Urbana-Champaign Asian American Cultural Center Archives.

99   *Asian American Artists Collective Newsletter*, 16.

100 University of Illinois YMCA, Communiversity Course Catalog, Fall 1993,
     Folder: Activism for Asian American Studies, University of Illinois at Urbana-
     Champaign Asian American Cultural Center Archives. The Communiversity
     program was established in 1976 and offered noncredit classes in special interests
     and social issues. "Communiversity: Providing Continuing Education for the
     University and Community," *Daily Illini*, 6 December 1977.

101 Richard Chang, "Learn Your History, Asian-Americans," *Crossroads: The
     Multicultural Magazine of the Daily Illini,* 17 November 1993.

102 Jonathan Berlin, "Building Bridges: One on Two with Reshma Saujani and Mark
     Harang, Co-Presidents of the Asian/Pacific American Coalition," *Daily Illini*,
     1 February 1995.

103 Ho Chie Tsai interview, 28 July 2008.

104 Melita Marie Garza, "NU Students Demand Ethnic Studies, Chanting 'No
     Program, No Peace,'" *Chicago Tribune*, 13 April 1995.

105 Ragini Shah, "A Piece of the Pie: The Unknown Story behind the Asian
     American Adviser Proposal," *Asian American Quarterly*, Asian American
     Advisory Board, Northwestern University, Evanston Illinois, vol. 1, issue 1,
     Spring 2003, Folder: Asian American Resources, National, University of Illinois
     at Urbana-Champaign Asian American Cultural Center Archives.

106 Boaz Herzog, "'We Will Not Be Ignored': About 150 Students Battle Cold to
     Demand Asian-American Studies Program from Cautious Administration,"
     Daily Northwestern, 13 April 1995.

107 Rebecca Winters, "Strike Gains National Support," *Daily Northwestern*, 21 April
     1995.

108 Robert Yap, "Making History by Fighting for Our History: The Real Story of
     NU's Protest for Asian American Studies," *Rice: The Staple for Asian American
     News and Entertainment* (formerly *Asian American Quarterly*), Spring 1996,
     Folder: Asian American Resources, National, University of Illinois at Urbana-
     Champaign Asian American Cultural Center Archives.

109 Brian Wasag, "NU Advisory Board Starts Student Fast: Asian American
     Demands: Group Asks for Representation in Faculty and Programming," *Daily
     Illini*, 18 April 1995.

110 Stacey Jackson, "Asian American Cultural Center Is Long Overdue," *Daily Illini*,
     26 April 1995.

111 Kendra L. Williams, "'Teach In': An All-Day Program Examines the Past and
     Future of Asian Americans," *Crossroads: The Multicultural Magazine of the Daily
     Illini*, 18 January 1996.

112 Vida Gosrisirikul to Bill Riley, Subject: "Proposal for an Asian Pacific Amer.
     Freshman Orientation," 19 April 1994, Folder: APAC 4 of 4 Asiantation, Univer-
     sity of Illinois at Urbana-Champaign Asian American Cultural Center Archives.

113 Gosrisirikul, "Proposal for an Asian Pacific Amer. Freshman Orientation."

114 Vida Gosrisirikul to Members of the Asian Pacific American Resource Board
     (APARB), Subject: "Proposal for Funding the Second Annual Asian Pacific
     American New Student Orientation—'What's in It for You?'" 10 February 1995,
     Folder: APAC 4 of 4 Asiantation, University of Illinois at Urbana-Champaign
     Asian American Cultural Center Archives.

115 Yuki Llewelyn, "Welcome Incoming Asian American Students," Fall 1994,
     Asiantation booklet, University of Illinois at Urbana-Champaign Asian
     American Cultural Center.

116 "Asian Is Not Oriental," Asiantation 1995 Asian Pacific American New Student Orientation, University of Illinois at Urbana-Champaign, University of Illinois at Urbana-Champaign Asian American Cultural Center.

117 Asiantation 1995 Asian Pacific American New Student Orientation, University of Illinois at Urbana-Champaign, University of Illinois at Urbana-Champaign Asian American Cultural Center. Emphasis in original.

118 Vida Gosrisirikul, "Asiantation Is Not Orientation," Asiantation 1996 Asian Pacific American New Student Orientation, University of Illinois at Urbana-Champaign, University of Illinois at Urbana-Champaign Asian American Cultural Center.

119 Karen Hawkins, "Asiantation Information: Orientation Program Lets Students Know What to Expect," *Daily Illini*, 31 August 1995.

120 Welcome, "Unseen Unheard Conference of Asian America" booklet, October 1997, University of Illinois at Urbana-Champaign Asian American Cultural Center.

121 "Unseen Unheard" conference program, 4 December 1999, p. 5, University of Illinois at Urbana-Champaign Asian American Cultural Center Archives.

122 "Unseen Unheard" conference program, 3; emphasis in original.

123 Patricia Askew (former UIUC vice chancellor for student affairs), interview by Sharon S. Lee, 9 July 2007 in Urbana, Illinois.

124 Wesley Rizal, "Interview: Philippine Student Association Maria Gutierrez Shares PSA's Goals for the Year," *Crossroads: The Multicultural Magazine of the Daily Illini*, 20 October 1993.

Chapter 5 Seeing and Hearing Asian American Students

1 Susan Yung Maul to Patricia Askew, 2 May 1995, Folder: APARB, University of Illinois at Urbana-Champaign Asian American Cultural Center Archives.

2 Patricia Askew to Michael Aiken, 22 December 1995, Folder: Asian American Staff Position, University of Illinois at Urbana-Champaign Asian American Cultural Center Archives.

3 Katherine Klimas, "Position Created to Address Asian American Affairs," *Daily Illini*, 28 February 1996.

4 "The Nightmare Has Begun . . ." *Newsletter of the Asian Pacific American Coalition* 1, no.1 (September 1996): 3, Folder: APAC 1 of 4, University of Illinois at Urbana-Champaign Asian American Cultural Center Archives.

5 Joan Mocek, "Asian Americans Drive for Studies Program," *Daily Illini*, 4 September 1996.

6 "What's New?" *Asian American Activist, the Newsletter of APAC—the Asian Pacific American Coalition* 1, no. 2 (November 1996), Folder: APAC 1 of 4, University of Illinois at Urbana-Champaign Asian American Cultural Center Archives.

7 Meeting minutes with assistant provost David Liu and professors willing to help on establishment of Asian American Studies, 6 May 1996, Folder: Early APAC documents, University of Illinois at Urbana-Champaign Asian American Cultural Center Archives.

8 Grace Uy, "Asian Program to Hire Professors," *Daily Illini*, 7 October 1996.

9 Email from Vida Gosrisirikul, 2 April 1997, Folder: Early APAC Documents, University of Illinois at Urbana-Champaign Asian American Cultural Center Archives. Emphasis in original.

10 George T. Yu (founding director of UIUC Asian American studies program), interview with Sharon S. Lee, 1 March 2007 in Urbana, Illinois.

11 Peter Monaghan, "A New Momentum in Asian American Studies," *Chronicle of Higher Education*, 2 April 1999; Karen Lam and Jim Cho, "A Higher Education: How Do Top Schools Fare on the A.-Dometer?" *A. Magazine*, August/September 1997, pp. 49–52, 54, 56, 58, 87.

12 Asian American Studies Program website, University of Illinois at Urbana-Champaign, 2007, http://www.aasp.uiuc.edu/p_faculty.html.

13 Grace Uy, "APA Students Fight for Center," *Daily Illini*, 10 March 1997.

14 Nancy Cantor, "Affirmative Action and Higher Education: Before and after the Supreme Court Rulings on the Michigan Cases," *Chicago Tribune*, 28 January 2003; Patricia Gurin, Jeffrey S. Lehman, and Earl Lewis, *Defending Diversity: Affirmative Action at the University of Michigan* (Ann Arbor: University of Michigan Press, 2007).

15 Ad-hoc Committee on Asian Pacific American Campus Life, University of Illinois at Urbana-Champaign Final Report, 30 April 2003, University of Illinois at Urbana-Champaign Asian American Cultural Center, Director's files.

16 Vasanth Sridharan, "Asian American Cultural Center Opens to Warm Greetings," *Daily Illini*, 12 September 2005.

17 Jeremy Bautista (UIUC alumnus), interview with Sharon S. Lee, 7 July 2007 in Chicago.

18 Bautista interview, 7 July 2007.

19 Kay Burgess, "Students Seek Place for Asian Awareness," *Daily Illini*, 16 October 1996.

20 Vida Gosrisirikul (UIUC alumnus), interview by Sharon S. Lee, 2 March 2007 in Urbana, Illinois.

21 Karin Wang (UIUC alumnus), phone interview by Sharon S. Lee, 8 September 2008.

22 Charles Chang (MAASU founder), phone interview by Sharon S. Lee, 8 October 2008.

23 Corinne M. Kodama, OiYan A. Poon, Lester J. Manzano, and Ester U. Sihite, "Geographic Constructions of Race: The Midwest Asian American Students Union," *Journal of College Student Development* 58 (2017): 872–890.

24 Jeffrey K. Grimm, Nue Lee, Samuel Museus, Vanessa S. Na, and Marie P. Ting, "Asian American College Student Activism and Social Justice in Midwest Contexts," *New Directions for Higher Education* 186 (2019): 30.

25 James D. Anderson (head of educational policy studies, UIUC), interview with Sharon S. Lee, 21 June 2007 in Champaign, Illinois.

26 Dana Takagi, "Asian Americans and Diversity Talk: The Limits of the Numbers Game," in *Diversity in American Higher Education: Towards a More Comprehensive Approach*, ed. Lisa M. Stulberg and Sharon Lawner Weinberg (New York: Routledge, 2011), 156.

27 Clarence Shelley (founding director of UIUC Special Educational Opportunities Program), interview with Sharon S. Lee, 22 March 2007 in Urbana, Illinois.

28 Sylvia Hurtado, Jeffrey Milem, Alma Clayton-Pedersen, and Walter Allen, *Enacting Diverse Learning Environments: Improving the Climate for Racial/Ethnic Diversity in Higher Education*. ASHE-ERIC Higher Education Report, 26(8) (Washington, DC: George Washington University, Graduate School of Education and Human Development, 1999).

29 Esther Chan, "Does Diversity Include Me? Colorblindness and Racial Triangulation among Asian Americans on Two College Campuses," *Ethnic and Racial Studies* 43 (2020): 2217–2235.

30 Christine Bennett and Alton Okinaka, "Factors Related to the Persistence among Asian, Black, Hispanic, and White Undergraduates at a Predominantly White University: Comparisons between First and Fourth Year Cohorts," *Urban Review* 22 (1990): 33–60; Chalsa M. Loo and Garry Rolison, "Alienation of Ethnic Minority Students at a Predominantly White University," *Journal of Higher Education* 57 (1986): 58–77; Alvin Alvarez, and T. Ling Yeh, "Asian Americans in College: A Racial Identity Perspective," in *Asian and Pacific Islander Americans' Issues and Concerns for Counseling and Psychotherapy*, ed. Daya Singh Sandhu (Commack, NY: Nova Science Publishers, 1999), 105–119; Samuel D. Museus and Julie J. Park. "The Continuing Significance of Racism in the Lives of Asian American College Students," *Journal of College Student Development* 56 (2015): 551–569.

31 Vida Gosrisirikul, "Why a Cultural Center Is Important . . ." Asiantation 1995 Asian Pacific American New Student Orientation, University of Illinois Urbana-Champaign, University of Illinois at Urbana-Champaign Asian American Cultural Center.

32 Tom Kim, "Asian Americans Wrestle with Minority Status: Resources Available to Other Minorities Overlooked for Asian Americans," *Daily Illini*, 2 August 2000.

33 Gabriel Chin, Sumi Cho, Jerry Kang, and Frank Wu, *Beyond Self-Interest: Asian Pacific Americans toward a Community of Justice: A Policy Analysis of Affirmative Action*, UCLA website, 1997), http://www.sscnet.ucla.edu/aasc/policy/beyond .pdf; Eugenia Escueta and Eileen O'Brien, "Asian Americans and Higher Education: Trends and Issues," *Research Briefs* 2 (1991): 1 (ERIC Document Reproduction Service No. ED381103); Shirley Hune and Kenyon Chan, "Special Focus: Asian Pacific American Demographic and Educational Trends," in *Minorities in Higher Education: Fifteenth Annual Status Report: 1996–1997*, ed. Deborah Carter and Reginald Wilson (Washington, DC: American Council on Education, 1997); Samuel D. Museus, "Asian Americans and Pacific Islanders: A National Portrait of Growth, Diversity, and Inequality," in *The Misrepresented Minority: New Insights on Asian Americans and Pacific Islanders, and the Implications for Higher Education*, ed. Samuel D. Museus, Dina C. Maramba, and Robert T. Teranishi (Sterling, VA: Stylus, 2013), 11–41.

34 About AANAPISIs, accessed 15 October 2019, https://www.aanapisi.net/about _aanapisis; Julie J. Park and Robert Teranishi, "Asian American and Pacific Islander Serving Institutions: Historical Perspectives and Future Prospects," in *Understanding Minority-Serving Institutions*, ed. Marybeth Gasman, Benjamin Baez, and Caroline Sotello Viernes Turner (Albany, NY: State University of New York Press, 2008), 111–126.

35 Karin Wang interview, 8 September 2008.

36 Ian Lovett, "UCLA Students' Video Rant against Asians Fuels Firestorm," *New York Times*, 15 March 2011, https://www.nytimes.com/2011/03/16/us/16ucla.html.

37 JoJo Baccam, "Cultural Incompetency: Racist Yik Yak Posts Target Asian Students on UI Campus," University of Iowa International Programs, 26 October 2015, accessed 29 November 2019, https://international.uiowa.edu/news/cultural -incompetency-racist-yik-yak-posts-target-asian-students-ui-campus.

38 Kathryn Rubino, "Former Biglaw Attorney Goes on Anti-Asian Racist Social Media Rant," *Above the Law*, 4 September 2018, https://abovethelaw.com/2018/09 /former-biglaw-attorney-goes-on-anti-asian-racist-social-media-rant/.

39 Emma Whitford, "When Asians Are Targets of Racism," *Inside Higher Ed*, 11 October 2018, https://www.insidehighered.com/news/2018/10/11/anti-asian -messages-spread-washington-university-st-louis.

40 Kevin Jin, "Racialized Aggressions and Sense of Belonging among Asian American College Students," Institute for Asian American Studies (Boston), 2019, https://scholarworks.umb.edu/cgi/viewcontent.cgi?article=1043&context=iaas _pubs.

41 Rachel Ramirez, "Asian Americans Need to Talk about Anti-Blackness in Our Communities," Vox, 3 June 2020, https://www.vox.com/first-person/2020/6/3 /21279156/george-floyd-protests-police-brutality-tou-thao-asian-americans.

42 A study in 2015 found that Asian Americans were six times less likely to be killed by police than African Americans. Kevin Cheng, "What Role Do Asian Americans Have in the Campus Protests?" *Atlantic*, 8 December 2015, https://www .theatlantic.com/education/archive/2015/12/asian-americans-campus-protests /419301/.

43 Sara Weissman, "Erasing Hate: Advocates Combat Anti-Asian Bias amid COVID-19 Pandemic," *Diverse Issues in Higher Education*, 14 May 2020, https://diverseeducation.com/article/177116/; Anna Purna Kambhampaty, "'I Will Not Stand Silent.' 10 Asian Americans Reflect on Racism during the Pandemic and the Need for Equality," *Time*, 25 June 2020, https://time.com /5858649/racism-coronavirus/; "National Report," Stop AAPI Hate website, 1 June 2021, https://stopaapihate.org/national-report-through-march-2021/.

44 Francie Diep, "What Asian American Student Activists Want," *Chronicle of Higher Education*, 6 April 2021, https://www.chronicle.com/article/what-asian -american-student-activists-want.

Selected Bibliography

Abelmann, Nancy. *The Intimate University: Korean American Students and the Problems of Segregation*. Durham, NC: Duke University Press, 2009.

Ahne, Joseph. "Koreans of Chicago: The New Entrepreneurial Immigrants." In *Ethnic Chicago: A Multicultural Portrait*, edited by Melvin G. Holli and Peter d'A. Jones, 463–500. Grand Rapids, MI: William B. Eerdmans Publishing Co., 1995.

Ancheta, Angelo. *Race, Rights, and the Asian American Experience*. New Brunswick, NJ: Rutgers University Press, 1988.

Ancis, Julie R., William E. Sedlacek, and Jonathan J. Mohr. "Student Perceptions of Campus Cultural Climate by Race." *Journal of Counseling and Development* 78 (2000): 180–185.

Anderson, James D. *The Education of Blacks in the South, 1860–1935*. Chapel Hill: University of North Carolina Press, 1988.

Badillo, David A. "From La Lucha to Latina/o: Ethnic Chicago, Political Identity, and Civil Rights in Chicago." In *La Causa: Civil Rights, Social Justice, and the Struggle for Equality in the Midwest*, edited by Gilberto Cardenas, 37–53. Houston: Arte Publico Press, 2004.

Ball, Howard. *The Bakke Case—Race, Education, and Affirmative Action*. Lawrence: University Press of Kansas, 2000.

Bell, Derrick. *Silent Covenants: Brown v. Board of Education and the Unfulfilled Hopes for Racial Reform*. Oxford: Oxford University Press, 2004.

Bowen, William, and Derek Bok. *The Shape of the River: Long-Term Consequences of Considering Race in College and University Admissions*. Princeton, NJ: Princeton University Press, 1998.

Bowman, Kristi L. "The New Face of School Desegregation." *Duke Law Journal* 50 (2001): 1751–1808.

Cardenas, Gilberto, ed. *La Causa: Civil Rights, Social Justice, and the Struggle for Equality in the Midwest*. Houston: Arte Publico Press, 2004.

Carney, Cary Michael. *Native American Higher Education in the United States*. New Brunswick, NJ: Transaction Publishers, 1999.

Cress, Christine M., and Elaine K. Ikeda. "Distress under Duress: The Relationship between Campus Climate and Depression in Asian American College Students." *NASPA Journal* 40 (2003): 74–97.

Dixson, Adrienne D., and Celia K. Rousseau, eds. *Critical Race Theory in Education: All God's Children Got a Song.* New York: Routledge, 2006.

Esquivel, Arisve. "Creando una Casa: Embracing Space, Containing Space in the Definition of a Latina/o Community at the University of Illinois at Urbana Champaign." MA thesis, University of Illinois at Urbana-Champaign, 2001.

Foster, Julian, and Durward Long, eds. *Protest! Student Activism in America.* New York: William Morrow & Co., 1970.

Fuertes, Jairo N., and William E. Sedlacek. "Using the SAT and Noncognitive Variables to Predict the Grades and Retention of Asian American University Students. *Measurement and Evaluation in Counseling and Development* 27 (1994): 74–85.

Geiger, Roger. *Research and Relevant Knowledge: American Research Universities since World War II.* New Brunswick, NJ: Transaction Publishers, 2004.

Golden, Daniel. *The Price of Admission: How America's Ruling Class Buys Its Way into Elite Colleges—and Who Gets Left outside the Gates.* New York: Crown Publishers, 2006.

Gonzalez, Kenneth P. "Campus Culture and the Experiences of Chicano Students in a Predominantly White University." *Urban Education* 37 (2002): 193–218.

Gordon, Leonard. "Race Relations and Attitudes at Arizona State University." In *The Racial Crisis in American Higher Education,* edited by Philip G. Altbach and Kofi Lomotey, 233–284. Albany: State University of New York Press, 1991.

Gotanda, Neil. "Asian American Rights and the 'Miss Saigon Syndrome.'" In *Asian Americans and the Supreme Court: A Documentary History,* edited by Hyung-Chan Kim, 1087–1103. New York: Greenwood Press, 1992.

Graham, Hugh Davis. *Collision Course: The Strange Convergence of Affirmative Action and Immigration Policy in America.* Oxford: Oxford University Press, 2002.

Gurin, Patricia, Jeffrey S. Lehman, and Earl Lewis. *Defending Diversity: Affirmative Action at the University of Michigan.* Ann Arbor: University of Michigan Press, 2007.

Hirsch, Eric. "Columbia University: Individual and Institutional Racism." In *The Racial Crisis in American Higher Education,* edited by Philip G. Altbach and Kofi Lomotey, 199–211. Albany: State University of New York Press, 1991.

Hurtado, Sylvia. "The Campus Racial Climate: Contexts of Conflict." *Journal of Higher Education* 63 (1992): 539–569.

Hurtado, Sylvia, Deborah Faye Carter, and Albert Spuler. "Latino Student Transition to College: Assessing Difficulties and Factors in Successful College Adjustment." *Research in Higher Education* 37 (1996): 135–157.

Iijima, Chris. "The Era of We-Construction: Reclaiming the Politics of Asian Pacific American Identity and Reflections on the Critique of the Black/White Paradigm." *Columbia Human Rights Law Review* 29 (1997): 47–89.

Institute for the Study of Social Change. *The Diversity Project: Final Report.* University of California, Berkeley, 1991.

Jo, Ji-Yeon. "Neglected Voices in the Multicultural America: Asian American Racial Politics and Its Implications for Multicultural Education." *Multicultural Perspectives* 6 (2004): 19–25.

Kaplowitz, Craig A. "A Distinct Minority: LULAC, Mexican American Identity, and Presidential Policymaking, 1965–1972." *Journal of Policy History* 15 (2003): 192–222.

Katznelson, Ira. *When Affirmative Action Was White: An Untold History of Racial Inequality in Twentieth-Century America*. New York: W. W. Norton and Co., 2005.

Kidder, William. "Situating Asian Pacific Americans in the Law School Affirmative Action Debate: Empirical Facts about Thernstrom's Rhetorical Acts." *Asian Law Journal* 7 (2000): 29–68.

Levine, David O. *The American College and the Culture of Aspiration, 1915–1940*. Ithaca, NY: Cornell University Press, 1986.

Lew, Jamie. *Asian Americans in Class: Charting the Achievement Gap among Korean American Youth*. New York: Teachers College Press, 2006.

Lewis, Amanda E., Mark Chesler, and Tyrone A. Forman. "The Impact of 'Color-blind' Ideologies on Students of Color: Intergroup Relations at a Predominantly White University." *Journal of Negro Education* 69 (2000): 74–91.

Li, Guofang, and Gulbahar Beckett. *"Strangers" of the Academy: Asian Women Scholars in Higher Education*. Sterling, VA: Stylus Publishing, 2006.

Lopez, Ian Haney. "Race, Ethnicity, Erasure: The Salience of Race to Latcrit Theory." *California Law Review* 85 (1997): 57–125.

MacDonald, Victoria-Maria, John M. Botti, and Lisa Hoffman Clark. "From Visibility to Autonomy: Latina/os and Higher Education in the US, 1965–2005." *Harvard Educational Review* 77 (Winter 2007): 474–504.

MacDonald, Victoria-Maria, and Teresa Garcia. "Historical Perspectives on Latino Access to Higher Education, 1848–1990." In *The Majority in the Minority: Expanding the Representation of Latina/o Faculty, Administrators, and Students in Higher Education*, edited by Jeanett Castellanos and Lee Jones, 14–43. Sterling, VA: Stylus Publishing, 2003.

Matsuda, Mari. *Where Is Your Body? And Other Essays on Race, Gender, and the Law*. Boston: Beacon Press, 1996.

McClelland, Katherine E., and Carol J. Auster. "Public Platitudes and Hidden Tensions: Racial Climates at Predominantly White Liberal Arts Colleges." *Journal of Higher Education* 61 (1990): 607–642.

McGee, Ebony O., Bhoomi K. Thakore, and Sandra S. LaBlance, "The Burden of Being 'Model': Racialized Experiences of Asian STEM College Students," *Journal of Diversity in Higher Education* 10 (2017): 253–270.

Morley, Kathleen M. "Fitting in by Race/Ethnicity: The Social and Academic Integration of Diverse Students at a Large Predominantly White University." *Journal of College Student Retention* 5 (2003): 147–174.

Morse, David. "Prejudicial Studies: One Astounding Lesson for the University of Connecticut." In *The Asian American Educational Experience: A Source Book for Teachers and Students*, edited by Don T. Nakanishi and Tina Yamano Nishida, 339–357. New York: Routledge, 1995.

Murata, Alice. "Stardust and Street of Dreams: Chicago Girls Clubs." *Chicago History*, Spring 2001, 21–35.

Mutua, Athena. "Shifting Bottoms and Rotating Centers: Reflections on LatCrit III and the Black/White Paradigm." *University of Miami Law Review* 53 (1999): 1177–1218.

Nakanishi, Don T. "Asian Pacific Americans in Higher Education: Faculty and Administrative Representation and Tenure." In *Racial and Ethnic Diversity in*

Higher Education, edited by Caroline Turner, Mildred Garcia, Amaury Nora, and Laura Rendon, 370–375. Needham Heights, MA: Simon & Schuster Custom Publishing, 1993.

———. "A Quota on Excellence? The Asian American Admissions Debate." *Change* (1989): 38–47.

National Asian Pacific American Legal Consortium, Asian Law Caucus, Asian Pacific American Legal Center, et al., Brief as Amicus Curiae Supporting Respondents, *Grutter v. Bollinger* 539 US 306, (2001) (No. 02-241) and *Gratz v. Bollinger*, 539 US 244, (2001) (No. 02-516).

Ng, Jennifer, Sharon S. Lee, and Yoon K. Pak. "Contesting the Model Minority and Perpetual Foreigner Stereotypes: A Critical Review of Literature on Asian Americans in Education." *Review of Research in Education* 31 (2007): 95–130.

Ogren, Christine. *The American State Normal School, "An Instrument of Great Good."* New York: Palgrave Macmillan, 2005.

Olson, Keith W. *The GI Bill, the Veterans, and the Colleges*. Lexington: University Press of Kentucky, 1974.

Omi, Michael, and Howard Winant. *Racial Formation in the United States: From the 1960s to the 1990s*. 2nd ed. New York: Routledge, 1994.

Onkst, David H. "'First a Negro . . . Incidentally a Veteran': Black World War Two Veterans and the GI Bill of Rights in the Deep South, 1944–1948." *Journal of Social History* 31 (1998): 517–543.

Osajima, Keith. "Racial Politics and the Invisibility of Asian Americans in Higher Education." *Educational Foundations* 9 (1995): 35–53.

Perkins, Linda. "The African American Female Elite: The Early History of African American Women in the Seven Sisters Colleges, 1880–1960." *Harvard Educational Review* 67 (1997): 718–756.

Pewewardy, Cornel, and Bruce Frey. "Surveying the Landscape: Perceptions of Multicultural Support Services and Racial Climate at a Predominantly White University." *Journal of Negro Education* 71 (2002): 77–95.

Reid, Landon, and Phanikiran Radhakrishnan. "Race Matters: The Relation between Race and General Campus Climate." *Cultural Diversity and Ethnic Minority Psychology* 9 (2003): 263–275.

Saito, Natsu. "Model Minority, Yellow Peril: Functions of 'Foreign-ness' in the Construction of Asian American Legal Identity." *Asian Law Journal* 4 (1997): 71–95.

San Miguel Jr., Guadalupe, and Richard R. Valencia. "From the Treaty of Guadalupe Hidalgo to Hopwood: The Educational Plight and Struggle of Mexican Americans in the Southwest." *Harvard Educational Review* 68 (Fall 1998): 353–412.

Shabazz, Amilcar. *Advancing Democracy: African Americans and the Struggle for Access and Equity in Higher Education in Texas*. Chapel Hill: University of North Carolina Press, 2004.

Smedley, Brian D., Hector F. Myers, and Shelly P. Harrell. "Minority-Status Stresses and the College Adjustment of Ethnic Minority Freshmen." *Journal of Higher Education* 64 (1993): 434–452.

Solmon, Lewis C., Matthew S. Solmon, and Tamara W. Schiff. "The Changing Demographics-Problems and Opportunities." In *The Racial Crisis in American Higher Education: Continuing Challenges for the Twenty-First Century*, rev. ed., edited by William A. Smith, Philip G. Altbach, and Kofi Lomotey, 43–76. Albany: State University of New York Press, 2002.

Solomon, Barbara. *In the Company of Educated Women: A History of Women and Higher Education in America*. New Haven, CT: Yale University Press, 1985.

Solórzano, Daniel. "Critical Race Theory, Race and Gender Microaggressions, and the Experience of Chicana and Chicano Scholars." *Qualitative Studies in Education* 11 (1998): 121–136.

Solórzano, Daniel, Miguel Ceja, and Tara Yosso. "Critical Race Theory, Racial Microaggressions, and Campus Racial Climate: The Experiences of African American College Students." *Journal of Negro Education* 69 (2000): 60–73.

Suzuki, Bob. "Revisiting the Model Minority Stereotype: Implications for Student Affairs Practice and Higher Education." *New Directions for Student Services* 97 (2002): 21–32.

Tierney, William. "The Parameters of Affirmative Action: Equity and Excellence in the Academy." *Review of Educational Research* 67 (1997): 165–196.

Tierney, William, and Jack K. Chung. "Affirmative Action in a Post-Hopwood Era." In *The Racial Crisis in American Higher Education: Continuing Challenges for the Twenty-First Century*, rev. ed., edited by William A. Smith, Philip G. Altbach, and Kofi Lomotey, 271–283. Albany: State University of New York Press, 2002.

Trucios-Haynes, Enid. "Why 'Race Matters': LatCrit Theory and Latina/o Racial Identity." *La Raza Law Journal* 12 (2000): 1–42.

Urban, Wayne J., and Jennings L. Wagoner. *American Education: A History*. 3rd ed. Boston: McGraw Hill, 2004.

Weinberg, Meyer. *Asian-American Education: Historical Background and Current Realities*. Mahwah, NJ: Lawrence Erlbaum Associates, 1997.

Williams, John B. "Systemwide Title VI Regulation of Higher Education, 1969–88: Implications for Increased Minority Participation." In *The Education of African Americans*, edited by Charles V. Willie, Antoine M. Garibaldi, and Wornie L. Reed, 110–118. New York: Auburn House, 1991.

Yamamoto, Eric. "Foreword: We Have Arrived, We Have Not Arrived." *Asian Law Journal* 3 (1996): 1–6.

Index

Figures and tables are indicated by page numbers in italics. Except for its main entry, the University of Illinois, Urbana-Champaign is referred to by its abbreviation, UIUC, throughout the index.

About the Author

SHARON S. LEE is a teaching assistant professor in education policy, organization, and leadership at the University of Illinois at Urbana-Champaign (UIUC). She earned her PhD in educational policy studies from UIUC, with a focus on the history of education, higher education policy, and diversity issues. She has worked in higher education administration since 1997, in academic and student services. Her research on Asian American college students and minority discourse has appeared in the *Asian American Law Journal* and UCLA's journal *InterActions*.

Printed and bound by CPI Group (UK) Ltd, Croydon, CR0 4YY

09/06/2025

14685735-0001